Exploring English Castles

Exploring English Castles

Evocative, Romantic, and Mysterious True Tales of the Kings and
Queens of the British Isles

Dr. Edd Morris

Skyhorse Publishing

Skyhorse Publishing books may be purchased in bulk at special discounts for sales promotion, corporate gifts, fund-raising, or educational purposes. Special editions can also be created to specifications. For details, contact the Special Sales Department, Skyhorse Publishing, 307 West 36th Street, 11th Floor, New York, NY 10018 or info@skyhorsepublishing.com.

Skyhorse® and Skyhorse Publishing® are registered trademarks of Skyhorse Publishing, Inc.®, a Delaware corporation.

Visit our website at www.skyhorsepublishing.com.

10 9 8 7 6 5 4 3 2 1

Library of Congress Cataloging-in-Publication Data is available on file.

Cover design by Jane Sheppard
Cover photo credit: ThinkStock

Print ISBN: 978-1-63220-348-9
Ebook ISBN: 978-1-63450-009-8

Printed in China

Table of Contents

Introduction: A Note for Castle Explorers

Like many of the greatest elements of modern-day England—from loose-leaf tea to chicken tikka masala curry—castles were a foreign import. The first of their kind arrived in England in 1051 and was built in rural Herefordshire—a sleepy place that's, strangely enough, the county where I was born.

A misty morning breaks over the ruins of Corfe Castle.

A beautiful tower within the Norman castle of Lewes, in East Sussex.

This founding fortification was a design sensation—imported directly from France, always a place of cutting-edge fashion. To our modern eyes, it certainly wouldn't have looked like much—it was likely just a mound of earth with scattered wooden fortifications across the top. Despite this, there would have been nothing comparable in Medieval England. As a result, its presence would have felt like an alien spaceship landing in the countryside. The contemporary chroniclers had no word for this new-fangled monstrosity, so they just plumped for the French term: they christened it a *castle*.

This castle was to be the first of many. Come 1066—some fifteen years later—the Normans would invade England from the continent and would build hundreds more of the things. Some would be built with care; others would be thrown together in haste. Either way, the Normans used castles to hold power over their conquered nation. These modern fortifications, in combination with devastating military skill and political cunning, meant that a force of just two thousand disciplined invaders commanded a nation of two million rowdy Anglo-Saxons, all in a matter of months.

Quite obviously, these first castles don't look at all like the castles of our imaginations. Indeed, if I asked you now to visualize a castle, I doubt you'd dream of a muddy hillock topped with a timber fence. Over time, this fortification evolved, and the word *castle* began to mean something quite different. The 1100s and 1200s signified a special species of gray stone monster: a structure bristling with grand towers, great keeps, curtain walls, jagged crenellations, fortified gatehouses, and swinging drawbridges.

The alluring path through Colton's Gate, in Dover Castle. Just beyond lies the Great Tower.

The central question, then, is what makes a castle a castle? After all, the earthen mound and gray stone enclosure are superficially very different beasts, yet we use the same word for each. Essentially—and I'd be quick to emphasize that this is my opinion from my own explorations, rather than the result of a lengthy academic endeavor—I believe a castle is an intriguing mix of high-status accommodation and hard-wrought defense. Those first Norman castles were called *motte and bailey*, where the *motte* was the defensive earth mound and the *bailey* was an enclosed courtyard for domestic use. Late medieval castles evolved to feature all those castle-y accoutrements we love so much (towers, arrow-slits, moats, and the like), but also housed grand tapestried rooms and gilded chambers fit for a king or queen.

8

The thick wooden door of Stokesay Castle in Shropshire.

Essentially, then, there's a tantalizing tension at the heart of a true castle. A castle isn't a fortress, and it's not a stately home. It's somewhere on the spectrum between the two, combining military prowess with unimaginable luxury. To put it another way, it's a place where you could sleep in a decadent four-poster one night and have your head chopped off and placed upon a spike the next (an eventful weekend, by any count). A true castle has a heady mix of violence and decadence, bloodshed and splendor, which is why, almost by definition, no real castle can ever be boring.

I should note, though, that many castles do carry an air of pretension. Building or refurbishing a castle would have been a devastatingly expensive exercise, suitable only for the grandees of early modern England. In return, an individual would have been blessed with a truly formidable status symbol; no one could doubt the societal standing of a man with a castle. In fact, the sheer appearance of a castle would have conveyed a great deal about its owner, his perceived self-worth, and his future aspirations.

The gatehouse of Carisbrooke Castle, upon the Isle of Wight. The castle was founded in about 1100, but this gatehouse was built in the 1300s. The castle is most famous for being the prison of King Charles I after his defeat in the English Civil War.

Chris Jenner/Shutterstock

As a result, do be warned: some English buildings that look distinctly castle-y can be a bit of a trick. Quite often, a social aspirant built what was really a grand house, and, with pretentions of greatness, disguised the outside with a few features of castle architecture to add a touch of ill-gotten grandeur. Consequently, I've been somewhat selective about the castles featured in this book. Everything within these pages is authentically medieval and truly fit to be called a castle.

I've also tried to approach writing about castles in a slightly different way. Many books about castles include a selection of fortresses and valiantly attempt to cover the thousand-year history of each one. I've taken a different approach: rather than cover a swathe of history for each, I've tried to take a snapshot of one of the most notable moments in the past: the Great Siege of Rochester Castle, for example, or when Queen Elizabeth visited Kenilworth. Hopefully this helps to bring some of the characters to life and also makes some of the underlying chronology a bit easier to understand.

The book begins with an important prologue: the Norman invasion. The year 1066 was probably the most important in the history of England, and it was the Normans who brought castles (indeed, sometimes even flat-pack castles) to our shores. From then on, I segue into how castles developed and evolved over the Middle Ages into formidable defensive structures—and then fell into decline and destruction.

Of course, I should note that there are literally hundreds of castles in England—and hundreds more in our neighboring countries of Scotland and Wales (see *A Snapshot of the Castles of Great Britain*, page 11). Evidently, although I'd love to, there's absolutely no way that I could cover them all. As a compromise, where relevant, I've tried to include tidbits, snippets, facts, and photos about castles that are somehow connected to the nine main ones I cover in depth. Hopefully this gives some taste of the amazing scale and variety of the castles scattered across Great Britain.

If you'd like to keep in touch—or if you're keen to tell me more about your own adventures to castles around the world—I'm always around at **www.exploring-castles.com**. I'd be delighted to hear from you.

A Snapshot of the Castles of Great Britain

K.Jakubowska/Shutterstock

The distinctive red-on-white cross of the English flag, flying over Warwick Castle.

England is one of the countries located upon the isle of Great Britain—alongside its neighbors of Wales and Scotland.* In the broadest terms, Wales is deep green and rugged; Scotland is crispaired and mountainous; and England is filled with hill and dale. The topographical differences between each country gave rise to different languages, cultures, and political structures, meaning that, during the medieval period, each country evolved quite separately.

As a result, the types of castles you'll encounter in England are quite distinct from those of Wales and Scotland. Castles in Wales are, by and large, formidable, fortress-like affairs: including an all-mighty "iron-ring" of fortifications built by the English king Edward I, constructed to consolidate his conquest of the country.

The fortifications of Scotland are no less awe-inspiring but built for a different political purpose. The social structure of the country, more closely aligned to bloodties of clan and family, resulted in smaller, nobler fortifications—occasionally classed as Tower Houses, which were a cross between castle and mansion.

Craigmillar, in Scotland, is part castle and part "Tower House"—a structure with a grander, residential purpose. Tower Houses aren't commonly seen in England or Wales.

By contrast, England's castles were most visibly forged by the Normans—indeed, the Norman conquest imported the castle to the isle of Great Britain, as these pages demonstrate.

Owing to the historic separation of our three nations, medieval castle builders focused their attentions upon political borders—where land was most closely contested. This is why castles tend to cluster along the border of Scotland and throughout the Marches—the medieval frontier land between England and Wales. The profusion of castles in southeast England are partly a consequence of the Nor-

man conquest from the continent, but were also built to protect the lands from further incursions from other European troublemakers.

_____

*It's a baffling topic, but when most people say *England*, they very rarely mean England (and I include a lot of fellow countrymen in this!). The United Kingdom (UK) is the political name for our country, which is formed of the union between England, Northern Ireland, Scotland, and Wales.

England, Scotland, and Wales are all located on an island known as Great Britain. This is a geographical distinction alone that evidently doesn't include Northern Ireland (as, obviously, it's located to the north of Ireland, on a separate isle).

A knight on horseback, as played by a medieval reenactor.

13

A selection of medieval-style weapons photographed during a battle reenactment in Italy

1066: A Story of Castles and Conquest

"They [the Norman commanders] wrought castles widely through this country, and harassed the miserable people; and ever since has evil increased very much. May the end be good, when God will!"

— *The Anglo-Saxon Chronicle*, 1066–7

It glowed near as bright as the moon—and all who looked upon it knew it bore ill. On April 24, 1066, the *fexedan steorra* (hairy star) appeared within the night sky—an omen never before seen by a living mortal. As the demon worked its way across the atmosphere, Anglo-Saxon England trembled below. The monk Eilmer of Malmesbury immediately understood its vile portents. "You've come, have you?" he reportedly wept. "You've come, you source of tears to many mothers, you evil. I hate you! It is long since I saw you; but as I see you now you are much more terrible, for I see you brandishing the downfall of my country. I hate you!" Eilmer was quite right. The year 1066 would see the end of the Anglo-Saxon rule of England. The Normans were coming.

In more modern times, this dreaded "hairy star" has been prosaically identified as Halley's comet, doing one of its 75/76 year laps through our solar system. But, in the absence of such scientific explanation, its appearance was seen as a potent omen. The Bayeux Tapestry records its devastating importance, showing Harold being crowned king of England—with a crowd of jubilant supporters to his left. But, on the right side, his comrades are distracted—pointing to the ominous shape of this star as it moves through the sky. In the next scene, one runs to tell Harold the terrible news; beneath him, the pattern of the tapestry depicts a small fleet of ships upon the sea. This flotilla would be the physical manifestation of the doom-filled prophecy.

And the ships would soon arrive. When Edward the Confessor died upon January 5, 1066, he didn't leave any obvious heir and so Harold of Sussex, Edward's brother-in-law, claimed that the old king had nominated him whilst lying on his deathbed.

William the Bastard of Normandy thought otherwise. William claimed blood connections to the old king, and thus England, he argued, was his own. But William was far away in Normandy and Harold was in England, and so Harold snatched the crown. It's said that, upon hearing this news, William was so angry he was unable to speak; he could only furiously pull at the fastenings of his cloak.

A French statue of William the Bastard (later, of course, William the Conqueror). There's obviously a fair amount of conjecture as to what William would or wouldn't have looked like—the statue's helmet, at least, is probably quite accurate.

William's anger was because—he alleged—Harold had deceived him. According to his version of events, Harold had come to France some years earlier and had promised not to stand in William's way of being the next king of England. For his part, Harold contested that he'd pledged friendship and nothing further. Unsure of who was the telling the truth,

England looked to the gods for help. And, sure enough, the hairy star proved (people said) that Harold was the liar.

To clinch matters, even the pope became involved in the disagreement. Upon William's plea, the pope judged that Harold had rescinded on an oath made upon a holy relic—an insult which condemned him and his supporters to burn in hellfire. On the basis of this prophetic comet and angry pope, William spent the hot summer of 1066 building boats and rounding up his forces to come and take England by force.

Things were looking particularly bad for King Harold, as other threats to his rule were emerging from unexpected locations. The king had made the error of falling out with his brother, Tostig, who had in turn fled to the arms of Harald Hardrada, the king of Norway. The pair claimed,

A medieval-style bow and arrow used by period reenactors.

K.Jakubowska/Shutterstock

through a Byzantine series of old agreements, that Hardrada was the true king of England, and so the duo set sail with a force of Vikings, intent upon capturing the city of York during September 1066.

It was a bold challenge, and Harold was forced to march north to York to defeat them. Here, he secured a spectacular victory at Stamford Bridge on September 25, using the element of surprise to wreak havoc upon the invaders. Harold's army pushed forward until the Vikings were fighting with their backs to the river; vast numbers were forced in and drowned. One particularly resilient Viking, it's said, captured a bridge and was such a ferocious fighter that he would let no one pass. One of Harold's enterprising men made a makeshift raft to float downriver and stabbed him from below.

Stamford Bridge was a bloodbath for the Vikings. Harold succeeded in killing his brother and also the king of Norway and sent the few survivors back from whence they came. The king had successfully defended the northern front.

Despite such success, however, something more ominous was happening in the South of England. Harold had known, long before he had decided to march north, that William the Bastard's army was biding its time on the other side of the English Channel—and was waiting for an opportune moment to pounce. Seeing the king so distracted, they did exactly that. On September 28, around seven hundred ships and between five thousand and ten thousand men arrived in Pevensey on the south coast (near modern Eastbourne). The Normans had arrived in Anglo-Saxon England.

David Fowler/Shutterstock

The evocative ruins of windswept, sea-splashed Hastings Castle.

David Hughes/Shutterstock

Pevensey Castle was built in 1066 by the Normans, upon the foundations of an old Roman fort. The external curtain walls were the work of the Romans; the Normans constructed a small, moated, innerbailey within the heart of these walls.

The Flat-Pack Castle

When the Normans arrived in England, they ate some roast chicken and then built a castle. Things were probably a trifle grander than those words might suggest, but the Bayeux Tapestry shows the Normans enjoying a grand feast on the beach to celebrate their safe arrival upon English shores. It's likely the food and drink were plundered from nearby villages, but the chicken on a spit is embroidered plainly for all to see: the Normans, it's quite clear, would have been appreciative of any modern fried chicken restaurant.

17

The gatehouse of Pevensey Castle—a castle crucial to the 1066 Norman invasion. Many centuries later, Turner (seemingly a fellow castle aficionado) produced a number of chalk sketches of the ruined structure.

It also appears that they were medieval connoisseurs of the IKEA model. On their second day in England—September 29—they quickly assembled a simple wooden castle on the foundations of the old Roman fortress at Pevensey. Although the wording of the chronicles isn't entirely conclusive, the strong suggestion is that the Normans brought precut timbers with them. This first castle, in effect, was assembled from a flat pack. The Norman poet Wace described it thus: "The carpenters . . . threw down from the ships and dragged on land the wood which the Count of Eu had brought there, all pierced and trimmed. They had brought all the trimmed pegs in great barrels. Before evening, they had built a small castle with it and made a ditch round it."[1]

---

[1] It's important to note that his writing wasn't contemporaneous; although Wace was Norman, his work *Roman de Rou* was probably completed some one hundred years after the conquest, and so we can't be entirely certain of its accuracy.

From a distance, this flat-pack castle sounds like a particularly strange state of affairs, but it was actually a pretty logical decision. The Normans had no way of knowing what resources—if any—they would encounter upon arriving in England. A common trick of medieval warfare (and one the Normans would use themselves) was to raze the ground surrounding an enemy, allowing foes no opportunity to forage for food, drink, or timber. With the risk of scarce resources, it made perfect sense to bring the timber they needed with them.

The flat-pack castle tells us other important things about the Norman technique of castlebuilding. It shows us that the fortresses the Normans built were broadly identikit—a standardized, predictable design repeated across the countryside they conquered.

This first castle also demonstrates to us that the Normans recognized that a castle equaled strength—and the sooner it was constructed, the stronger their position. As soon as this first fortress was finished—and Wace (quoted above) plus other chroniclers seem to concur that the majority was assembled within a day—the Normans filled it with stores and provisions, left it in the hands of a garrison, and then proceeded to build two further prefabricated castles slightly farther down the coastline.

On September 28, there had only ever been one castle in the whole of England. Now, on September 29, there were three. And just one day later—on September 30, 1066—the Normans marched on toward Hastings, a deeper port slightly to the east of Pevensey, which was better suited to harbor large ships from

Paul J Martin/Shutterstock

The rough stone remains of Canterbury Castle. A wooden motte and bailey castle was built here in about 1066.

Lance Bellers/Shutterstock

William the Conqueror was quick to fortify Pevensey Castle, although the castle was extensively adapted over the medieval period.

Paul J Martin/Shutterstock

The flint and sandstone walls of Canterbury Castle were added by King Henry I in the early 1100s.

the continent. Here, they founded castle number four. Indeed, wherever the Normans went, they founded a castle. It was a military strategy that would help them take control of England.

The southern coast of England was not just a convenient spot for the Norman military landing. Their presence in the area was one of the oldest tricks in the book of medieval warfare. King Harold was earl of Wessex—an English territory that incorporates Pevensey and Hastings. Occupying his lands was provocative. In addition, by terrorizing his people—and the Normans wasted no time in pillaging and plundering surrounding towns and villages—the forces sought to send a deliberate message to the rest of the English population. "If the King can't protect his own lands and his own people," they implied, "how can he ever claim to protect the rest of England?"

Harold, therefore, was left with little choice but to fight. A more desirable solution to the Norman problem would have been to trap the invaders in a small corner of England and burn everything in the vicinity, effectively starving them out over the winter. Such action would have required few men and limited force. Instead, the Normans were goading him into an early battle. Their troops were fresh and ready for war; his men were tired and battle-worn and would need to march the length of England to reach their foes. Harold, of course, would have known the topography of his territories of Wessex, but the Normans would have been able to scout out every inch of the land to prepare themselves for the fight. Harold was already upon the back foot.

Nonetheless, Harold was an impetuous man, perhaps rather intoxicated by his exceptional victory in the North. His strategy, he decided, would be to take the Normans by surprise by arriving as soon as possible. Accordingly, he allowed his troops little time for rest and marched his forces south—recruiting fresh men enroute. After the briefest of pauses in London, he proceeded at full speed from the capital, along the Dover road, via Rochester, and finally reached the outskirts of the Norman encampment on October 13. His troops barely had a night to rest—battle began at 6:30 a.m. that following morning.

Ron Ellis/Shutterstock

The remains of Hastings Castle—one of the very first castles built in England. This archway is thought to have been the entrance to the old chapel.

The Death of Harold, and the Norman Conquest of England

According to the Bayeux Tapestry, Harold died from an arrow to the eye. Whether that's true, our assumption is that the battle was even sided, lasting well into the afternoon of October 14. Historians suppose that the death of Harold spelled the defeat of the Anglo-Saxon side; however, we know surprisingly little about

A beautiful modern embroidery of the Bayeux Tapestry, decorating the hem of a skirt.

the course of the battle, as many of the primary sources contradict themselves. The only fact that we can be quite sure of is that the Normans won. And, with the last Anglo-Saxon king dead, William the Conqueror could stake a dramatic claim to England.

It didn't mean that the Anglo-Saxons had surrendered, however. In the immediate aftermath of battle, their leaders refused to recognize William the Bastard as the true king, instead declaring that the throne should fall to Edgar the Atheling (a distant blood relative to deceased King Harold). William, therefore, needed to flex his military muscle to consolidate his conquest of England. To succeed, he needed to capture London.

The rough stone ruins of Berkhamstead Castle. It was one of the first Motte and Bailey castles to be built in England, just after the 1066 invasion.

His route to London, however, would be intentionally circuitous: he wished to gain control of surrounding ports and adjacent towns to force the hand of the Londoners. Resultantly, he made progress first to coastal Dover, where he founded a castle (see page 70), then to the important cathedral town of Canterbury, which he captured and—guess what—built a castle.

He then dispatched a section of his men to test the defenses of London, brushing Southwark with his fingertips, where he was rapidly rebuffed. Undeterred, his forces circled around London, passing counterclockwise to its western side, where they crossed the Thames at Wallingford (and built a castle), progressing then to Berkhamstead, on the northwestern border of London, where, again, they built a castle. By the time he'd reached Berkhamstead, the Anglo-Saxon leaders realized the game was up: an envoy galloped out to meet him, swore oaths of fealty, and presented William with hostages as a guarantee of good behavior.

On Christmas Day 1066—approximately two months after the Battle of Hastings—William was crowned king of England in Westminster Abbey, London. William the Bastard lost that rather uncomplimentary epithet and became William the Conqueror. Of course, with London surrendered, William did what he knew best to consolidate his control over the capital: he built a castle. The White Tower—as it's known nowadays—is at the heart of the Tower of London. You can visit it today.

The impressive shape of the White Tower, at the heart of the Tower of London. William the Conqueror laid the first timbers in 1066.

atiger/Shutterstock

Detail from the White Tower. Although we don't know the exact date, the first stones were probably laid in about 1078.

Fedyaeva Maria/Shutterstock

The Motte and Bailey Castle

This isn't just a hillock in an English field; it's the mound of abandoned Yelden Castle, a Motte and Bailey fortress in Bedfordshire.

It's thought that King William and the Normans managed to build around five hundred motte and bailey castles between 1066 and 1086. That's a pretty impressive pace of work, equal to one castle every two weeks: a testament to the speed and ease of building these fortifications.

As the name might suggest, a motte and bailey castle always included two key elements: the motte (a man-made mound, perhaps in the range of twenty-five to eighty feet in height) and the adjacent bailey (a raised, flat-topped courtyard, often kidney shaped, which nestled against one face of the motte). Both elements would be encircled by a deep ditch, which was generally a fortunate by-product of the earth excavations required to construct the motte.

Thick, wooden, palisade-style fencing, Scandanavian in style. Palisade fencing was commonly used within Motte and Bailey castles.

Each motte and bailey castle was finished with a sprinkling of wooden fortifications. At the apex of the motte, one would encounter a sizable wooden tower, built as a defensive vantage point and stronghold. Spiky wooden palisade fencing encircled both the summit of the motte and the perimeter of the bailey, adding an additional line of protection.

The bailey would have functioned as the residential part of the castle. In early days of the Norman conquest, this flat-topped plinth was used as a temporary military encampment, but as time wore on, more permanent wooden buildings—things like kitchens and stables—were built on top of it. Depending on the overall size of the castle, a bailey could even extend to acres.

A number of factors contributed to the strength and success of the motte-and-bailey design. The predominant advantage was height: The wooden tower was a terrific vantage point, and anyone attempting to scale the sides of the castle would be greeted by a hail of arrows. The motte also functioned as the central stronghold. Even if the bailey was breached, the steps up to the summit of the motte could be intentionally burned away, hampering the efforts of any attacker.

In the hands of the enemy, of course, fire was the greatest vulnerability of any motte and bailey fortress. Fire could devastate the wooden palisade fences, the buildings upon the bailey, and even the tower on top of the motte. As a consequence, if time permitted and a castle appeared particularly important, Norman commanders would build structures from stone. Stonework was a lengthy, expensive building process, but one which rendered castles much less vulnerable to an inferno. Indeed, some years after the initial frenzy of conquest, the Normans would return to many of their most valuable motte-and-bailey castles and re-create the timber buildings in rock.

With so many motte and bailey castles built in England, some were evidently destined to emerge into political prominence and others would fade to insignificance. Of those that rose into prominence, an excellent example is Windsor Castle. Windsor is presently one of the residences of the Queen of England (throughout the years, it's evolved into something that more resembles a palace than a true castle). Nonetheless, the first structure at Windsor was a motte and bailey, built by William the Conqueror in the 1070s. The Round Tower—at the heart of the modern castle—is built on a hill that used to be the old motte, and, over the years, the royal palace grew around it.

Daniel Dent/Shutterstock

The beautiful shape of Clifford's Tower, York. Built on top of a Motte and Bailey mound, Clifford's Tower would once have been a part of the greater complex of York Castle; sadly, this has long since disappeared.

Tamworth—in the Midlands—is another brilliant example of a surviving stone castle situated upon a visible motte. In addition, Clifford's Tower in York is quite obviously constructed upon an old motte. It used to form a part of a large castle complex; sadly, it's been destroyed.

Evidently, it's hard to see remains of those motte and bailey castles that were undeveloped and forgotten; these timber-topped earth mounds were never likely to endure 950 years of the British weather. Nevertheless, you'll stumble across some remnants as you travel around England; suspicious small hillocks, poking out of otherwise flat fields, can often be a clue that you're looking at the remains of a motte.

Anastasiia Kucherenko/Shutterstock

Windsor Castle, England—an official residence of Queen Elizabeth II and the biggest occupied castle in the world (although I'd personally argue that it's more of a palace than a true castle). The Round Tower, upper right, was built upon the original Motte and Bailey mound.

Knyazeva Ekaterina/Shutterstock

The keep of Cardiff Castle, Wales. You'll win no prizes for guessing that this structure was built upon an old Motte and Bailey foundation.

Robert Hackett/Shutterstock

Tamworth Castle, in the English Midlands, mushrooms up from the earth below. As its appearance suggests, the fortress started out as a Motte and Bailey castle; in more modern times, residential buildings have been crammed behind these grand walls.

The Age of the English Castle

Evidently, castles developed a great deal from their origins as motte-and-bailey earthen mounds. Those fortresses with the greatest perceived strategic importance—including Corfe (page 160) and Rochester (page 116)—were built from stone from the off: vast towers of carefully hewn rock, wrought into mighty structures designed to overawe the grumbling Anglo-Saxon populace.

Whereas Southern England adapted rather quickly to its new rulers—probably simply due to the sheer proximity to London—those in the North of the country were rather less enamored with William the Conqueror. Rumbling discontent evolved into outright rebellion, and William was surprisingly lenient in his efforts to quell those initial uprisings. The discontent lingered, however, and so the new king decided to use unprecedented force to subdue the troublesome Northerners. His campaign of "harrying the North" took place between 1069 and 1070 and was a show of exceptional brutality: his forces burned and pillaged vast swathes of countryside, resulting in the starvation of as many as one hundred thousand people (a tremendous figure, perhaps as much as a twentieth of the population of England at that

Ruined walls of Canterbury Castle. Canterbury was one of the three Royal Castles of Kent, but it quickly became overshadowed by Dover Castle—the pet project of King Henry II.

time). Castles—including those at York, Richmond, Durham and, well, "New Castle" (now, of course, the modern city of Newcastle)—cemented his conquest of the region.

England was an unstable place during the high medieval period. The result was that anyone who built a castle would be predominately concerned with defense. The original fortresses—which started out as grand stone towers—were speedily fortified and strengthened, in response to attack, siege, and other external threats.

The following pages explain the defensive features common to almost every medieval fortress. I've chosen to separate out this section as it provides a useful reference when reading almost every other chapter of the book. It also makes it a bit easier to understand the evolutionary development of the castle.

Of course, English castles were not built for defense alone. As I've described before, every fortress was a cunning amalgamation of residential luxury and military might. The chapter on Goodrich Castle (page 46) is an explanation of what life was like in a medieval castle; it's the perfect setting for us to discover the luxuries and challenges of everyday life in a fortress.

27

Probably the most famous "castle" in England—the Tower of London. The White Tower—the work of the Normans—lies at the heart of the complex. Much of the Tower really functioned as a Tudor prison.

Built to Bristle: Attacking and Defending a Medieval Castle

From murder holes to trap-filled barbicans, medieval castles were built to withstand attack. The apex of defensive castle design took place within the high medieval period (c.1100–1300)—a time when England was a relatively unstable place and when craftsmen were skilled enough to render nightmarish designs into stone.

Every defensive innovation within a castle—from the deep moat to the perilous gatehouse—developed in response to a past threat. It's not as though designers plucked these ideas from the air; instead, they studied the Achilles heels of other fortresses and attempted to out-think the flaws and weak spots that had led to the capture of other castles.

One of the first—and most obvious—defensive developments was the curtain wall. Back in the early days of motte and bailey castles, wooden palisade fencing surrounded the flat-topped bailey. The curtain wall was a stone re-rendering of this simple enclosure. A looped curtain wall protected the buildings at the heart of the fortress from attack, and a walkway along the apex of the wall provided a lookout for those defending the castle (occasionally, you might hear such walkways poetically called *allures*).

Pretty much every castle I feature in this book enjoys some form of curtain wall, obviously in varying states of repair. However, a curtain wall was, by no means, just a plain stone face; it came fully loaded with defensive elements designed to wreak physical or psychological havoc upon an enemy.

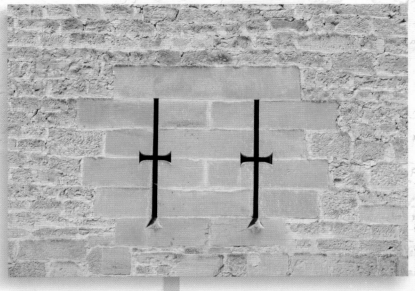

An arrow loop in a cruciform shape, photographed in Puymartin, the Dordogne, France. Note the two "feet" at the bottom of the arrow loop; these gave an archer a wider range of vision.

The simplest defensive element was the arrow-slit. An arrow-slit was a thin, vertical slice in the castle wall, through which an archer would be able to shoot his longbow at those attacking the fortress. Some arrow-slits were shaped like the Christian cross: the horizontal crack permitted a wider field of vision of the oncoming forces, and the religious motif took on particular significance when used in the crusader castles of the Middle East.

As time passed, arrow-slits grew increasingly complex. On the internal wall of the castle, the walls surrounding the arrow-slit were cut away at an oblique angle to maximize the field of vision of the archer firing within. Small embrasures (hollows) were built to provide archers with stone benches and greater elbow room, and, in later medieval times, these provided the opportunity to rest a heavy crossbow upon the floor.

29

Incidentally—as a little aside—arrow-slits were sometimes known as *arrow-loops*. Although you might wish to take the story with a pinch of salt, there's a persistent rumor that the modern expression *loophole* derives from the name of these defensive structures. The story says that, in the same way that a loophole is a narrow means of release from a weighty legal contract, an arrow-loop (thus *loophole*) was a means of release of a projectile through a weighty castle wall.

Part and parcel of every fortress would have been the battlements that crowned the walls; also known as crenellations, these jagged teeth really define medieval defensive architecture. The sticking-up bits are technically called *merlons* (the gaps are *crenels*), and those defending the castle could shelter behind the merlon while reloading their bows. As medieval times wore on, the notorious crossbow rose in popularity (it boasted quite lethal accuracy and range—for more

information, see the chapter on Rochester, page 116) and, as a result, arrow-slits were cut into many merlons; it would have been too dangerous to even step into the unprotected territory of the crenel.

An arrow loop built within a merlon (a merlon is one of the sticking-up bits within a range of crenellations). As aim of attacking archers improved, it became too dangerous to step out from the protection of a merlon to fire back down; the solution was to build an arrow-loop within.

Those attacking castles devised all manner of ingenuities to overcome the obstacle of the curtain wall and those archers stationed along it. Most obviously, one could try to use brute force: perhaps a stone-flinging trebuchet (a pulled-taught catapult that lobbed rocks of up to 250 pounds, potentially punching a vast hole in the brickwork). At the simpler end of the scale, an attacker could try and use a battering ram to bash down a wooden door. Attacks from these, however, were relatively easy to circumvent; in the Great Keep of Dover, the wooden entrance doors were situated up a series of steps at the first floor of the castle. Unlike noble visitors, battering rams couldn't climb stairs.

A series of crenellations upon the castle of Sao Jorge in Lisbon. The sticky-up bits are technically called "merlons," and the gaps are "crenels."

A reconstruction of a medieval battering ram. Some battering rams would have been vast, but such size would have made them unwieldy to transport.

A rickety-looking castle drawbridge from France.

If those attacking a castle were unable to get through a curtain wall, there was the potential to climb over it. One could ascend a wall using makeshift hooks, ropes, and ladders—although woe betide the first unlucky assailant to scale the wall and encounter the enemy within. An alternative to a ladder would have been the siege machine: a bit like a long-necked giraffe on wheels, this contraption could have been trundled up to the castle walls. A handful of attackers would have ridden upon its upper levels, ready to jump down into the enemy's territory.

If you couldn't get through the curtain wall, and you couldn't get over it, either, the next viable strategy was to go underground. Teams of unlucky men would be forced to dig tunnels toward the castle foundations; their ultimate aim would have been to undermine the foundations of a square tower, leading to its collapse. You'll discover much more about this technique within the chapter on Rochester Castle, page 116.

As a result of these techniques, the curtain wall was a good deal more vulnerable than it might have initially appeared, but those designing a fortress could construct additional defensive features to augment the castle's strength. Digging a moat was a perfect strategy. Moats made it very difficult to get up close and personal to the castle walls with a ladder or siege machine. In addition, the sodden earth beneath a moat would have made tunneling difficult. Of course, if drainage or water supply made a moat impractical, a deep, ragged ditch afforded similar advantages. Additionally, attacking forces couldn't intentionally drain the putrid waters within.

The passage into the castle naturally became a defensive weak spot; after all, a wooden door was a much weaker barrier than a stone wall, and wheeling a battering ram up a prebuilt road would almost have been a bit too easy.

The gatehouse was the logical response to this problem: a grand, fortified entranceway, protected by multiple portcullises, wooden doors, arrow-slits, and those infamous murder holes in the ceiling (more about these in a moment).

A gatehouse could be further fortified with the addition of a barbican. Effectively, a barbican was a protruding part at the front of the fortress that acted as an extra layer of protection before the gatehouse. Conceptually, the building acted as a funnel, often forcing a vulnerable visitor through a winding pathway of tricks and traps, where those defending the fortress had a definite upper hand. Most often, barbicans were added some time after the original gatehouse was built, solely to ratchet up the strength of the preexisting castle.

The barbican at Lewes Castle, near Sussex (as seen on page 43) is a particularly impressive example of such design: it boasted functional machicolations, a portcullis, and two large turrets. It was added during the 1300s, whereas the remainder of the castle was completed during the Norman period. Despite such might, the castle's defenses were breached during the Peasant's Revolt of 1381—albeit only by a gang of ne'er-do-wells who managed to break in and drink approximately $160 (£100) of wine.

This is what I call a moat! The spectacular aerial view of the medieval castle of Muiderslot in Muiden, the Netherlands.

Evidently, no matter the strength of the curtain wall or the depth of the moat, there would need to be some form of entrance into the heart of the castle. Medieval people couldn't airlift in supplies or parachute in from a helicopter.

The distinctive shape of a wrought metal portcullis. Many castles would have been fortified with multiple portcullises.

An impressive series of mostly decorative machicolations upon Tarascon Castle, Provence, France.

On a more grisly note, gatehouses and barbicans frequently contained murder holes: a suitably ghoulish name for a dastardly innovation. These holes studded the ceilings of the outer buildings, and all manner of nastiness could be poured, thrown, or fired through these holes to defend the castle. Indeed, you'll often hear that boiling oil was the weapon of choice, and would have been tipped onto an unfortunate enemy.

It's a gory story that everyone loves but, unfortunately, it's not strictly true. Although boiling oil would certainly have been used on occasion, it would have been too difficult to deploy routinely. Imagine the sheer logistics of obtaining the oil, boiling it, and pouring it during a frenzied battle—the hassle almost certainly outweighed the damage done.

Instead, those defending the castle would have thrown everything at hand onto those below—usually including jagged rocks and chunks of metal, not to mention carefully aimed arrows.

Incidentally, as the medieval period wore on, those attacking the castle became increasingly aggressive and lit fires within locked corridors—the aim was to burn down wooden doors and to fill the fortress with smoke and confusion. Luckily, then, these murder holes had a dual purpose: water could be poured down to quench any fire started below.

The murder hole was the sibling of another defensive feature—the machicolation. These were little, deathly balco-

A form of machicolations, upon Lewes Castle in East Sussex. The word "machicolation" seems to derive from the French—"to break a neck."

nies that ran along the top of castle walls. Machicolations were studded with holes in their floor, meaning that defenders could drop stones through them onto any enemy below.

You won't find many working machicolations within England, although there are a couple of good examples in Wales and France (pictured on page 33). However, you'll

The distinctive design of functional medieval machicolations, seen within the castle of Franco de Toledo, Valladolid, Spain.

find decorative machicolations on a vast number of castles (indeed, they're so common that you'll even see them on Cinderella's Castle in DisneyWorld). In medieval times, however, their purpose would not just have been aesthetic. Machicolations were a fearsome feature of any fortress—their name roughly originates from the French words for *crush* and *neck*—and even "decorative" versions would have had a psychological impact.

Anyone attacking a medieval castle resultantly faced an unpleasant variety of different ways to die. I, for one, wouldn't wish to get too close to a series of machicolations. One might therefore make a strategic choice and decide to engage in a siege. Siege was a common technique in medieval times—at its most simplistic level, those besieging a castle only required a more abundant supply of food and patience than those on the other side.

Despite this, siege was mentally and physically exhausting for both parties (see Rochester, p. 116 and Corfe, p. 160) and an impractical strategy if time was limited. Don't assume, also, that every standoff would result in siege; at its outset, both sides would weigh up their potential of success. If those in the castle had very little food and those approaching appeared strong and disciplined, the best solution was often to surrender there and then; on the other hand, if those in the castle were flaunting their vast stores of food, those approaching the fortress might simply decide not to waste their time. Siege was distinct to every other form of medieval warfare in that the psychological aspect was paramount.

Prisoners and Dungeons

Surely dungeons have always been pitch black, underground lairs filled with shackled, forgotten prisoners?

Well, you might be somewhat surprised. If you've ever read or watched the series *Game of Thrones*, you might have realized the importance of prisoners in early modern warfare. The son or daughter of a rival family was an invaluable bargaining tool in any struggle for power. Many prisoners—in early medieval times at least—were the children of fellow nobles who had to be held securely but were undeserving of cruel or inhumane treatment.

These prisoners were often confined to respectable rooms in the most secure towers of the castle—usually the castle keep. The French name for such towers was the *don-jon* (effectively meaning "stronghold"). Over time, as medieval warfare developed and more of the peasantry came to be captured and imprisoned, the dungeon (an Anglicization of the French words) came to mean the secure part of the castle where prisoners were held.

Eventually, the dungeons of modern imagination developed—cold, cruel, dark cells filled with rogues and unfortunates.

An illustration depicting the entrance to Carlisle Castle, Isle of Wight. Photo credit: Morphart Creation/Shutterstock

The innards of Restormel Castle in Cornwall. It was first built in about 1100, as a Motte and Bailey castle.

Decline and Decay: The End of an Era

The English castle-building season lasted from 1066 until the early 1300s. From the late fourteenth century onward, castles across the country fell into decline.

Political considerations were the primary reason behind the rise and fall of the castle. By the late 1200s, England was a much safer, more stable country than it had been following the Norman invasion. As a result, nobles did not need to hole themselves up in little fortifications, surrounded by every conceivable defensive technology. Instead, a different type of power had emerged: soft power. A castle needed to visually demonstrate the power and might of its master, but it increasingly didn't need the working defensive mechanisms to actively assert its strength.

Bodiam Castle is a great example. From the outside, it was a terrifying late medieval castle, but under the external bluster, it's really a pussycat that couldn't have inflicted much more than a scratch upon anyone attacking it. You can discover more on page 138.

Social reasons also led to the decline of the castle. As England edged toward the glorious years of the Tudors, national wealth and prosperity were on the rise. Nobles wanted luxurious homes; a castle, encumbered with so much heavy, defensive armor, was full of compromises and design flaws (a turret tended to be draughty, rather than whimsical). As a result, the rich dedicated their attentions to building new, luxurious residences, now believing the castle to be a mongrel born of less refined times.

Some military academics have also argued that castles fell out of favor because they just weren't strong enough any longer. It's a view I don't agree with. One on hand, it is true that, as the medieval age drew to a close, gunpowder was becoming

Stephen Mulligan/Shutterstock

The glorious appearance of Hampton Court, inextricably linked to King Henry VIII. During the Tudor period, the popularity of castles declined; the age of the palace had arrived.

increasingly popular, and cannon and mortar would have a devastating impact in decimating castle walls. However, cannon and mortar weren't in common use until the English Civil War in the 1640s, and English castles declined long before then.

An illustration of the Tower of London.

Castles enjoyed their last hurrah during the English Civil War of the 1640s. At that time, most castles were possessed by rich landowners who generally supported the king. The unexpected result was that these decaying fortresses enjoyed a brief resurgence into military significance; they generally became garrisoned in favor of the Royalist side and resisted extended siege by the opposing Parliamentarians (see page 183 for more on the role of castles during the English Civil War).

When the Parliamentarians won the Civil War, they gleefully proceeded to destroy or damage the defenses of most of those castles that had eluded them (such a technique was called *slighting*). In the case of some of the most formidable castles—such as Pontefract, in the North—they razed the entire thing to the ground. The outcome was that, by about 1660, the vast majority of castles in England had been reduced to forgotten, ruinous states and would remain that way for approximately the next 150 years.

Between 1300 and the mid-1600s, therefore, most castles in England languished. They were left to decay, seen as relics of a bygone age. Often, the stones of ruined castles were scavenged and reused to build new mansions and palaces. Sometimes, even if the bulk of the castle survived, the draughty older chambers would have been mothballed. In their place, new residences were added to the castle complex, filled with luxurious rooms more befitting of those sophisticated early modern tastes. An excellent example is Leicester's Residence in Kenilworth Castle, which was built to host Queen Elizabeth I (see page 254).

By the 1600s, the majority of castles were forgotten and untended. If they were falling into ruin—and many would have been quite dilapidated—it's unlikely that anyone would have restored them. Indeed, back then, old English castles would have attracted little admiration or nostalgia—they would have been perceived to be archaic junk.

The Renaissance of the English Castle

The castle renaissance began in the early 1800s and continues until this day. In the early nineteenth century, England modernized and industrialized, and the increasing complexity of modern life created a yearning for older, simpler times. Medieval literature became fashionable again. Romantic poets and authors became fascinated with the specters of wild mountains, rough seas, and evocative ruins. England underwent a transport revolution. As a result, the first tourists crept into the staggering, overgrown, creeper-infested ruins of old castles. What they saw captured many an imagination, and the craze of the castle began again.

40

of the castle changed: no longer an irrelevant relic, it became a vision of mystery, romance, and subtle British power.

Pretty soon, England's richest were building themselves stately homes and, according to the latest vogue, calling the things "castles." Most of these were built during the mid-nineteenth century and constructed according to the latest styles of Gothic Revival architecture. Nowadays, historians would refer to such castles—not unkindly—as being called *follies*. Indeed, one of my friend's families owns such a folly—Banwell Castle in Somerset, England. The mansion was designed by one of the greats of Gothic Revivalism, Pugin—the man responsible for the Palace of Westminster (British Houses of Parliament). Today, you can pop in for a cream tea or stay the night in a four-poster bed.

The perfectly circular outline of Restormel Castle, Cornwall. It's Britain's best example of a "shell keep" castle—the stone wall was built as a jacket, wrapping around the old, wooden motte and bailey buildings.

Romantic artists such as Turner and Constable then painted castle ruins, depicting jagged remains amidst sweeping countryscapes. Tennyson wrote epics upon King Arthur in Tintagel. At the same time, gothic literature emerged as a genre; a common motif became the ruined, lightning-lit castle, replete with shimmering ghosts and dastardly mysteries. Popular perception

Banwell Castle in Somerset, England—a "folly," and a great example of Gothic Revivalism.

41

Ivy creeps across the ruins of Gleaston Castle, Cumbria. During the Victorian period, every English castle would have been covered in foliage. Ivy, although romantic, is a disaster for conservationists.

Although the emerging, frantic interest in castles prevented many fortresses from destruction, it didn't necessarily protect these places from well-meaning but misguided attempts at reconstruction. Many wealthy Victorian benefactors decided to "restore" castles, rebuilding sections with an idealized, fairytale view as to what the castle should have looked like. They often exaggerated battlements, aggrandized gatehouses, and added witches-hat roofs to turrets. Many of the castles featured in this book suffered some degree of such "restoration"—victims include

Tintagel and Dover. But they got off lightly; some castles in the United Kingdom (Dolwyddelan in Wales springs to mind) were extensively remodeled at the expense of their authenticity.

Indeed, during the Victorian period, castles were interpreted in a very different manner to which we see them today. The Victorian vogue was to wander around the romantic ruins in a state of reverie, marveling at their otherworldly appearance. One of my favorite examples of such whimsy took place within

The path to Dolwyddelan Castle, in Snowdonia, Wales. Dolwyddelan is a spectacular little castle, but its present-day appearance is the result of modern reimagination; the distinctive battlements, which define its profile, were added in the nineteenth century.

The barbican of Lewes Castle, East Sussex. The building boasts great views and has an interesting attached museum.

Beeston Castle, North-Eastern England, where a wealthy Victorian businessman chose to import a number of kangaroos who'd hop through the ruined rooms, presumably to the delight (rather than terror) of his guests.

Happily, in the early twentieth century, proper academic interest turned toward castles. University teams excavated ruins to research historical connections. Aggressive "restoration" became eschewed, with conservation becoming the key. A visit to a castle became a chance to engage with its history, rather than a chance to spot a kangaroo.

In recent years, the ongoing care of English castles has fallen into the care of not-for-profit bodies. Most in this book are exceptionally well looked after by English Heritage (**www.english-heritage.org.uk**), an organization dedicated to preserving England's historic past. A smaller portion is looked after by the National Trust (**www.nationaltrust.org.uk**), a custodian of vast proportions of Britain's countryside.

Resultantly, there's a wealth of amazing castles for you to discover, all scattered across the beautiful hills and dales of green England. Here are stories from nine of my favorites. I hope you enjoy them.

43

THE CASTLES

Goodrich is built of a unique red sandstone that beautifully complements the blue sky on a sunny day.

Life in a Medieval Castle: Goodrich

I couldn't write a book on castles without featuring Goodrich. Goodrich is an arresting little fortress, neatly tucked away in the rolling green countryside of Herefordshire—the county where I was born. I guess there's an element of bias in my enthusiasm for the castle, but there's no doubt that it qualifies as one of England's most alluring; with its ragged ochre walls and verdant surroundings, visiting Goodrich in the summertime is an eye-poppingly colorful experience.

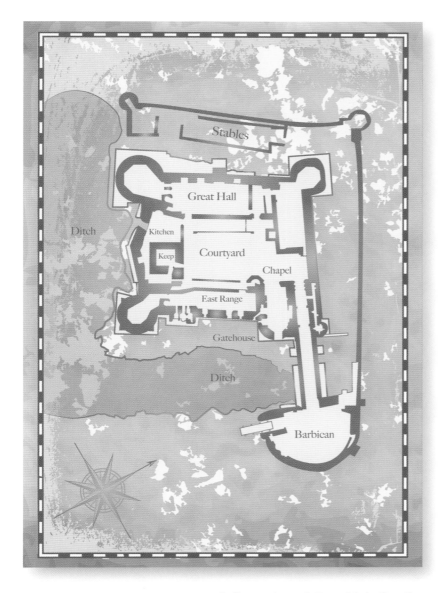

A floor plan of Goodrich Castle.

delighted in the luxuries of its light, airy rooms and decadent banqueting hall.

In fact, the lingering charm of Goodrich is that it feels eminently livable. Even as a modern visitor, standing amongst the ruins of the fortress, the place feels, well, *cozy*. The red sandstone walls exude warmth; the residential chambers are grand without being overbearing; and the barbican gives that nod of reassurance that, if you were to bed down for the night, you'd be well protected.

This feeling of self-contained security isn't an accident. Goodrich isn't like the majority of medieval castles in England that evolved over time; for these fortresses, their grand new rooms and chambers were added as extensions as the years passed by. Goodrich, by contrast, was 90 percent planned and built in one fell swoop around 1280. The consequence is that the castle coheres beautifully—hardened defenses flow into residential rooms. And it's for this reason that Goodrich is the perfect base to explore and understand exactly what life would have been like in a castle during medieval times: the smells, the sounds, the food, the luxuries, and also the deprivations.

Exploring Godric's Castle

G oodrich is much more than a pretty facade, though. As castles go, it's the perfect amalgamation of military strength and residential luxury—in fact, it's pretty much a textbook example of what makes a medieval castle so interesting. Its grand chambers must be viewed alongside its deep ditch and impressive gatehouse. A guest to Goodrich, visiting in the late 1200s, would have

It initially looks so simple—but the more you consider it, the more the mystery grows. If you were to peruse the listings of Herefordshire within the 1086 Domesday Book, you'll notice that it catalogs a certain "Godric's Castle," positioned close to the present-day fortress of Goodrich. It seems almost certain that the old record and its modern ruin bear some connection,

Goodrich is seated upon a natural sandstone plinth, and the ditch (now grassed) runs along the south and east sides.

The approach to Goodrich through the Herefordshire countryside.

Contrast the window-studded red brickwork of the 1290s castle to the relatively plain, gray face of the 1160s keep. Larger windows epitomised developments in medieval architectural technique.

and that the name "Godric's Castle" morphed into "Goodrich Castle" over the years.

That's pretty neat and easy, right? Well, not really—this throws up a number of intriguing questions. There's limited evidence for any fortifications dating back to 1086, and historians have struggled to discover anything about this mysterious Godric. Even his name poses a puzzle—as the name originates from Old English. In 1086, we'd have assumed that the only men in England who could have held a castle would have been from Norman bloodlines. How on Earth could an Englishman ever have laid claim to a fortress?!

It's a puzzle that we'll probably never be able to solve; Godric has been lost to the mists of time. In fact, the entire history of his castle remains rather foggy until about the mid-1100s when the blue-green keep was constructed.

The keep is virtually the only surviving part of the fortress that wasn't built in the late 1200s. Visiting Goodrich today, you can see that this building is quite distinct from the remainder of the castle: it's rendered from a rougher, blue-hued stone; it has a straight-edged, square design that contrasts with the smoother, rounded edges of the later buildings; and it's studded with small, black windows, less extravagant in size than those in the remainder of the castle. The keep is obviously the earliest and most rudimentary part of the fortress; the rest of the castle was built around it and later consumed it.

The bulk of Goodrich, therefore, is shaped like a lopsided parallelogram, with a tower at each of the four corners. A fifty-foot-long barbican, its endpoint shaped like the letter D, protrudes from the eastern face of the fortress. The northern and western sides are naturally protected by the River Wye and a steep cliff; the other two aspects of the castle are secured

49

The entrance to the castle—that is, standing upon the barbican and looking in toward the gatehouse. You can see the modern stained glass window of the castle chapel on the left side of the entrance; further left again you can glimpse some fantastic arrow-loops.

with a deep, man-made ditch, which snakes underneath the drawbridge and causeway of the projecting barbican. The aforementioned early medieval keep has been consumed within the southern face of the castle; as it measures just twenty-eight feet in length, it now forms only a small part of the 160-foot side of Goodrich.

The four sides of the castle enclose a small but important courtyard, which would once have been full of the mud, bustle, and wandering dogs that typified medieval life. An ominous, black well—thought to be three times deeper than the keep is tall, although we don't quite know for

sure—supplied the castle with water, and would have proved essential during the siege of 1646.

The Life of William de Valence: A Medieval Morality Tale

The Goodrich we see today was built for one man: the rather dislikable William de Valence. Powerful but eminently unpleasant, de Valence's life story is made all the more satisfying for the twist in its tale: he received his final comeuppance.

De Valence was born in around 1230 near Poitiers, France. During his sixty-six-year existence, he was almost universally distrusted as an "alien" by the English, although he was a particular friend and favorite of King Henry III.

William was born in 1225 into the Lusignan family. The Lusignans had once been powerful nobles in France but, by the 1240s, their star was rather waning. In 1247, King Henry III—William's half-brother—invited the family to England, ostensibly to strengthen strategic alliances between the two countries. As it happened, Henry and William got on like a house on fire and, as a token of friendship, the king orchestrated a grand marriage between William and the beautiful Joan de Munchensi. The monarch then gifted the newlyweds with extensive properties in England, including Goodrich Castle.

Although King Henry may have liked him, William was a flawed man. He was impetuous, violent, and quick to temper, with a persistent disrespect for the rules of the land. Even so, he was skilled in tournaments and adept at warfare, and the king quickly knighted him.

It's obvious why a newcomer like William would evoke jealousy within the Royal Court, but the behavior of his family won him no new friends. The Lusignans were greedy and acquisitive—foreigners who had suddenly been gifted vast swathes of English countryside and who were unafraid to quarrel and bicker to obtain any additional acre. Perhaps paranoid after their previous fall from grace within France, the family would do anything to protect their regained wealth, and so employed a selection of bruisers and strongmen to collect the taxes and tithes their tenants owed. One of their

The gray stone keep is at the center of the image. Note the base of the tower upon the right—to modern eyes, it looks something like the fins of a rocket, but these spurs bear a great similarity to a number of contemporaneous castles, including Caerphilly Castle in Wales. It's thought that they were built to prevent the towers from being undermined.

stewards was a man named William de Bussy, whose lack of manners rubbed pretty much everyone the wrong way.

The Lusignans also had a natural tendency toward arrogance and, due to the king's favoritism of William, thought themselves above the law. Indeed, a 1256 order made by the king effectively exempted the entire clan from the English legal system—decreeing that no writ could be served against them. It was a potent mix of petulance and privilege—and, as a result, the king's court quickly split between Lusignan and the queen's family, the Savoyards, and the two opposing sides squabbled for years.

William's chickens, however, would come home to roost. In 1258, King Henry III was becoming increasingly distrusted by his people, and the fractured court implied—probably with good reason—that the widely distrusted Lusignans had

51

Despite being the oldest part of Goodrich, the light gray keep is the tallest surviving section. It spanned around three floors and the base is around twenty-five square feet.

caused the schism between king and country. Channeling this ill-sentiment—and with few friends at court to protect him— de Valence was exiled to France that July, painted as the primary cause of the king's ills.

Although the court disliked William, the king's enthusiasm was not greatly reduced and so, in 1261, Henry invited his friend back to England. His wings, however, would be severely clipped. The Savoyards now held political power in the realm, and, over the next thirty years, William was reduced to a state of dutiful, unquestioning obedience—first to Henry III and then to his half-uncle, Edward I, whom he assisted during this fearsome king's conquest of Wales between 1277 and 1283. William's vicious temperament was

certainly a perfect match for King Edward's similarly violent worldview: the two men were the perfect pair to subdue and subjugate Wales.

In fact, it's quite likely the conquest of Wales provoked the construction of most of Goodrich Castle. Herefordshire is technically in Marcher country—the turbulent frontier land between England and Wales. Although the fortress was never severely threatened by any Welsh marauders, it was on the sidelines of conflict and so received a lot of important visitors. The castle needed to be luxurious enough to sustain large parties of demanding guests but simultaneously have the strength to defend itself should things with the Welsh get a little sticky. William undoubtedly poured money into the project—after all, the appearance of the castle reflected his status as a lord, and he'd never exactly received much respect in England.

Edward I was undoubtedly aware of his half-uncle's dismal social standing. As a result, during 1296, the king chose to make a "thank-you" gesture, and records suggest that the monarch leased his royal builders to work upon Goodrich Castle for a short while. Perhaps they were helping out with the finishing touches.

It was ironic timing as, that very same year, de Valence would meet the end that some may say he deserved. Traveling with his son, the pair went to Cambrai, northern France, to act as an envoy for King Edward. The diplomatic expedition was a disaster and, on his return trip, de Valence became embroiled in an armed skirmish. We don't know exactly what happened; perhaps battle-hungry William let a trivial argument escalate into violence. Nonetheless, de Valence was grievously injured. His son, Aymer, managed to drag his wounded father back to Dover, where his wife, Joan, arranged for him to be carried, by litter, to his manor in Brabourne, Kent. William died there in May of that year.

The widowed Joan was no less formidable than her husband. On his death, his estates—including Goodrich—passed on to her. She maintained the portfolio of properties with characteristic vigor, spending most of her time at Goodrich but moving between her other possessions at alarming speed, accompanied by a vast retinue of advisors and servants. William may have died, but the ambitious Lusignan bloodline undoubtedly lived on.

Nicholas Peter Gavin Davies/Shutterstock

Looking onto the southern face of the castle. You can clearly see the 1160s light gray keep on the left side of the photo—this is the oldest section of Goodrich and contrasts in style and stone to the remainder of the fortress, built around 130 years later.

Goodrich Castle in Feudal England

Modern media would have us think that medieval times were marked by unyielding bloodshed. It's certainly true that England in the Middle Ages was a good deal more violent and dangerous than England in the twenty-first century, but Medieval England was, by no means, in a state of constant war. Then (as now!), land equaled money and power. Those with land were the baronial classes, who had been granted their estates by the owner of most of England—the king. As long as the barons held their grounds (or even increased their shares), money and power would flow in their directions. The human psyche meant that although a baron would almost certainly take up arms to defend his property, few would be willing to

53

risk their estates on unwise wars or ill-planned violence. This pure self-interest kept England in a state of relative tranquility.

The underlying system—feudalism—had arrived in 1066, alongside the Normans. It all boiled down to a simple pyramid of power. The king owned all the land in the country and granted it to his barons in exchange for military support. The barons required crops and income, and so the land had to be tilled and harvested—a task dedicated to the peasants. The peasants worked the land in the name of their barons, with the condition that he would provide them with support and protection in the event of war. The system was imbued with many different forms of taxation and reciprocity, but the network of self-interest remained the same.

Feudalism therefore meant that the land of England was parceled up into easily managed chunks, each administered by a baron. (It was generally more deviously complex than this suggests—for example, a baron often sublet his land to a knight.) A castle acted as the base of feudal power within a region. From William de Valence's Goodrich, power radiated to his surrounding lands on the Wye borders. The castle was the seat of administration for taxes, tithes, and justice; a place of aggrandizing feasts and banquets; a very visible demonstration of the baron's prestige and military strength; and a safe sanctuary for those on the lower rungs of the ladder in the event of medieval war. Feudalism spread its tentacles from Goodrich, just as power similarly radiated from many other medieval castles.

However grand Goodrich may have been, it was just one of the properties owned by William de Valence. In common with

Even today, Goodrich maintains an imposing appearance. It's easy to understand why it held such status in feudal England, and why it posed such a headache to the Parliamentarians during the English Civil War.

the majority of medieval barons, William possessed lands and property across much of Great Britain; he was the lord of manors in Bayford and Essenden (and, confusingly, in Hertfordshire—as a Herefordian, I'll take offense if you mix the two up), the Earl of Pembroke, and the guardian of lands in Wexford (Ireland). Evidently, he couldn't be in all those places at once and, without the ability to conference-call his sheriffs in each of his properties, needed to constantly travel around the country to perform duties of administrating, serving justice, and maintaining an aura of control.

A baron like William would have been constantly on the move, but traveling around the country would have been a tricky business. In general, English roads would have been little more than pot-holed dirt tracks. To make matters worse, although I previously said that Medieval England was relatively free of outright war, this certainly didn't

David Hughes/Shutterstock

Goodrich, looking onto the southeastern tower. You can see the great ditch in the foreground.

have been too costly to keep such a luxurious bed in each destination—man power, by contrast, was cheap.

In the baron's absence, each castle or manor would have been kept ticking by a handful of domestic staff, protected by a small military garrison of a few loyal men. On the baron's approach to the castle, however, everything would have whirred into life. With any luck, a member of the household would have written in advance to warn of the entourage's arrival, meaning that the castle kitchens would be fully stocked with supplies; rooms would have been cleaned and aired; and water would be have been freshly drawn, ready for bathing and washing. Often, on the final approach to the castle, the cooks and bakers from the household would have ridden ahead of the main party to help with the preparations for the

mean that the countryside was a haven of tranquility; some stretches of road were rendered perilous by opportunistic thieves and petty robbers.

A baron traveled between properties with his entire household, and there was certainly no conception of traveling light. Countess Joan de Valence (the wife of William) traveled with a household of up to 196 (from the records we have today, there never seemed to be fewer than 122 in her entourage), and those with her ranged from stewards to treasurers, cooks to porters. The household would have been a procession of stray dogs, carts, and wagons, often transporting items of furniture we'd naturally assume to be nonportable—for example, records show that some households even traveled with a four-poster bed and feather mattress. It seems unwieldy to us today, but it would likely

This causeway (right) crosses the great ditch of Goodrich, running from the barbican to the gatehouse.

55

The southwestern round tower—to the left of the image—connects to the Great Hall. The lower levels were used to store food; the upper levels would have housed grand accommodation.

welcoming feast and to ensure that the lord and lady were greeted with the smell of fresh-baked bread.

Everyday Life in Goodrich Castle: Business and Banquets in the Great Hall

On the arrival of William and Joan de Valence, Goodrich Castle would have awoken from its slumbers. Every room in the castle would be a hub of noise. No place in the

fortress would have been busier, noisier, or more vibrant than the Great Hall.

The Great Hall dominates the western aspect of Goodrich and similarly dominated everyday life in the castle. In common with nearly every medieval castle, the Great Hall was the site for administration and business and also for feasting and entertainment. When designing Goodrich, the architect almost certainly sited the Great Hall first and then slotted in every other room around it.

The Hall is around eighty feet in length and would have been flooded with light through three extravagant windows, which extend almost to its full height. Beneath the windows is a long stone bench, which was where William and Joan de Valence, alongside their most important of guests, would have been seated during a feast. The closer a guest was seated to the noble pair, the greater one's status in society (a very literal demonstration of the modern expression *out in the cold*). Those with higher statuses were also served their food first and also enjoyed the use of more permanent furniture. Less dignified guests would have been seated on the medieval equivalent of a trestle table.

Although we live in times of excess, a modern feast would pale in comparison to a true medieval banquet. Medieval society placed great weight upon lavish hospitality and conspicuous consumption (little has changed, then), and the tables of an average medieval banquet would have groaned beneath platters of spit-roast mutton, venison, and game; jellies died a saffron yellow or boiled-blood black; hearty stews and consommés; and diced boiled vegetables (it was believed that raw greens caused sickness).

To our modern taste buds, the flavors of medieval food would have been overwhelming; sweet and savory dishes were served at the same time, and many of the most popular foods mixed the two flavors. In addition, cooks utilized vast quantities of herbs and spices—likely to disguise that the meat had been cured or salted, as it couldn't be frozen or refrigerated. This culinary cornucopia would have been washed down with weak ale or poor wine; the drinks were

This image—from another medieval castle, rather than Goodrich—shows a typical fireplace.

chosen because they were safer to consume than water, not because of their taste or alcohol content.

A tremendous effort was required to procure and prepare such a quantity of food, and so the castle kitchen was invariably positioned adjacent to the Great Hall, as is the case in Goodrich. (Rather unexpectedly, though, the Goodrich kitchen isn't connected to the Great Hall via a direct doorway; one would have had to walk between the two via the courtyard.) Little survives today of the Goodrich kitchen, but the space is tiny: enough for one great hearth and not much else. Despite its diminutive size, it was room enough to prepare some mighty feasts, including one for Easter 1297, the ingredients for which included half a boar, two veal calves, six hundred eggs, and at least twenty-four pigeons. That little kitchen would have been a pressure cooker.

Evidently, a great number of servants would have been required to prepare such vast quantities of food. In medieval times, many had alarmingly specific jobs—as well as the expected butchers and bakers, it's likely that the castle would have been home to an ale wife (a woman charged with brewing for the fortress), candle makers, scullions (low-rung kitchen servants), and bottlers (those who managed the wine and ale). The largest feasts could employ hundreds of servants, and sometimes, out of necessity, temporary kitchens were built inside the castle courtyard or outside the curtain walls.

Goodrich's Great Hall—in common with many other Great Halls of the period—was directly linked to two important storerooms located in the base of the southwestern tower. The first of these was the pantry, where bread and dry goods were held; the second was the buttery, which, counter-intuitively, was actually the store for wine and ale (see boxout, page 67). On the upper level of the southwestern tower, there's a grand residential room that boasts a fireplace, a washbasin, and direct access to the Great Hall. It was undoubtedly reserved for the most important guests.

The Great Hall was not only used for the pomp and ceremony of feasting. The hall was the political and administrative heart of the castle—where, of a morning, William de Valence would have heard reports from his stewards upon domestic affairs, his knights and armored men would have reported upon matters of defense, and he would have adjudicated disputes and disagreements between those lowly men toiling his lands. We tend to think of medieval life as being filled with feasts and leisure; in actual fact, the day-to-day running of a feudal castle and its surrounding lands would have been a significant administrative burden—particularly as most lords toured between properties, so work would pile

58

Viktor 1/Shutterstock

The highest-status members of the castle would have enjoyed hunting and eating game, including wild boar.

up in their absence. If a baron was lucky and the day's workload was light, he might be able to snatch a few hours of an afternoon for hunting or other sports—if not, the administration might continue until nightfall.

After nightfall, within earlier medieval castles, the Great Hall would have been transformed into a sleeping chamber, with the majority of the castles' inhabitants bedding down upon the straw-strewn floor. Goodrich enjoyed a comparatively large number of residential rooms, so it's likely the Great Hall wasn't routinely used for sleeping (although when it was inundated with visitors, there was probably little other option). However, on the opposite side of the castle was the lower-status East Range, which was likely a dining hall for less important guests. It's very likely that the East Range was routinely used as sleeping quarters, and we can only imagine the dark, drafty chamber with a hard stone floor, which would have afforded zero privacy.

In the late medieval period, when England was secure enough for some of the household to sleep outside the castle walls, the East Range was transformed into a three-story building of residential chambers, affording some privacy and luxury for those able to lodge within.

Even though the Great Hall of Goodrich was of much higher status than the East Range, its interior decor would still have been remarkably plain. During the 1290s, tapestries would have been unaffordable and expensive, and the walls would more likely have been whitewashed—perhaps, if money allowed, accented with thin red or green borders. The floor of the hall would have been stone, covered with reeds or straw; the straw mopped up the grubby mess of everyday life and would be sprinkled with herbs to keep things vaguely sweet smelling.

Prayer and Reflection within the Castle Chapel

The stained glass window inside the church of Carisbrooke Castle, England. As most in Medieval England would have been illiterate, windows like these were an important way to visually narrate religious tales.

Chris Jenner/Shutterstock

If the Great Hall was the heart of Goodrich Castle, the gatehouse chapel must represent the castle's soul. Medieval England was, understandably, a God-fearing place, and almost every castle included some place of Christian worship. The richest and grandest of castles—and within these, we can include Goodrich—boasted their own chapels, of varying sizes. Smaller castles, or rural manor houses, may only have had smaller rooms dedicated to prayer, although some enjoyed their own altar.

Worship was integrated into the everyday fabric of castle life. Every day would begin with the lord and lady attending mass in their chapel, usually alongside some of the higher-status members of their retinue. Grander sermons were held upon Sundays and religious festivals, and the medieval calendar would have been punctuated with special services for christenings, funerals, weddings, and saints' days.

Of course, during the medieval period, England was a Catholic country (the seismic shocks to English religion would occur some years later under Henry VIII). As befitted the Catholic faith, the chapel of a medieval castle would have included ornate and intricate internal decorations, which marked it apart from the main bulk of the fortress. Some of this grandeur is still visible in Goodrich, although the chapel has been significantly remodeled over time. There's a particularly grand trefoil-shaped priest's seat and a delicate sink that was used to wash the holy vessels used during Mass.

You'll discover Goodrich's chapel within the castle gatehouse—and, although it might seem a rather strange choice of location, a significant number of medieval fortresses positioned their

59

own churches in a similar place. It seems curious to locate a chapel in one of the defensive hotspots of the castle—a priest amongst the portcullises, if you like—but historians have come up with a number of theories to try and explain this oddity.

One theory relates to thanksgiving for a safe journey. As I mentioned previously, travel was a treacherous business during medieval times. Positioning the chapel at the entrance to a castle allowed any arriving visitors to pay their thanks for safe passage to the fortress. In the forebuilding to the Great Keep of Dover Castle (see page 76), there was a small an-techapel that was seemingly used for this exact purpose.

Other theories point to a symbolic importance of a gatehouse chapel. As the medieval period wore on, castle gatehouses grew progressively more ferocious, but they still represented a defensive liability. (For obvious reasons, one couldn't build a gatehouse facing a cliff edge: it had to provide access to the castle during peacetime.) Placing a chapel in a gatehouse might have made any attacker think twice before bombarding the building with stones and rocks from a trebuchet—in doing so, were they implicitly attacking God?!

There was one further element of symbolism to the gatehouse chapel. Should the castle be under attack and the gates closed, it meant that the chapel—and thus God—were physically upon the same side as those defending the fortress. Those attacking the castle became the heathens outside the gates.

The everyday significance of medieval faith was not solely derived from the grandeur and setting of the chapel.

60

In early medieval times, at least, priests were distinguished from much of society, as they were able to read and write. As a result, the clergy were often called to serve as advisors

Jeff Gynane/Shutterstock

A medieval reenactor, dressed as a jousting knight, goes into battle.

and stewards for castle barons. Indeed, Countess Joan often traveled with a small number of priests, who were likely to have assisted in matters of administration and organization.

During the late twelfth century, the castle chapel also played a role within an important medieval rite—the ceremony of knighthood. Knights enjoyed a rarefied status, below a lord but above the hoi-polloi of medieval society; a knight was trained in warfare but would also understand the codes and conceptions of chivalry and medieval romance. In times of trouble, a knight would ride to the side of a lord (or king, if bidden by his master); otherwise, he would have been responsible for peacekeeping, while peasants toiled his allocated fields.

As a result, "knight school" was a lengthy, challenging process. Boys from families of some means set to work early as squires—cleaning armor, tending to the horses, and observing and practicing combat and archery. Those who excelled would be able to progress to becoming knights at around their fifteenth or sixteenth birthdays.

The ceremony of knighthood was complex and filled with symbolism: the young man would hold a night's vigil in the chapel before the big day, would attend morning Mass with his family and friends, and then would prepare for the dubbing ceremony. Here, the candidate would declare his oath of fealty and would then receive a symbolic blow (usually a pretty mighty whack) from his father—symbolically the last knock he should receive. At the end of the ceremony, the new knight would be granted his sword, as blessed by the priest of the chapel, and, after a mighty feast, would be fit to do his honorable work.

A medieval reenactor in the garb of a mighty knight.

The Trials of the Medieval Toilet

In my experience, modern visitors to medieval castles are fascinated by medieval toilet facilities, and the good news is therefore that Goodrich has some of the most complete latrines of any castle in England. In the Middle Ages, such toilets were referred to as *garderobes*—a euphemistic term, as it was the French word for a cupboard or wardrobe. There's a persistent myth that the word originated from a cry of "Guard your robe!" shouted by those using the toilet to anyone in splash distance below, but let's put that wild story to rest. (Conversely, there's some truth in the tale that medieval people used to hang their clothes close to toilets, under the belief that the stench deterred fleas and moths.)

In Goodrich—as in the majority of medieval castles—latrines tended to be cupboard-sized spaces, either built into the thick castle walls or as small outpouchings upon the side of the fortress.

A medieval latrine, a design consistent in castles across Europe. (The iron bars are to prevent curious modern visitors from falling through!)

Bil McKelvie/Shutterstock

They were built in the fabric of the richest residential chambers (for example, into the luxurious environs of Goodrich's northwest tower), and waste generally just dropped downward into a cesspit below. As medieval times advanced, designs grew more sophisticated, and chutes or simple pipes could have been used to discharge the effluent directly into a pit or the moat. Most castle moats would have been truly fetid and, although medieval hygiene was pretty horrifying when judged by modern standards, those in high society would have at least dipped their hands in water before eating a meal.

Goodrich, of course, boasted no moat, but its toilet arrangements were really quite innovative. During the 1450s, part of the East Range was converted into a "guarderobe tower," which functioned as the sewage system for the entire castle. The Toilet Tower—as I prefer to call it—boasted three waste chutes, which fed down to a still-visible waste outlet on the outer wall of the castle. To mitigate the smell—and to keep the chutes unclogged—some poor soul (named, oddly, the "gong farmer") had to shovel the waste away from the bottom outlet into the castle ditch. The next time you have a bad day at work, do remember that things could always be worse.

In fact, there's much more to be thankful for. In medieval times, there was no real conception of personal privacy; almost every aspect of life was communal and that included using the toilet. It wasn't uncommon for a guarderobe to consist of one long wooden bench with multiple holes in it, with no partition to separate yourself from your neighbor. Indeed, although we can't be entirely sure, it appears that the latrine chamber in Goodrich contained two seats to each waste chute—at least you'd never be short of

The front elevation of the castle—the gatehouse is to the right of the photo. Around one-third from the left, you'll see a ruined tower—this is the "toilet tower." If you've got eagle eyes, look for a small hole at the base, just above the rocky foundations—this is the chute for the waste.

someone to chat with while going about your business. If you weren't already dissuaded from time traveling back to medieval times, I should also mention that toilet paper certainly didn't exist yet; however, you'd have the choice between hay, leaves, or moss.

If I haven't entirely grossed you out yet, there's one further icky story on which to end. During the 1203 siege of Château Gaillard (in Upper Normandy, France), the forces attacking the castle discovered a rather innovative route in. Yep, you guessed it right: they climbed up an unguarded garderobe chute, which granted them access to the inner fortress. The castle fell shortly afterward, and the garrison of 140 men were taken prisoner. We can only hope those soldiers who scaled the sewer were suitably rewarded.

This photograph isn't from Goodrich—it's actually from a French castle—but it's a typical medieval guarderobe, poking out from the castle wall.

63

The Ruins of Goodrich, and the English Civil War

The Civil War wrought vast damage upon the castle, but this jagged scar does enable you to understand the thickness of the castle walls.

"I humbly conceive it [Goodrich Castle] as useless," wrote Colonel John Birch in 1646, "and a great burden to the country." His emphasis was clear: Goodrich Castle had to be destroyed.

Being modern castle enthusiasts, we probably don't share Colonel Birch's desire for the utter destruction of Goodrich, but it's possible to empathize with his frustrations. Akin to the siege of Corfe during the English Civil War (see page 160), Goodrich became a flashpoint of conflict between the Royalists and the Parliamentarians and endured six long weeks of hard-fought siege between the two sides.

Unusually, in 1642, it was the Parliamentarians who first garrisoned the castle—English castles were almost invariably held by the Royalist side. It was a particularly strange turn of events when you consider that rural Wales and tranquil Hereford were devoutly loyal to the king, and, likely as a result, the castle was recaptured by the Royalists in early 1644. The Royalist commander, Henry Lingen, made the fortress his headquarters.

Although Lingen had secure hold of Goodrich, he had a faltering grip over the neighboring city of Hereford. In late 1645, despite his best efforts, the city fell to the Parliamentarians. King Charles knighted Lingen in

A replica of an English Civil War cannon—the sort of device that was used to wreak havoc upon castles like Goodrich.

recognition for his bravery during the lost battle, and the newly titled Sir Henry then employed every resource to frustrate and worry the conquering Parliamentarians, while his own forces were still based in Goodrich Castle.

As a consequence of the relentless skirmishes, the leader of the Parliamentarian side—the formidable Colonel John Birch—chose to unleash his wrath upon Goodrich during March 1646. In the pitch-black of the night, his men set a distraction at the castle gates while they scaled the castle walls, stole all the horses, and then torched the stables to the ground. The Parliamentarians then rode elsewhere, thinking that the resistance in Goodrich was over.

Theirs turned out to be a symbolic victory: by no means did it stop Sir Lingen's men from continuing to wreak Royalist havoc in rural Herefordshire. Exasperated,

A vast mortar, similar to the indomitable Roaring Meg.

Colonel Birch rode back to the county in the summer of 1646 and wrote a series of genteel letters to Lingen, kindly suggesting that he should stop what he was doing and surrender the castle. When Sir Henry refused to budge, Colonel Birch responded that he had "really desired your welfare," and signed the final epistle, "In honour, sir, your loving friend. John Birch." The subtext was clear: now, Birch would literally bring out the big guns to break Goodrich.

Indeed, few could have imagined the sort of weaponry to which Birch would resort. The colonel commissioned the construction of a vast mortar—a huge cannon that was, according to Birch's secretary, "the biggest in England," with a 15.5-inch diameter across its barrel. This terrifying machine was nicknamed Roaring Meg (an unexpectedly common name for a Civil War cannon), and the machine was capable of firing 200-pound shells at any unfortunate target. To speed its success, Colonel Birch requested eighty barrels of gunpowder from Parliament—and then set his monster to work on Goodrich Castle.

However resolute the Royalist garrison, and however strong the walls of Goodrich, neither was a match for Roaring Meg. The mortar was merciless—punching vast holes in much of the fabric of Goodrich, but saving special wrath for the northwestern tower (perceived to be the weakest spot of the castle). Folktales tell that Sir Birch was so fond of his pet monster that on July 31, 1646, he personally fired the last nineteen shells at Goodrich before threatening to storm the castle. The Royalists were utterly overcome by the efforts, and Sir Lingen was forced to raise the white flag of surrender.

Birch later wrote that "I thought not fit to grant, neither to give them [Sir Lingen's garrison] any thing beyond mercy for their lives." He ordered them to march out as prisoners, without their firearms, and, as the crowd of 170 left the castle, the Parliamentarian men played a little ditty on makeshift instruments, the tune of which was later known as "Henry Lingen's Folly." The song was apparently used to accompany village dances in southern Herefordshire over the next two hundred years. It has, unfortunately, been lost to time.

Roaring Meg wreaked destruction upon Goodrich, and further slighting took place during the next year. The castle was rendered indefensible and virtually uninhabitable by the actions, becoming the picturesque ruin that exists to today. Despite this—and as a rather amusing twist of fate—the mighty mortar of Roaring Meg similarly withstood the test of time, and now resides within the ruined castle walls. It remains impressive to this day, with a persistent, bristling menace.

Booze and the Buttery

You'll often hear that grand castles boasted their own butteries. This might conjure up images of industrious dairy maids, churning vast amounts of fresh butter to supply the hungry nobles. Well, this may have happened in some castles—but this would have taken place in the dairy. The buttery, counter-intuitively, was the store for alcohol.

The confusion arises because the term *buttery* derives from the French *boutille*, which means "small barrel" or "bottle." The buttery would usually have been a small storeroom adjacent to the Great Hall of the castle and would have been filled with containers of wine and ale. Wine, of course, was the higher-status drink—whereas ale was generally consumed by the lower orders.

Consequently, barrels of beer may have been stored in an underground section of the buttery. Don't forget that medieval water was effectively undrinkable, meaning that the inhabitants of even a small fortress would have consumed significant quantities of drink—making the buttery one of the busiest rooms of any castle.

The location of Goodrich Castle.

Goodrich Castle

Castle Lane, Goodrich, Ross on Wye, Hereford-shire, HR9 6HY

+44 (0)1600 890538

Managed by English Heritage

Official Website: **www.english-heritage.org.uk/daysout/properties/goodrich-castle/**

My Website: **www.exploring-castles.com/goodrich_castle.html**

Open every day in spring and summer; closed most weekdays during winter—check before you travel

The castle literally dominates the town of Dover, which lies beneath it. The Great Keep is clearly visible upon the skyline, but also note the prominence of the Anglo-Saxon church and the old Roman lighthouse. The emblematic white chalk cliffs lie below.

Dover Castle and the Cult of a Murdered Archbishop

Dover Castle was built to resist medieval siege and adapted to survive a nuclear war. It's physically and symbolically the strongest castle in the whole of England and has defended the realm for more than 950 years. Of course, its formidable defenses have adapted over time—morphing from a medieval stronghold to an army control center during World War II, and, most recently, to a nuclear bunker, should a third world war break out.

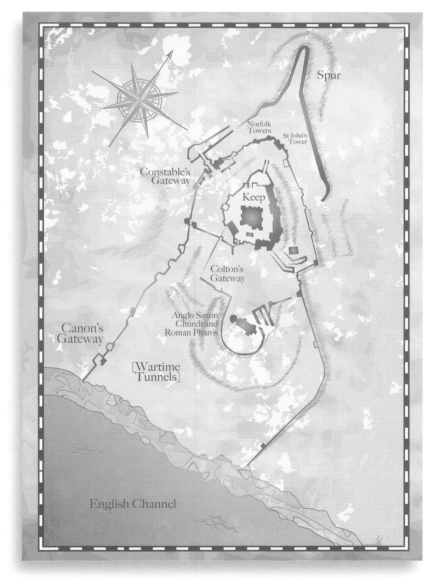

A floor plan of Dover Castle.

Much of Dover's importance stems from its location. The castle is positioned at the narrowest point of the English Channel, where only twenty-one miles of sea separate us from Continental Europe. Although such proximity to France is tantalizing to modern tourists, it was unsettling during medieval times—and frankly terrifying during the German occupation of France in WWII.

On account of its gargantuan size, important position, and symbolic significance, Dover Castle is often called the "key to England"—an epithet coined by chronicler Matthew Paris in the thirteenth century. And although many forces have shaped Dover throughout the years, no man had a greater influence than Henry II—the king who commissioned the Great Keep in 1180. Henry had many reasons to impress with his new Great Keep. But one of these reasons—rather unexpectedly—may have been the gory murder of one of his once-close advisors: Archbishop Thomas Becket.

It's a bloody story of squished brains and prickly personalities. But first, we need to explore the foundations of Dover. After all, it was one of the very first castles in England.

Norman Dover: "The Front Door to England"

Following William the Conqueror's success in the battle of Hastings, the Normans took a rather circuitous route to London. Rather than proceed directly to the capital, William's army took a route resembling a clockwise spiral—first capturing

Dover, and then Canterbury, before traveling through Newbury, Wallingford, Oxford, and then Berkhamstead. They finally reached London on December 25, 1066—more or less two months after their victory in Hastings.

The Normans realized the practical and symbolic importance of securing Dover early in their campaign. Their continued success depended upon the ready supply of men and equipment—and holding a port such as Dover ensured unhindered links to their lands in Northern France.

As a result, the Normans arrived around seven days after their victory at Hastings. And, although Dover was fortified, many sources record that it yielded to the invaders without much of a fight. A cynic would point out that, shortly prior to the Norman arrival, a surprisingly destructive fire mysteriously erupted in a nearby settlement; perhaps this had something to do with Dover's willing surrender.

Even so, the town was quite a prize. Its fortifications were Anglo-Saxon in origin: a large burgh, made of man-made soil embankments, surrounded the outskirts of the habitation, and these mounds had been somewhat heightened in the years prior to 1066. We can't be sure, but there may have even been rudimentary wooden towers positioned atop some of the earthen mounds—a precursor to the later fortifications, which were rendered in stone.

It's commonly said that William and his troops paused in Dover for eight days before proceeding on their conquest. According to William of Poitiers—a Norman chronologer—

English Heritage (red on white flag, top) presently care for the castle.

the pause was chiefly "to add the fortifications which were wanting"—that is to say that it took them slightly more than a week to build the first castle. Others have asserted that the pause was actually due to sickness among William's troops—after all, the first castles in Hastings and Pevensey had been thrown together in more or less a day.

Almost wherever you go in Dover town, the castle is visible; it's equally prominent as you approach England by ferry across the Channel.

Whatever the reason for eight days of respite, the Normans would have sought to crown the fortified burgh of Dover with one of their own motte-and-bailey castles. In all likelihood, this simple wooden citadel would have been built between the Saxon church and the Roman lighthouse (within the confines of the existing curtain walls, although there's little evidence to pinpoint the exact spot). If this first structure was indeed built beside the Roman remains, such positioning was likely purposeful. On many occasions during William's conquest of

England—most notably within the castle of Colchester—he actively sought to build upon Roman remnants, reappropriating the grandeur of past colonizers to his own name.

When William and his forces left Dover to proceed onward with the conquest, they left the castle in the hands of a garrison. Ultimate control of the fortress fell to Bishop Odo, William's half-brother—an unpleasant little man who, in later years, was tried and imprisoned over a mysterious plot to overthrow the

73

pope. Despite his personal failings, the crooked bishop was one of the most powerful men in the whole of Norman England—second in command to King William.

The importance of Bishop Odo's garrison at Dover would be quickly—and amply—demonstrated. In 1067, an anti-Norman rebellion took place within Kent. Put simply, the Anglo-Saxons were not pleased with their new leaders. Indeed, Odo was a particularly harsh and unjust ruler, described as being a "ravening wolf" for others' money and properties. Consequently, the people of Kent appealed to all who would listen in Europe, asking for assistance in over-throwing their Norman overlords.

Indeed, it appears that the Kentish were so desperate for help that they scraped the barrel of European nobility, enlisting the support of Count Eustace of Boulogne. Back in 1051, Eustace had attacked the town of Dover and had killed twenty men while doing so; in 1066, he had fought at the Norman side within the battle of Hastings. Eustace had since fallen out with William the Conqueror—hence his willingness to side with the Kentish rebels—but he was undoubtedly an unnatural ally to their cause.

In the autumn of 1067, Bishop Odo and the majority of his garrison were away from Dover, doing business near London. The Kent locals therefore urged Count Eustace to sail his ships to England, take the castle, and become king in lieu of William. (Clearly, *anyone* was better than the incumbent.)

Although there were few men within the fortification of Dover, its design (and the skill of those inside) overwhelmed

74

The scale and ambition of the outer curtain wall is breath-taking (as is the view, of course!).

Dover Castle, and the town below.

Count Eustace's undisciplined troops and the inexpert locals who had joined them. Eustace "feared a shameful defeat," one chronicler said, and so ordered a hasty retreat. The garrison inside the castle decided to press their advantage and unexpectedly sallied out of one of the gates, causing panic and chaos among the rebels—and a hefty death toll. Count Eustace himself survived the onslaught and fled back to France; his nephew, however, was captured and taken as a political prisoner.

This sorry affair at Dover was the first rebellion against the Norman rule of England—and it was an abject failure. It amply demonstrated the strength and importance of Norman castles. One castle—even a castle with a limited garrison—could comfortably resist an English uprising. Over the next few years, there would be many similar rebellions as the Anglo-Saxons struggled against their new masters. None of these would be successful.

The Transformation of Dover under Henry II

It's time to jump forward more than one hundred years to the reign of Henry II. From 1067 until around 1160, we know very little about what happened to Dover Castle. There's little archaeological evidence for any building work during the period and equally limited documentary evidence of any particular events within the castle. However, after roughly a century of slumber, Dover was to be transformed by King Henry II—one of the most prolific castle builders in the whole of English history.

Henry was a formidable king. His personality was something of a tightly coiled spring; unable to sit still for even the briefest period, Henry restlessly rode the length and breadth of his lands, keeping a close eye upon its everyday governance. His red, wiry hair and sharp features led to many chroniclers

approximately $10,500 (£6,440) on works upon the fortress (likely a tad more, as we know that some records are missing). This was a vast sum of money, as, late in his reign, average annual returns to the exchequer only amounted to around $35,000 (£20,000). The cost of Dover Castle was therefore more than a quarter of the English crown's annual income.

As a consequence of such a sizable financial outlay, Henry got a significant quantity of castle. The works were planned and executed by Maurice the Engineer—one of the greatest castle architects of medieval times and, sadly, a figure who remains mysterious to us today. Maurice oversaw the construction of the walls that form the loop of inner bailey and also part of the outer curtain wall. However, it was the Great Tower—the vast keep at the heart of the inner castle—that represented both Maurice and the king's most remarkable achievement.

Exploring Dover Castle's Great Keep

Even today, the Great Keep is a revelation. It's a mighty tower that stands more than ninety-five feet tall and is wrought out of an imposing gray stone. The external style is rather plain and unadorned—perhaps to cut an intentionally imposing figure or perhaps to form an intentional contrast to the spectacular furnishings held inside.

Today, if you were to walk toward the tower, you might not realize that its footprint is virtually a square—the base of the keep measures ninety-six by ninety-eight feet. Here at ground level, you might also not appreciate that the four external walls of the keep

Henry II of England (1133–1189). Engraved by Bocquet and published in the Catalogue of the Royal and Noble Authors, United Kingdom, 1806.

describing his appearance as "lion-like," and, in old age, he developed bowlegs from spending so much time in the saddle. In the annals of English kings, Henry is recognized as a reformist and pragmatist who renegotiated the royal settlement with the barons, overhauled the justice system, and tried (unsuccessfully, as we will see) to exert some control over the church.

He was also responsible for the construction, or renovation, of a great number of important castles—including Arundel, Hastings, and Kenilworth. But, for some reason, he seems to have held a particular fascination with the construction of Dover. It's documented that Henry spent a minimum of

are quite phenomenally thick, measuring twenty-one feet in width. Owing to medieval building techniques, the walls taper slightly as they ascend, decreasing in width to eighteen feet—a necessary concession to structural integrity. Likewise, a thick cross-wall slices through the middle of the building, so that the inner chambers of the castle are rectangular, rather than square,

The protected entrance to the Great Keep. Walking directly through the visible door leads you into the basement; more distinguished visitors would have taken the stairs (which run through the shadowed area of the photograph) to the grander rooms on the higher levels.

in shape. This cross-wall provides additional structural support, but contains three large mural arches to permit passage between the rooms within the upper levels of the keep.

Standing at the foot of the keep, if your eyes are drawn upward to the perfect-looking crenellations, it's worth mentioning that these (sadly) aren't entirely authentic. In Henry II's time, the tower would have been a little shorter than it stands today. In the 1790s, the ceiling of the upper floor was rebuilt in vaulting brick, designed to support rooftop gun placements installed in the 1800s. (During WWI, anti-aircraft search lights were installed on the keep roof.) In the 1930s, possibly due to a concern that the roof of the tower was no longer "authentic," a project began to incrementally heighten the tops of the walls, perhaps to conceal the architectural devastation of the gun placements. The existing crenellations are part restoration and part reimagination; although they look evocative, they should be appreciated with a pinch of salt.

Raj Krish/Shutterstock

Returning to ground level, the ceremonial entrance to the keep would have been through the squat, rectangular forebuilding, which nestles against the northeastern face of the tower. This forebuilding contained everything a noble might have needed upon reaching Dover after a long trip, including a robing room and a small chapel, used for prayers of thanks for a safe journey. The predominant purpose of this forebuilding was to act as a grand conservatory: the sizeable staircase permitted a noble guest direct access to the state rooms on the second floor of the castle without the need to walk through the basement level (which was most likely used for stores) or the first floor (which was most likely used as the garrison).

The feeling of ascending directly to the second floor would have been the medieval equivalent of turning left to the business class cabin when boarding an international flight. "Economy" status guests would most likely have entered via the lower level and ascended to higher levels of the keep using one of the two 114-step spiral staircases positioned at the south and north corners of the building.

Despite such grandeur, the forebuilding was not solely designed to provide an elegant entrance. Like the rest of the keep, it was a sensational marriage of luxury and defense. The ascending passageway through the forebuilding was fortified by two gate-towers and a drawbridge, with a further, final gate at the main entrance to the tower. Positioning the main entrance above ground level was a crucial design trick, as it protected the wooden door from being beaten down by a battering ram. Another defensive feature was the absence of a roof over the ascending stairs; this open-air arrangement allowed archers to easily pick off any unwanted guests. (It's worth noting that during the Tudor period, many of these features of medieval defense were adapted or removed in response to the castle blossoming into something that more resembled a palace.)

Let's imagine that we were noble guests of 1190, ascending those forebuilding stairs in peacetime, about to enjoy a state visit to the keep. What would we have found within? Well, a $4.05 million (£2.5 million) recent restoration project by the curators of Dover

The spectacular restored interior of the Great Keep, replete with grand tapestries and elegant hangings.

fires flicker in the grand fireplaces. On the ground floor of the keep lies an expansive medieval kitchen, where cooks would have prepared spit-roast game and fresh saltwater fish for the guests upstairs. But the centerpiece of all this grandeur is the decadent, central throne room, with its noble, five-foot-tall blue throne, backed by a vast crimson and gold tapestry of a snarling lion.

It's quite obvious that this luxuriant interior and spectacular exterior were intended to impress any noble visitor to Dover. But the central question remains: Why did Henry II choose to lavish money on building it all *here*, as opposed to any other site in England? Why suddenly resurrect a castle that had been studiously ignored for more than a century?

Modern scholars have argued that the answer to this puzzle lies in a small enclave on the second floor of the castle. Boasting an ornate vaulted ceiling and richly decorated walls, this little sanctuary is a chapel dedicated to a recently canonized medieval saint—the murdered Thomas Becket.

Castle, English Heritage, answers that question most effectively: King Henry II's keep would have been a riot of medieval colors—yellows, blues, and reds of eye-popping vibrancy.

Today's restoration is true to extravagant, eclectic medieval taste: the keep walls are covered by fabrics and bedecked in tapestry, sinuous embroidered drapes hang from the ceilings, and the soft beds are dressed with feather-fluffed pillows and rabbit-fur blankets. Vast, creaky oak doors separate the chambers, crouching lions are carved into wooden furniture, and log

The Bloody Death of Thomas Becket

It was a horrendous death, even by medieval standards. Not content with just stabbing the archbishop at the altar, one knight hacked clean through the victim's skull. The final assailant stood on the neck of the corpse and stepped down, hard—squirting brains and blood across the sacred floor of Canterbury Cathedral. "We can leave this place, Knights," this final tormentor then gloated, no doubt with gore-stained boots. "He will not get up again."

Golden engraving depicting the murder of Thomas Becket, taken from a French reliquary.

It's no exaggeration to say that the violent death of Thomas Becket sent shockwaves through medieval Europe. What made the blood-stained episode all the more sensational was that the murder, every whisper said, had been commissioned by the king. The entire messy affair was a personal and political disaster for Henry II—and it would take every ounce of his political skill to rehabilitate his shredded reputation.

First, a bit more about the victim, Archbishop Thomas Becket. Becket was born in 1118, the son of an up-and-coming family of merchants. He had enjoyed a good education, rudely cut short when his father's business burned to the ground. Tall, pale, ambitious, and exceptionally good at dealing with details, he quickly rose to become Archdeacon of Canterbury.

80

It was there he met King Henry II. It was an unlikely pairing, but the two men immediately hit it off, and Becket became Henry's right-hand man—taking care of the minutiae that this broad-brush, big-ideas king tended to miss.

So how did a best friend transform into a potential murder victim? The friction between king and king's hand began when Henry made the mistake of overpromoting Becket, in 1162, to the position of archbishop of Canterbury. Henry's motivations were logical but misguided. Becket had been invaluable to him in smoothing the path of governing the country. But the king still clashed all too frequently with the Church—with each accusing the other of becoming over-mighty. If he promoted his friend to a high position in the Church, Henry reasoned, such conflicts would be solved.

Not so—in fact, Henry had made two fundamental misjudgments. The first was Becket's legitimacy for the role of archbishop, as he was neither a priest nor a bishop. No problem for a king like Henry II—with one swoop of his hand, he made Becket a priest one day and a bishop the very next. The technicalities were dealt with, but Becket nurtured a persistent sense that he was an outsider, resented by the flock of clergy beneath him.

Henry's second mistake was to gravely misunderstand his friend's pysche. Becket was details obsessed and a stickler for rules. This hadn't been a problem when he had worked for Henry—he simply dotted the i's that his master had missed. As archbishop, however, he was in charge of an organization that vied with the monarchy for power over the English people. Rather than roll over and accept what his

B.S. Karan/Shutterstock

A replica trebuchet stands beside the Great Keep; although these mighty machines were rightly feared during the medieval period, it looks rather puny in comparsion to these vast, thick walls.

king wanted, Becket chose to play exactly to the rules—using his position to challenge and scrutinize the king.

Becket's enthusiasm for orthodoxy probably arouse, too, from something of an inferiority complex. He probably wanted to prove to his bishops and clergy that he wasn't just a stooge to Henry, and he relished challenging, debating, and nit-picking every single issue as a matter of proud independence. To Henry, however, this about-turn from pliant assistant to spiky adversary was utterly incomprehensible. Literally overnight, Becket had transformed from the king's closest advisor to an infuriating thorn in his side.

The relationship was to worsen even further. Both men were known for their haughty pride and intractable stubbornness. Now that they had cause to disagree—and this was something

81

that happened with alarming frequency—the duo managed to entrench themselves in opposing positions, grinding the wheels of governance to a halt.

By 1164, the situation was at its breaking point. After one of their characteristic squabbles—which had even involved an appeal to the pope—Henry claimed victory, and, rather than win graciously, chose to make Becket look like a fool in front of his own flock. It was too much for Becket to bear. He voluntarily exiled himself to France for six years, where he tortured himself with cold baths and sack-cloth clothing and wrote self-serving, petulant letters about his mistreatment by Henry II to pretty much every notable in Europe.

Perhaps out of guilt—or sheer boredom with the long-running conflict—Henry attempted to call peace in 1169,

but Becket, with his intractable stubbornness, scuppered the chance of reconciliation. This broken peace deal did, however, embolden Becket to return to England, where he immediately waded into another ecclesiastic mess, condemning a group of bishops who'd participated in a ceremony dedicated to King Henry's son.

On hearing this news, Henry II is said to have uttered that infamous rhetorical question: "Oh, who will rid me of this meddlesome priest?" It was a lesson that one should never speak in jest. Very soon, four knights plus an assistant rode down from Yorkshire and slaughtered Becket in cold blood.

Henry almost certainly never meant to have Becket murdered. And even if he had, it's pretty unthinkable that he would have sent a troop of men to slice up an archbishop in a cathedral, while the monks chanted evening vespers. The knights were probably working on an assumption that their king would have them rewarded for their services; instead, Henry was as aghast at the brutality as the rest of Europe. It's said that, on hearing the news, he locked himself away in his chamber for three days and spoke to no one. Realizing they had made a grotesque mistake, the knights then ran into hiding. Rather than serving their king, they had plunged his reign into a dire political crisis.

Indeed, quite quickly, most of England perceived Henry to be a murderer. Such animosity even extended to the continent where, it's said, the pope refused to even speak to an Englishman for weeks after Becket's death. For a while, it even appeared that Henry would be unable to continue as king of England. But the monarch dealt with the crisis in a

An illustration of the murder of Thomas Becket taken from an 1864 book.

typically shrewd manner. Henry decided to keep a low profile—leaving England to attend to "pressing" affairs in Ireland, hoping that time and absence would help heal the wounds.

Despite Henry's best efforts to forget the sorry affair, however, the scandal of Becket's death didn't appear to be going anywhere. Miracles were said to have occurred upon the spot where Becket died, and a Becket-worshipping cult accordingly emerged from the woodwork. Thousands of pilgrims trooped to Canterbury Cathedral every year to pay their respects, and the archbishop became canonized as a saint. We can only imagine Henry's frustration. The cult of Becket undermined his position as monarch.

Henry realized he needed to gain the upper hand over the specter of this endlessly troublesome priest. In 1174, with his characteristic savvy, he chose to make his own, very public, pilgrimage to Becket's shrine at Canterbury, some four years after the archbishop's murder. It was an intentionally theatrical affair. Henry traipsed all the way to Canterbury barefoot; he invited each of the cathedral's seventy monks to flog him (three lashes for each monk, five for each prelate), and he then spent a cold, uncomfortable night crouching beside the tomb, reciting psalms and prayers without a single break.

The very next day, something quite incredible happened: Henry's long-term nemesis, King William of Scotland, was captured at Alnwick, a town on the border of Scotland and England. For the rationally minded, it was a sensationally serendipitous turn of events—but most of Medieval England interpreted this as a message from God that Henry had been forgiven.

But Henry wasn't going to stop there: he was one who would press home his advantage. Becket was still remembered and revered as a man who died standing up to the king. To really cement his control over England, Henry needed to reappropriate the image of Becket for himself. Under the guise of continued piety and penance—but likely with the real political intention of controlling popular memory of the martyr—Henry built the image of Becket into the very fabric of Dover Castle. That troublesome priest was to become a symbol of the status quo.

B.S. Karan/Shutterstock

Window detail upon the Great Keep. Evidently, this is a modern addition.

A Very British Misconception

The story of troublesome Becket is well-known across England. As a result, you'll find pubs, streets, and tourist shops bearing his name; although, rather curiously, you might see it rendered as "Thomas à Becket." (You'll often hear people use that *à* when saying his name and—shudder—you might even spot it in a history book or two.)

So, where did this mystery *à* come from?! Well, Becket was never known as Thomas à Becket during his lifetime. The *à* is a strange verbal tic, which appears to have been adopted by renaissance writers who were inspired by another monk named Thomas who enjoyed that fancy *à*.

The intention of those writers appears to have been to make Becket sound a bit grander than he really was— meaning the added *à* is entirely a falsehood. Reading it aloud, however, does give his name a pleasing ring and is perhaps why this rather odd mutilation has persisted for the last few hundred years.

Thomas Becket's name is commonly, and incorrectly, rendered "Thomas à Becket" throughout the United Kingdom.

Building Becket into Dover Castle

Canterbury is a short distance from Dover: about eighteen miles, as the crow flies. The town was rapidly emerging as a holy hotspot for pilgrims anxious to pay their respects to Becket, and, as such, the place was beginning to prove a

political problem for Henry II. Indeed, from 1175, the monks of Canterbury Cathedral—who were emboldened by the growing antimonarchical sentiment and enriched by the donations of the pious—rapidly set to extend and aggrandize their magnificent church, adding the glorious Trinity Chapel and Corona as a very visible shrine to their fallen archbishop.

The onion-skin layers of defense would have made Dover close to impenetrable. There's one line of walls around the keep that forms the Inner Bailey; also note the outer ring of curtain walls that front onto the steep hillside slopes.

The rolling Kent countryside surrounding the castle is a spectacular place for a walk.

Of course, such structures had symbolism beyond the simple memory of Becket. Canterbury was beginning to exemplify the strength and preeminence of the Church over the English monarchy. Whereas Henry had sought to clip the wings of religion by appointing Becket in the first place, the reverence of the deceased archbishop was helping the Church assert moral superiority over the English monarchy.

Henry's headache was to worsen as the shrine attracted international attention. In 1177, Philip I, Count of Flanders, decided he'd like to travel to England and pay a visit to the priest's tomb, and Henry could do little but accompany him. When Philip wished to return to France, he then had to pass through Dover, and, there, Henry could only offer embarrassingly poor accommodation within which his guest could spend the night.

Things were to get even more awkward in 1179 when the terminally ill King Louis VII of France decided he'd like to pay his last respects to Becket. Again, following Louis's pilgrimage to the glorious surroundings of Canterbury Cathedral, Henry had little to offer his most-distinguished guest but some rather shoddy accommodations close to the port of Dover. It would have been plainly obvious that the memory of the long-dead archbishop was still able to upstage this floundering king, and this, of course, would not do. As a result,

85

barely a year later, Henry II commissioned the development of Dover's Great Keep.

It bears mentioning that there were other castles in Kent that Henry could have chosen to extend, aggrandize, or rebuild. There was (and still is) a castle in Canterbury, for example, and Henry could quite happily have chosen to devote his attentions to souping up this spot. However, the king probably realized that such efforts would have been insensitive and obvious. Dover was close enough to Canterbury to deflect attentions from Becket's shrine, but far enough away to maintain an aura of good taste.

As a result, construction of the Great Keep of Dover began in 1180—five years after the monks at Canterbury started work

The Great Keep stands more than 95 feet tall. Impressive today, it would have been a sensation during the time of Henry II.

A reading seat within a window recess in the Great Keep. It's a deep alcove, giving some sense of the tremendous thickness of the keep walls—around 18 feet at this section of the tower.

upon their cathedral. In the design and construction of his ostentatious new fortress, Henry sought to render in stone everything the English monarchy stood for: order, grandeur, glory, and ceremony. It was an obvious riposte to what those religious men were doing down the road. But there were other advantages to the location of Dover beyond its sheer one-upmanship. Its coastal position meant the new tower would serve as a dramatic welcome to England, and its chambers would be a luxurious abode for any distinguished traveler arriving from the continent.

Henry's masterstroke, however, was to appropriate the imagery of Becket within the very walls of his castle. Upon the second floor of the Great Keep, he commissioned a small chapel dedicated to the memory of the fallen archbishop. Architecturally, the chapel bears great similarity to Canterbury Cathedral: it has a grand, ribbed, vaulted ceiling and decorative chevrons that run across the chancel. It boasts, too, a tiny nave, and a diminutive adjacent alcove was likely designated as a Royal Pew—the perfect spot for a conspicuously pious king.

Under the guise of piety, Henry therefore had absorbed the image of Becket into his monument to monarchical power. The power of the Church was symbolically subsumed to the authority of the state: a masterstroke of a particularly canny king. Dover would not only be able to receive distinguished guests in luxury but it would also demonstrate to the world that Henry was a man firmly in charge of England. The king had brought his old friend back into the fold.

A Vast and Mighty Fortress

Dover Castle is gargantuan: one of the few castles in England that requires an entire day to explore properly. For clarity and brevity in this book, I've chosen to focus on the jewel in its crown: the Great Keep at the heart of the fortress. But there's much more to Dover: a profusion of towers, turrets, and protective walls; a Roman lighthouse; and an officers' barracks.

These sheer slopes would have made it desperately difficult for any assailant to the fortress. Note that the visible windows, and the brickwork beneath the arch, were added in the nineteenth century.

The entire fortress is situated upon "castle knoll," a naturally raised spur of land. The southern boundary of the spur is formed by the emblematic white cliffs of Dover; the western side of castle knoll falls down into a steep valley, where you'll encounter the modern town.

This fortuitous spur measures around one thousand yards from north to south and five hundred yards from east to west. The entire castle is enclosed within a mighty curtain wall, studded with evocatively named towers, from Godsfoe to Avranches.

At the northernmost point of the spur (that is to say, the furthest point from the cliffs), the castle tapers into a point like the bow of a ship. This face was once the weakest aspect of the castle, but it was transformed in the early 1200s into a truly formidable defensive barrier. The old northern entrance was bricked up, forming the present Norfolk Towers, and a round satellite tower—St John's Tower—was built in the moat. An underground passageway allowed men to pass between the towers out of the range of enemies and allowed an unprecedented field of attack while aiming arrows from atop the satellite tower.

The curtain walls of the castle enclose another interesting sight: the old Roman "pharos," built in

The spectacular Roman Lighthouse and the adjacent Ango-Saxon church, with its cruciform shape. The church was extensively restored in 1862 after previously being used as a coal-store.

approximately the second century AD. Today, it stands much shorter than its original height, and its uneven flint finish forms a dramatic contrast to the delicate stonework of the Church of St. Mary-in-Castro, built not a foot to the east. The Church of St. Mary was Anglo-Saxon in origin and is cruciform in shape; it sadly decayed considerably following the Saxon period and, in the early 1800s, was used as a coal-store. The church was painstakingly restored from 1862 onward, a delicate soul amidst the rougher stone walls of the rest of the fortress.

Skipping through the centuries, a smattering of nineteenth-century military buildings stud the enclosure of Dover, attesting to the significance of the fortress during modern warfare. Such buildings include the officers' barracks and admiralty lookout, the radar base at the cliff's edge, and the antiaircraft gun emplacements. An Englishman's home is his castle, and, for many troops stationed in the fortress, the castle literally became their home. As a result, the silhouette of Dover assumed a symbolic significance for members of the forces returning to England—visible from afar as they sailed across the Channel.

The view from the top of the Great Keep, looking down onto the triangular spur of the castle.

Going Underground: The Hidden Strength of Dover

Not many fortresses in the Western world can claim to have safeguarded their country for more than 950 years. Indeed, the majority of castles in England had no real defensive purpose after the end of the medieval period. A smattering of castles (including Corfe and Goodrich, as featured elsewhere in this book) assumed some role in the English Civil War of the 1640s. Dover's status—as the guardian of a country for almost a millennium—is truly remarkable.

Curiously, however, Dover's strength comes as much from its mighty walls as from the ground that lies below it. The towering "white cliffs of Dover" plunge into the English Channel and are a clue that the soil here is

The Anglo-Saxon Church and Roman Lighthouse can be seen in the top left corner. The more modern building, in the foreground, is one of a selection added during the nineteenth century, when Dover Castle became a military garrison.

formed primarily of soft white chalk. It's a friable, pliable material and is easy to dig down into.

On a couple of occasions, the fine soil has been a defensive disadvantage to Dover. During the 1216 Great Siege of the castle, Prince Louis and the French forces discovered that the best threat to the fortress was to burrow beneath the northern barbican and then underneath the eastern gate tower. Their subterranean offensive meant that vast chunks of the castle walls tumbled to the ground—leading to frantic efforts to defend Dover using tree trunks and sheer force.

From that moment on, those inside the castle realized the defensive potential of going deeper underground. Hubert de Burgh immediately set out to build a complicated series of underground tunnels connecting a series of new defenses—linking the new Norfolk Towers to the satellite of St John's Tower (see "A Vast and Mighty Fortress," page 87).

In 1797, however, the technique of tunneling truly came into its own. Faced with a new French threat in the shape of the Napoleonic wars, the Royal Engineers burrowed deep into the grounds of the castle, building a barracks fit for two thousand men.

Constable's Gateway, built between 1221 and 1227 to strengthen the approach to the castle. The gateway is a profusion of five towers, designed to give the maximum possible field of vision over any intruder. The gateway was somewhat redeveloped in the late 1800s, explaining why the windows don't look in the slightest bit medieval.

Andrzej Sowa/Shutterstock

This first web of underground passages came to be known by a code name—Casemate. From 1941 onward—when Britain was most gravely threatened by Nazi invasion of World War II—two subsequent levels of tunnels were added. One, named Annexe, was constructed at a higher level within the cliff; the next, Dumpy, was dug even deeper underground.

This multilevel maze of underground tunnels is dark, confusing, and extremely claustrophobic. It's said that English Heritage, the present-day managers of the castle, have been unable to map every twist and turn of the network. Others whisper of long-concealed tunnels that hold classified state security secrets.

Whatever the truth, this underground lair would have been a perpetually gloomy home to many brave servicemen. Its fear-inducing underground hospital could have treated hundreds in cramped conditions, and its profusion of bunk beds, radio-transmitters, and army and naval control rooms became the setting for one of the bravest missions of British wartime: the 1940 evacuation of Dunkirk.

Operation Dynamo—as the mission was code-named—was a desperate rush to evacuate Allied troops from France in the face of an inexorable German advance. Later hailed as a miracle of deliverance, the mission originally sought to rescue 40,000 men—in actual fact,

The location of Dover Castle.

more than 330,000 were repatriated by a flotilla of ships, some as simple as citizen-sailed fishing boats. The entire operation was coordinated from the darkened bowels of Dover Castle, as war raged in the sky above.

The evacuation of Dunkirk is one of the golden achievements of British history: a time when volunteers and citizens pulled together for communal good. In the 1960s, however, a new man-made horror threatened the world: nuclear war. Foreseeing a nuclear strike that would wipe out London, the British government designated the tunnels to be a seat of power for a region of postapocalyptic Britain. This makeshift bunker was equipped with an air-purifying device, a generator with fuel, and vast stores of food and water. It was also to contain a broadcast chamber for BBC radio to inform and educate what was left of the nation. We can only be thankful that it never needed to be used.

Dover Castle

Castle Hill, Dover, Kent, CT16 1HU
+44 (0)1304 211 067
Managed by English Heritage
Official Website: **www.english-heritage.org.uk/daysout/properties/dover-castle/**
Official Facebook: **www.facebook.com/EHDover-Castle**
My Website: **www.exploring-castles.com/dover_castle.html**
Open every day in spring and summer; closed most weekdays during winter—check before you travel

David Hughes/Shutterstock

Tintagel Castle, and the Legend of King Arthur

A cold sea air swirls around the remains of Tintagel. The rough stone castle walls crouch low against the cruel weather: huddling over secrets long lost or legends too-soon forgotten.

Of what little we know about Tintagel (and the reality is, it's surprisingly little) we can confidently say that the place is less a castle and more a legend rendered in failing rubble. Indeed, if you were flicking through this book and trying to pick the odd-castle-out, Tintagel is undoubtedly the sore thumb: it never housed any noble family, it certainly never defended itself in siege, and no moment of major historical importance ever played out within its walls.

Tintagel's setting is rough and rugged; a profusion of bridges and staircases connect the various sections of the castle. Erosion may eventually make some of these parts impassable.

A floor plan of Tintagel Castle.

Quite rightly, then, you might be wondering if my inclusion of Tintagel is the proof required that I've finally lost it. If it's not architecturally much of a castle, and it was never the site of anything that castle-y, then why feature Tintagel in a book about English castles? The answer is that Tintagel is a solid-stone rendering of the legend of King Arthur—layers of folklore and literary tradition have created something as close to Camelot as anything you'll find on earth.

95

Of course, there was—and still is—something of a castle at Tintagel, alongside a plethora of remains from the Dark Ages and a palpable sense of history. However, it's the expectant aura of mystery that tends to grab tourists and produces such eulogistic accounts of almost every visit. Some have claimed that the site boasts spiritual significance; die-hard rationalists like me believe that the stunning natural setting and 1,500 years of history are responsible for bowling people over.

To truly understand Tintagel, you need to know a little more about the creation of the cult of King Arthur, a figure who, I guess, you'll know a little about already. But first, it's important to delve into the spectacular Cornish setting of the fortress and its strategic importance within Britain's Dark Ages.

The Salt-Soaked Setting of Tintagel

Cornwall isn't like the rest of England. The county boasts its own Celtic language (Cornish, of course) and proud black flag, etched with a distinctive white cross. In part, you might reason its fierce independence from just glancing at a map: Cornwall sticks out from the rest of the country like the point of a boot. It is a sea-splashed peninsula most famous for trawler-net fishing, crab catching, tin mining, and sunny childhood holidays.

Choppy seas have nurtured the indomitable Cornish identity, and these rough waters still break against its 422 miles of shoreline. The coast itself is spectacular: rough and rocky, pocked with protected bays and windswept bluffs. Fingers of

The black and white flag of Cornwall.

rock reach from the main headlands into the turbulent seas beyond, with the spaces between them render into sheltered coves and protected bays.

Tintagel is situated on one such rocky outcrop, poking out from the northern Cornish shoreline. From simply studying the geography of the area, it's easy to fathom the early importance of Tintagel: the peninsula offers the perfect mix of defensive strength and trading potential, with rough seas to the north and south but a sheltered bay ("the haven") tucked into the eastern aspect. Modern academics think that there's evidence for limited late Roman occupation of the land, but the first real settlement developed during the Dark Ages (500–700 AD). The now-ruined castle was built during the 1200s.

The relentless erosion of the sea explains the somewhat scattered and disparate appearance of the existing castle remains. In medieval times, the castle entrance was located upon the mainland, and the fortification stretched along the peninsula. The thinnest section of the peninsula was at its neck, giving the castle a natural defensive advantage; should an attacker break through the exterior entrance, the narrow rocky isthmus leading to the central courtyard would have been easy to obstruct or to defend.

Over the past seven hundred years, however, the sea has eaten away this rocky causeway, removing the continuity that once existed between the two sections of the fortress. As a result, many modern visitors may not realize that Tintagel was once seated upon a peninsula; it appears that the castle is scattered

The Upper Courtyard of Tintagel Castle, situated on the mainland side. This defensive shell is the most intact section of the castle, although many of the buildings once within the courtyard have since eroded away or tumbled into the sea.

Andreas Juergensmeier/Shutterstock

across a small island and the adjacent shoreline, with a 1970s bridge connecting the two sections.

The ceaseless, erosive power of the sea is a recurring theme when exploring Tintagel. From the photographs upon these pages, it should be abundantly clear that the fortress is extensively sea-worn and ruinous; in parts, the castle is reduced to little more than ragged walls of piled rubble. The most complete sections (and I speak comparatively!) are probably the upper and lower courtyards, which nestle alongside the castle entrance on the mainland.

These connecting courtyards appear to have had a primarily domestic purpose and so would once have been filled with the comings and goings of medieval castle life. Although there's limited evidence of it today, both courtyards are likely to have contained timber residences, and stone latrines are built into some of the sea-facing walls. The upper courtyard boasts the largest and most complete wall in all of Tintagel: a sweeping defensive shell that faces the mainland and would have proved a barrier to attack. Despite the apparent completeness of this one wall, the present-day appearance of both courtyards is far removed from their medieval shape and size: significant sections of both have fallen into the sea.

From the lower courtyard, one can cross the bridge to the island, where you'll encounter what would once have been the heart of the castle: the Island Courtyard. The courtyard was home to the Great Hall and other accommodations, and the entrance would have been guarded by a grand gate tower. Many of these buildings have since slipped into the sea; the majority of the gate tower, chunks of the Great Hall, and even

97

To the right, in the foreground, you can see the shell of the Upper Courtyard on the mainland. It hunches away from the approaching road, serving to protect the entrance to the castle complex. The bridge (mid photo) runs to the Island Courtyard, where you can just make out some of the remnants of the fortress.

the old pantry and buttery have tumbled into the oceans. Only evocative sections remains intact, such as the ragged stone gateway, which once communicated with the gate tower.

Outside of the Island Courtyard, you'll discover much more upon the little peninsula, including a worn, part-medieval chapel and cold, dark cave, once assumed to be a larder for the castle kitchens. However, the island is most intriguing for its plethora of low-stone remains, now covered in dense grass that rustles in the sea winds. Ever mysterious and incompletely excavated, these ruins date to the Dark Ages and are fundamen-

tal to understanding some of the secrets of Tintagel and help explain why a medieval castle was built here in the first place.

The Dark Age Remains of Tintagel, and the Myth of King Arthur

Dark Age remains are scattered across the island of Tintagel. In the majority, these remains form rough geometric shapes: stretched squares and elongated rectangles of rough stone foundations, which nowadays reach just ankle height.

Some of the numerous Dark Age remains that are scattered across the Tintagel island. These remains generally reach to ankle height and are thought to be the foundations of old buildings.

Andreas Juergensmeier/Shutterstock

The present archeological assumption is that these remains represent the foundations of long-lost buildings; their walls and roofs were likely formed of rough stone or hewn timber and have melted away over the last 1,500 years.

Nowadays, the primary puzzle is to establish the exact nature of this Dark Age settlement. In the 1930s, archeologists assumed these weathered remains were part of an early monastery; evidence was derived from Christian crosses etched upon surviving shards of pottery. In modern years, however, researchers have been able to analyze the composition of such pottery in more depth. Detailed studies have suggested that some of these pots were wine jars originating in the Mediterranean; others were oil jars that came from the North Coast of Africa. The resultant theory is that Tintagel was a trading post and port with maritime links to much of Europe; native Cornish goods (perhaps including tin) would likely have been exchanged for these foreign luxuries.

Despite its assumed prosperity, this early settlement at Tintagel appears to have collapsed between 600 and 700 AD. We don't know the exact reason for its failure: perhaps the withering of trade links or the collapse of a local power system. (There's some evidence that Tintagel may have been a place of renown in Dumnonia, an early kingdom of the English southern counties.) Whatever the cause, the site quickly fell into decay and ruin and captured the imagination of one medieval author, writing around five hundred years later.

The author in question was Geoffrey of Monmouth, creator of the 1136 *Historia Regum Britanniae (The History of the Kings)*. His book purported itself to be a sweeping, academic history of the British people; the reality was that it was a cunning hybrid of historical snippets and wild legends (see boxout, page 101). Nonetheless, this text was the first to tell the story of King Arthur to the medieval masses, and our wily author imbued the tall tale with enough historical nuggets to make the whole thing seem factually plausible. Geoffrey had paid a visit to the Dark Age remains at Tintagel (or, at least, knew someone who had) and conjured these remnants to be the long-forgotten fortress of a dastardly villain named Gorlois. In Geoffrey's telling of the now-famous tale, the then-king of Britain, Uther Pendragon, manages to sneak into Gorlois's fortress using the magic of Merlin. He then seduces Gorlois's wife, Ygraine, and the pair conceive Arthur.

Surviving rough stone buildings, which likely had a domestic purpose. Many of these were built upon the Dark Age remains that were scattered across the area.

It was Geoffrey's work of fiction that made the first connection between Arthur and Tintagel, and we might wonder why he chose this particular spot to be the place of the king's birth. The answer is likely more straightforward than you'd imagine: Geoffrey was probably as seduced by Tintagel as any modern visitor. With its stunning natural backdrop and ancient ruins (and remember that medieval people would have perceived Dark Age ruins to be ancient!), Tintagel probably felt as mystical to an early modern author as it does to a twenty-first-century tourist.

Nonetheless, it's important to emphasize that there's no factual or anecdotal evidence that can otherwise link anyone called Arthur to this place in Cornwall. Even so, this hasn't stopped the conspiracy theorists from working overtime. As recently as 1998, the international media was briefly gripped by an Arthurian frenzy following the discovery of an intriguing

fragment of slate upon the eastern aspect of Tintagel Island. A number of names are scratched, graffiti-style, into the surface of the stone; one of those included is Artognou. According to one of the experts who discovered the stone, it was the "find of a lifetime."

Seeing as the name Artognou looks a bit like Arthur, the British media (and Arthurian enthusiasts worldwide) decided that two plus two equals twenty-two, and that the stone finally proved the link between a fabled Arthur and the Dark Age ruins at Tintagel. The reality is that the stone proves nothing of the sort, as Artognou was a common Celtic name (and, in any case, there were plenty of other Celtic names that began with A-r-t). Indeed, the so-called Artognou stone, although interesting, would have been consigned to a historical footnote if not for its semantic coincidence. The whole event highlights the danger of imposing modern expectations upon historical evidence.

The path leads up to the Island Courtyard (mid photo). As you can see, the island is made up of quite sheer, steep slopes; much of the castle has since tumbled into the sea.

The Makings of a Legend: The Origins of King Arthur

Low tide in The Haven, alongside the castle. According to Alfred, Lord Tennyson, this is where Merlin plucked the baby Arthur from the foaming sea.

Today, you'd be ridiculed for believing that the stories of King Arthur, Queen Guinevere, and Lancelot are factually true. Modern audiences understand the tales of Arthur to be the work of romantic folklore—medieval legends, well-worn over time.

In early modern times, however, King Arthur was palpably real. Arthur was revered as an exemplary king of Britain who had, many years before, ruled the territories of the British Isles with strength, wisdom, and courage. To contemporary Englanders, Arthur was as real a monarch as King Henry II or William the Conqueror. Although a medieval cynic might doubt some of the taller tales of Arthur's achievements, he would never dream of questioning the *existence* of this legendary king.

Nowadays, conversely, you might struggle to find any evidence that Arthur even existed. The legends most commonly assert that Arthur's glorious exploits took place between 500 and 600 AD; historians, on the other hand, haven't uncovered any evidence for a king or knight of this name. The suggestion (which we may still need to whisper rather quietly) was that Arthur was a creation of folklore. Rather than being a figure of British history, Arthur was a legendary character to whom historical details were later attached. To use the correct lingo, he was historicized.

So where did these Arthurian legends spring from in the first place? Well, like many of the greatest things in the modern United Kingdom, the Arthurian myth originated from Wales (my arm was twisted to say this—my partner's from Cardiff). In the old Welsh oral tradition, Arthur was a tremendous warrior who fought the Anglo-Saxons (a real threat to the early Welsh) alongside dragons, mystical boar, and monsters with the heads of cats and dogs (likely less real). Although Arthur would have been well-known in Welsh folklore, he would have been relatively unheard of within England until the breakout success of a rather devious book: Geoffrey of Montgomery's *History of the Kings of Britain*.

The *Historia Regum Britanniae*, to give it its Latin title, described the history of Britain before the arrival of the Normans and was, according to the author, based upon a secret Celtic document that he could share with no one else. The book was an instant publishing sensation, spawning 215 surviving medieval manuscripts (only the Bible boasts more), and Geoffrey's stories captured the imagination of most of England.

As you might have guessed from the author's preposterous claim of a "secret lost manuscript," the text was firmly a work of fiction. Although Geoffrey seasoned his book with just enough historical detail to make things look plausibly accurate, the reality was that the text was a lengthy fable of imaginary kings and impossible occurrences. This didn't stop most of Medieval England from swallowing the entire thing as fact—but, to be fair, scholars didn't realize that the book wasn't an entirely accurate historical source until the sixteenth century, and modern academies still struggle to sift the nuggets of truth from the swathes of fiction.

Some sections of the Island Courtyard survive, but, over the years, vast sections have fallen into the sea.

A view of The Haven, the sheltered bay on the north side of the island. You can see the entrance to Merlin's Cave within the rock face.

Of all the characters featured within Geoffrey's medieval con-trick, however, Arthur is undoubtedly the most notable. Geoffrey's epic is split into twelve books, and the exploits of Arthur and associates pretty much fill books eight to twelve. Within these tales, Geoffrey positions Arthur as a British monarch of the 500s and 600s and introduces the characters of Merlin, Uther Pendragon, and Guinevere. During the text, Arthur battles first against the Anglo-Saxons and later against the evil of his nephew Mordred, who, during book twelve, inflicts severe wounds upon our hero. As a result, Arthur is shipped off to the mysterious Isle of Avalon, where, rather than dying and passing to the underworld, he slumbers gracefully, waiting rise again—the once and future king.

Although Geoffrey's work was the first Arthurian text, it was by no means the last. The story of King Arthur ignited the imagination of western Europe, and the king became the focus of innumerable stories of medieval romance. These later tales added new details to the emerging legend—they introduced Knight Lancelot, the sword Excalibur, and the all-enduring round table. Within them, the character of Arthur mutated slowly; whereas Geoffrey's Arthur was but a ferocious warrior, the Arthur of medieval romance was a wise and kind king who let his array of knights do the fighting for him.

Building the Legend of Arthur: The Castle at Tintagel

In the mid-1200s, Richard, Earl of Cornwall, rendered the myth of Arthur into physical existence. Richard was born in 1209, the second son of King John. His brother—barely fifteen months older than him—would soon become King Henry III of England following his father's death in 1216.

We don't know a great deal about Richard. He was, by some accounts, a sickly child, whose tutors focused upon lessons of diplomacy and accountancy rather than upon physical strength and warfare. We can assume that he was a reasonably bright

The castle is built from locally quarried stone and slate. Although some outer walls exist, many of the inner buildings appear to have been temporary wooden huts.

scholar, given that Richard was one of a tiny minority of medieval English barons who could actually speak English (the language of the gentry was, of course, Norman French). Like all of England at that time, he would have been raised on those Arthurian legends popularized by Geoffrey of Monmouth.

Richard's big moment arrived at his sixteenth birthday. To celebrate, his big brother gave him a whopper of a present: the earldom of Cornwall and, therefore, the vast revenues from within. It was a gift that would help transform Richard into one of the richest men in the whole of medieval Europe, but it wasn't just luck that helped fill the earl's coffers. Richard was cunning and acquisitive and played off political allegiances to gain land and money.

As well as being greedy, it appears that the newly minted earl was rather proud and haughty. He commissioned a medieval chronicler to write exaggerated tales about his personal success in the Crusades and also had a penchant for expensive clothes (he was briefly imprisoned following the Battle of Lewes and would wear only robes of scarlet whilst held as a prisoner). To use a modern phrase, it's rather clear that Richard had delusions of grandeur, and the construction of a castle at Tintagel represented the ultimate exercise in vanity.

The Rise and Fall of the Castle at Tintagel

We don't know much about the process of building Richard's castle at Tintagel, and we don't even have a decent approximation of the dates. The best guess is that construction began in

A surviving archway within the Island Courtyard of the castle. This section would have once housed many of the residential functions of the castle, including the Great Hall.

about 1240, and the raw materials were quarried from nearby. In the main part, Richard's architects used Dark Age remains as the foundations for their buildings, appropriating the stones of Arthurian legend for their own use.

Indeed, the construction of Tintagel Castle owes more to symbolic significance than to any defensive need. Earl Richard's political control of Cornwall was never challenged, but this younger brother had an inferiority complex. Buying the land of Tintagel and building upon its remains meant he was building a Cornish connection between himself and the supposed greatest king of England.

The entrance doorway to the small castle complex upon "the island." Although the castle was built in around 1240 at the command of Richard, Earl of Cornwall, there's little evidence he actually ever stayed here.

Tintagel Castle, however, remained little more than the pet project of a rich man. There's no record that Richard ever really spent any time in the place—his main residence was Wallingford Castle—and it appears that he didn't ever stay the night in Tintagel (indeed, it's quite possible that he never even visited). As a result, it's unlikely that this little fortress ever witnessed grand medieval banquets or hosted distinguished guests; it languished, quickly forgotten, upon this windswept corner of Great Britain.

Tintagel fell from Richard's fickle favor because the earl was redirecting his attentions to the European continent, where he calculated that he had his best chances of seizing some form of power. Indeed, owing to his considerable wealth and an impressive skill for diplomacy, he was in 1256 rewarded with the exceptional title of the king of the Romans (effectively king of Germany). The ambitious man died at age sixty-two of a stroke that paralyzed his right side and left him unable to speak, and Tintagel passed forward to his son, Edmund. Edmund, in turn, lavished little attention upon the fortress and died in 1300. As a result, the unloved castle of Tintagel fell into the hands of the English state.

As we've glimpsed already, the Cornish shore is a cruel environment—especially for an already unloved castle. Just sixty years after the first stones were laid, Tintagel fell into disrepair. In 1337, the roof came off the Great Hall; some years later, its courtyards were used for sheep grazing. Without residents or regular visitors, Tintagel became purposeless and sea-worn, briefly used as a fourteenth-century prison and later as a sheltered landing place for the sixteenth-century tin miners. This soon-ruined fortress hardly reflected the grandeur and chivalry of Arthurian legend.

Excerpt from Tennyson's *Idylls of the King*: Depiction of a ruined castle, as discovered by the knight Geraint

"Then rode Geraint into the castle court,
His charger trampling many a prickly star
Of sprouted thistle on the broken stones.
He looked and saw that all was ruinous.
Here stood a shattered archway plumed with fern;
And here had fallen a great part of a tower,
Whole, like a crag that tumbles from the cliff,
And like a crag was gay with wilding flowers:
And high above a piece of turret stair,
Worn by the feet that now were silent, wound
Bare to the sun, and monstrous ivy-stems
Claspt the gray walls with hairy-fibred arms,
And sucked the joining of the stones, and looked
A knot, beneath, of snakes, aloft, a grove . . ."

The Resurgence of Tintagel: Of Artistic Interpretation

As the ruins of Tintagel slowly eroded from England's landscape, the memory of the legendary king also faded from the nation's consciousness. In 1485, the last significant medieval work upon Arthur had been published: Sir Thomas Malory's *Le Morte d'Arthur (The Death of Arthur)*, a bumper edition of all the greatest existing Arthurian stories, mixed in with a couple of new ones of Malory's own invention.

Le Morte d'Arthur would be the last Arthurian epic for a few hundred years. The Renaissance was well underway, and with it came a fascination with the ancient societies of Greece and Rome. Medieval chivalry and romance looked tired and dated in comparison to this new emphasis upon science and rational thought—the stories of Arthur appeared as irrelevant as the haggard remains of the castle at Tintagel.

Until the late eighteenth century, anyway. At that time, England was industrializing and urbanizing, and, in response, the Romantic movement flourished. Medievalism returned to vogue and—rather tellingly—*Le Morte d'Arthur* was reissued in 1815. It was to prove potent inspiration. In 1859, one of the greats of English literature—Alfred, Lord Tennyson—published *Idylls of the King*, a soaring, blank-verse retelling of the Arthurian legend. The poem remains as one of his most enduring works.

A statue of Alfred, Lord Tennyson, photographed outside Lincoln Cathedral.

For a Romantic like Tennyson, there could be little more evocative than the spectacle of rough waves, a rugged shoreline, and a half-ruined, wind-wrought castle. Indeed, the poet had visited the Cornish coastline in 1848 and had explicitly searched for the fragmentary remains of the legendary King Arthur. As a result, Tintagel plays a starring role within his lengthy *Idylls*—it is the place of Arthur's coming.

Excerpt from Tennyson's *Idylls of the King*: Merlin's Discovery of Arthur

"When Uther in Tintagel past away
Moaning and wailing for an heir, the two [Merlin and Bleys]
Left the still King, and passing forth to breathe, Then
from the castle gateway by the chasm
Descending through the dismal night . . .
. . . And then the two
Dropt to the cove, and watched the great sea fall,
Wave after wave, each mightier than the last,
Till last, a ninth one, gathering half the deep
And full of voices, slowly rose and plunged
Roaring, and all the wave was in a flame:
And down the wave and in the flame was borne
A naked babe, and rode to Merlin's feet,
Who stoopt and caught the babe, and cried "The King!
Here is an heir for Uther!"

His poetry has made a lasting impression. There's an impressive cavern on the eastern aspect of the isle of Tintagel—a black grotto that drips with saltwater and passes through the bedrock of the island. It's very likely that Tennyson's works gave the cavern its modern nickname of Merlin's Cave, and it's not hard to imagine a wizard emerging from the blackness, guided only by the conjured light at the end of his staff. Visitors today can tiptoe along its wet stones and try to sense the aura of magic for themselves. The only caution is that the cavern is at sea level and is filled with rushing, foamy seawater come high tide.

Tourism and the Arthurian Myth

Late nineteenth-century Britain became bisected by the railways, and, thanks to industrialization, the middle classes were blessed with spending money and sufficient time to holiday. The result was an explosion of national tourism—and Tintagel would quickly become a favored destination.

The castle ticked every requirement of Victorian fascination: evocative ruins, medieval romance, Arthurian legend, and connections to Tennyson's fashionable poetry. As a result, Tintagel attracted a cult-like following, and, until the early twentieth century, the ruins were uncritically interpreted to be the "real" birthplace and castle of King Arthur. Even the natural environment became appropriated within Arthurian myth; eroded hollows and nooks of stone upon the island became known as King Arthur's seat or Arthur's footprint.

As the tourists flocked to Tintagel, the legend of Arthur became self-sustaining; a railway hotel opened nearby with the name Arthur's Castle, and shops peddling Arthurian relics mushroomed within the small village. In the 1950s, MGM studios filmed scenes from *Knights of the Round Table* upon the ruined castle, transporting the frenetic grandeur of Hollywood to this remote, rural corner of England.

The dazzling buzz of Hollywood meant that serious academic study of Tintagel became overlooked by its visitors. Even

The sea-worn "Merlin's Cave," which nestles in the bay beneath the castle. The cave probably gained its name from Tennyson's poetry, but you can easily imagine a wizard emerging from the gloom.

The old railway hotel at Tintagel (now, rather creatively, dubbed the Camelot Castle Hotel) is an institution in itself— partially responsible, in the age of the steam train, for attracting mass tourism to the fortress.

CnOPhoto/Shutterstock

Rolf E. Staerk/Shutterstock

today, despite the best attempts of English Heritage (the custodians of the castle), it's difficult to disavail some visitors of the notion that Tintagel is an Arthurian relic.

Nonetheless, despite the adjacent profusion of plastic swords, Arthurian trinkets, and local restaurant meal deals named Lancelot's Ham Sandwich or Guinevere's Cream Tea, the castle ruins hold a special, evocative magic for almost every visitor. There's a unique sense of place: an "otherworldly" atmosphere, some say. (Indeed, the British tabloid the *Daily Mail* ran a recent story on the "face in the moss" of Tintagel: a natural apparition that apparently resembled Lord Voldemort from Harry Potter.) A visit helps one understand the symbiotic power of the legend of Arthur and the allure of Tintagel; both have sustained each other and will do so for some years to come.

Geoffrey of Monmouth's King Arthur and the Pig-Guzzling Giant

Geoffrey of Monmouth wrote of an Arthur who was conceived in Tintagel Castle and who soon succeeded his father, Uther Pendragon, king of England. Of his coronation, Geoffrey writes, "Arthur was then fifteen years old, but a youth of such unparalleled courage and generosity, joined with that sweetness of temper and innate goodness, as gained him universal love."

In Geoffrey's story, Arthur quickly proves his prowess in war. Bedecked in "a coat of mail suitable to the grandeur of so powerful a king" and toting Caliburn, "an excellent sword made in the isle of Avalon," Arthur quickly rides into battle with those pesky Saxons and inflicts grand damage: "[he did not cease] the fury of his assault until he had, with his Caliburn alone, killed four hundred and seventy men."

Arthur would prove to be a military hero. After defeating the troublesome Saxons, he pardons the Picts and the Scots, effectively uniting Great Britain. He doesn't stop there, though, as he also manages to grab control of Ireland, Iceland, Norway, Aquitaine, and the Orkney Isles. Under Arthur, Geoffrey describes a kingdom at its zenith: "For at that time Britain had arrived at such a pitch of grandeur, that in abundance of riches, luxury of ornaments, and politeness of inhabitants, it far surpassed all other kingdoms. The knights . . . were famous for feats of chivalry . . ."

Of course, every king needs to be kept busy. Geoffrey tells that, all too soon, the Romans got uppity, but, before them, Arthur had to defeat an altogether more unusual foe who came to hide out upon the isle of St Michael's Mount in Cornwall. (The island has long been a place of religious pilgrimage since the Archangel St. Michael appeared in 495.) Upon the isle, wrote Geoffrey, was "a giant of monstrous size . . . from the shores of Spain." It was a monster who kidnapped damsels and ate pigs whole: "his face [was] besmeared with the clotted blood of swine."

The king, however, made short work of this terrible imposter. "Arthur, fired with rage . . . lifted up his sword, and gave him a wound in the forehead, which . . . made the blood gush out over his face and eyes, and so blinded him . . . [he] gave the giant no respite till he had struck it up to the very back through his skull. At this the hideous monster raised a dreadful roar, and like an oak torn up from the roots by the winds, so did he make the ground resound with his fall."

Frankfurt Dave/Shutterstock

The Cornish coastline is spectacular; it's easy to understand why evocative legends have sprung from these magnificent surroundings.

King Edward the Castle Builder, A Round Table, and the "Corpse" of King Arthur

The Arthurian Round Table, as commissioned by King Edward I in about 1290. It weighs around 2,650 pounds, was repainted during the reign of Henry VIII, and presently hangs in the Great Hall of Winchester.

One of the greatest Arthurian enthusiasts was Edward I, king of England between 1272 and 1307. Edward I was one of the most fearless and ruthless of English kings—nicknamed Longshanks because he was at least six feet two inches tall (a medieval giant).

Edward was a long-term aficionado of King Arthur and it's said that, as a youth, he galloped into crusade carrying a book of Arthurian stories with him. Nonetheless, the most enduring relic of Edward's obsession is a vast round table made in 1290 in the style of the Arthurian legends and built of 2,650 pounds of English oak. Arthur, of course, chose to seat his men around this egalitarian design, and Edward's decision to commission such a table

The legend of King Arthur quickly became an obsession of the British people—and the British monarchy. Since the medieval period, no less than seven children of the British Royal Family have been named Arthur: the most recent Arthur was the grandson of Queen Victoria. The monarchs of Medieval England expended the most enthusiasm upon this legendary king—the early modern nation state relied upon the motifs of battle, of conquest, and of chivalric ideal, and many rulers attempted to hijack the cult of King Arthur to aggrandize themselves and their rule.

Looking onto "the island," but this time across the rougher, unprotected bay on the southern side of the castle.

was a conscious allusion to King Arthur's chivalry. This mighty piece of furniture became the ceremonial centerpiece of multiday jousting tournaments and mass dubbings of new knights: a new type of medieval tournament that came to be called, of course, a *round table*.

(Should you be curious, Edward's one-ton round table survives today and hangs in the Great Hall of Winchester, Hampshire. The gaudy striped decorations visible in the adjacent photograph were added during the reign of Henry VIII, who wanted a piece of the Arthurian action for himself, too.)

Edward's enthusiasm for Arthur was doubtlessly genuine—after all, most of Medieval Britain seemed to be swept up into the cult—but there were certainly elements of the Arthurian legend that he sought to appropriate for himself. In the early stories of Arthur, our hero was represented as a fearless warrior-knight who sought to unite the disparate peoples of Britain under his rule. Although King Edward's motivations were probably much less altruistic than those of Arthur, the monarch was an avid conqueror. Edward almost certainly thought that Arthurian legend granted him the legitimacy to capture all the territories of Great Britain, and the later part of his reign was defined by his successful conquest of Wales and failure to capture Scotland.

Ironically enough, it's the failure in Scotland for which Edward is best remembered. You'll probably recall him to be the "Hammer of the Scots"—the villain in the movie *Braveheart*. Over time, the king has gained extra-special notoriety for his vengeful rage at his Scottish failure—he ordered the bodies of patriots, including William Wallace, to be ripped apart in public. Such cruelty got him nowhere. Now infamous, Edward died before he saw Scotland conquered, a rare failure of an exceptionally ferocious king.

Edward was successful, however, at capturing Wales some years earlier during his reign. A vicious individual, his victory came with significant bloodshed—he employed a devastating military campaign to wrest control from the last of the Welsh princes. Unsurprisingly, the Welsh people were not pleased with this conquest of brute force, and rebellion simmered throughout the territory. To subdue his newly captured lands and discontented peoples, Edward encircled the country with an "iron ring" of fortresses that, to this day, remain as some of the mightiest in Britain. These monolithic beasts include Beaumaris, Harlech (pictured, page 197), and Caernarfon—an unrivaled demonstration of military might.

(It's important to realize that Edward I was one of the greatest castle builders of all the kings of England. The fact that his greatest works are in Wales means that he is, rather ironically, only a footnote within this book of English castles.)

There was to be one twist in the tale of the story—which would all be down to King Arthur. Despite Edward's best efforts to position himself as an Arthurian monarch, the Welsh had interpreted the story in a very divergent fashion. You see, by almost all accounts, Arthur was a Welshman—the first tales of Arthur were from the oldest Welsh folklore. According to the legends, King Arthur had never died (he'd just gone to Avalon to rest up for a bit), and the prevailing belief throughout Wales was that their legendary king would soon return to save them.

This persistent belief in salvation irked King Edward, but also proved to be a political liability: the belief of King Arthur's imminent return meant the Welsh kept on rebelling. As a result, Edward was keen to disavail the Welsh of any hope of salvation, and, in April 1278, made the trip to Glastonbury Abbey, Somerset, alongside his queen. Why Glastonbury? Well, some hundred years prior, the Abbey had burned down, and the monks hadn't the money to rebuild. With a flash of marketing cynicism that wouldn't be out of place nowadays, the monks jumped on the Arthurian bandwagon and conveniently unearthed two skeletons in their graveyard, which they heralded to be the remains of Arthur and Guinevere. The resulting stampede of pilgrims brought ample funds to Glastonbury (and likely ignited the aura of mysticism that persists in the area to this day).

Not all were convinced by this early medieval marketing ploy, and the Welsh were still holding out for their hero at the end of the night. Determined to prove that King Arthur was certainly not coming back from Avalon, Edward's trip to Glastonbury, which was advertised as a deferential pilgrimage to pay respects to the king, actually formed an attempt to control the symbolism of Arthur.

The remains of Glastonbury Abbey—the supposed tomb of King Arthur, and the site of King Edward I's calculating reburial ceremony in 1278.

Chris Dorney/Shutterstock

With an impressive knack for theater, Edward ordered a grand twilight ceremony where the grave of Arthur and Guinevere would be reopened. (The purported purpose for this grave digging was to create a grander tomb for the multitude of pilgrims.) As the sun set on the Abbey, and with the old tomb prized from the ground, the king grasped the freshly disinterred bones of "Arthur" and wrapped them delicately in white silk; his queen paid the same attention to the remains of Guinevere. After a long series of prayers, readings, and devotions, the majority of the remains were placed in a grand new tomb outside the Abbey; although, the two skulls were placed to one side. Edward and his queen paid further respects to these relics, with the king then commanding that both should be held back and displayed openly in public "on account of popular devotion." What he undoubtedly meant, of course, was "to prove that Arthur's actually dead."

The Welsh had met their match in Edward I; it appears that the king won. In 1284, an envoy of war-worn Welsh subjects traipsed to Westminster Abbey with a peace offering. With them they brought a collection of now-lost national treasures, including fragments of a fabled crown that, oral tradition said, belonged to King Arthur. There could be no conquest more complete: the Welsh had surrendered the mythology of Arthur to this cruel and unstoppable English king.

The location of Tintagel Castle.

Fulcanelli/Shutterstock

"The Haven"—the sheltered bay situated alongside Tintagel. Note that the coastline is pockmarked with small, dark caves.

Tintagel Castle

Castle Road, Tintagel, Cornwall, PL34 0HE
+44 (0)1840 770328
Managed by English Heritage
Official Website: **www.english-heritage.org.uk/daysout/properties/tintagel-castle/**
Official Facebook: **www.facebook.com/tintagelcastle**
My Website: **www.exploring-castles.com/tintagel_castle.html**
Open every day in spring and summer; closed most weekdays during winter—check before you travel

The rough stone appearance of Rochester Castle.

Paulina Grunwald/Shutterstock

Forty Fat Pigs, and the Siege of Rochester Castle

What would you do with forty big, fat pigs? Your initial answer, I'd assume, would not be "blow up a castle." But during the Great Siege of Rochester Castle in 1215, desperate times called for desperate measures. It was one of the longest and boldest sieges to ever take place upon English soil.

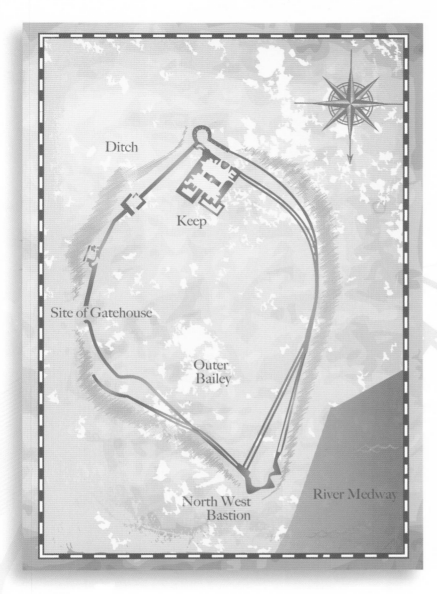

A floor plan of Rochester Castle.

William d'Albini was the leader of the opposition. English barons and their sympathizers formed his band of followers, all rebelling in exasperation at the extravagant demands of their grasping king. Stoic and long suffering, the men would have to overcome famine and claustrophobia within the twelve-foot-thick walls of Rochester Castle.

Both sides of the battle were matched in their stubbornness. Each party was equipped with the latest medieval technologies. And quick-thinking Baron William was an equal match to the calculating cunningness of King John. It was to be an almighty showdown in one of England's most distinctive early medieval castles: the fortress of Rochester in Kent, southern England.

Exploring Charles Dickens's Rochester

Some forty miles to the east of London, Rochester is a small city most famous for its connection to Charles Dickens. During the mid-1800s, Dickens lived close by, and, it's said, found inspiration for his novels in Rochester's architecture. Theories abound that Miss Havisham's house was modeled on Satis House, a stately home here, and the city's Guildhall is perhaps the spot where Pip became Joe Gargery's apprentice in *Great Expectations*.

By all accounts, Dickens was extremely fond of rambling around the city. Despite his enthusiasm, however, the ruins of Rochester Castle were mysteriously absent from his writings: described only once within the *Pickwick Papers* by a confidence-trickster tour guide, Mr. Alfred Jingle. Mr. Jingle isn't exactly an expert on English castles, and

As well as featuring this profusion of pigs, the siege was a battle of strong-willed characters. On one side, we have a true villain—King John of England. Although no historical figure can be painted in pure black or white, John had very few redeeming qualities: he was a mean, greedy, sniggering man, an intelligent but unpredictable king with a dark streak of cruelty.

A cold winter's morning in Rochester. Note the silhouette of the adjacent Cathedral, hiding behind the tree to the left of the picture.

what he does know is expressed only in mangled English: "glorious pile—frowning walls—tottering arches—dark nooks—crumbling staircases." Mr. Jingle's ignorance also extended to the adjacent Rochester Cathedral. Addressing a party of tourists standing upon the Rochester bridge, peering at the vista of the city through a telescope, our unreliable tour guide continued, "The old cathedral too—earthy smell—pilgrims' feet wore away the old steps—little Saxon doors . . . match-locks—sarcophagus—fine place—old legends too—strange stories: capital."

Mr. Jingle's knowledge of historic Rochester was quite clearly limited, perhaps not unusual in Victorian England, when medieval ruins seemed irrelevant to an industrializing society. Conversely, to modern visitors to Rochester, it is generally only its historic buildings that hold any interest; the plague of 1960s concrete and traffic-choked main roads are not, with the kindest of intentions, the most alluring features of the city.

Quite unexpectedly, however, Rochester Castle looks perfectly at home within this industrial landscape. Unlike the majority of early medieval towers, Rochester Castle has a rough-hewn, rag-stone, dirty-gray finish. At its upper levels, its windows are ragged black holes that, from a distance, appear uneven; its preponderance of straight edges is somewhat uncompromising; and the fortress is, unexpectedly, at its most photogenic when posed against dark skies. Rochester Castle seems to relish its gritty location.

It also dominates the skyline of the town. Although the castle is positioned directly beside the cathedral, it towers over it; likewise, it attracts attention from the river and also from the modern highstreet. Although it's far from being one of the most visited castles in England, Rochester has always commanded attention: holding physical, and symbolic, control over one of the most important routes into London.

Architecturally, Rochester Castle has a good deal in common with the earliest medieval towers, which include the White Tower within the Tower of London. (The Great Keep at Dover is of an extremely similar design, but built a little later.) The castle is a tall, relatively slender tower, with a square footprint measur-

Mark A Bond/Shutterstock

A view of the adjacent Rochester Cathedral, through one of the windows of the castle.

ing twenty feet by twenty feet. The building measures 113 feet in height, with each corner crowned with a turret of a further twelve feet. On three sides of the castle, the turret is a sharp, square shape; on the fourth southeastern side, it's a curved drum tower. We'll come back to this mysterious asymmetry a little later.

Within the castle—as in the Great Keep of Dover—a cross-wall runs through the middle of the building, splitting each of the four stories into a north and south chamber. The cross-wall was five feet six inches thick, primarily designed to provide structural support to the fortress—but it would play a surprisingly important role within the 1215 siege.

It bears saying that Rochester Castle consists of more than just the Keep—the fortress was surrounded by a curtain wall (now incomplete) and is seated upon a sizable bailey, which overlooks the wide, muddy estuary of the River Medway. The bailey itself may have been a pre-Norman earth-mound (it's built upon old Roman remains); however, the majority of the castle is firmly early Norman in origin and dates to 1088 when it was built for Bishop Gundulf.

Rochester is close to Canterbury, London, and the trade routes to France, granting the fortress significant strategic importance. The desire to wield control of Rochester, and thus the terrain around it, explains the ferocity of the 1215 siege between the rebellious barons and the dastardly King John.

The Road to the Baron's War: The Vagaries of King John

"Foul as it is," sniffed the monk Matthew Paris in the thirteenth century. "Hell itself is defiled by the fouler presence of King John."

Mark A Bond/Shutterstock

Most of the castle is built from Kentish ragstone—hence the irregular appearance. Note that the vertical lines along the corners are made of a finer rock; in fact, this was probably sourced from Caen, Normandy.

Paris was never a man to mince his words and indeed, throughout history, King John has never enjoyed salubrious reputation. Almost universally known as the "bad King of England," John—with his bulging eyes and penchant for expensive jewelry—has been portrayed as the classic villain in countless books, movies, and TV series. He was, popular culture tells us, the nemesis of Robin Hood, the ineffectual lion in a Disney film and the subject of one of Shakespeare's lesser-performed history plays.

There's no doubt that, during the passage of English history, some kings have been unfairly demonized and others unfairly revered. Unfortunately, most of the opprobrium leveled at King John is likely to be quite just. John almost certainly ordered the secret killing of his nephew, Arthur of Brittany, and in a fit of particularly unpleasant vengeance, condemned the wife and child of an overmighty baron to die of starvation in a castle dungeon. (Folktales say that when the bodies of

Rochester Cathedral, pictured behind some of the ruinous curtain wall that surrounds the castle.

Matilda and William were recovered, bite marks were found upon the boy; the mother had been driven to madness by hunger, and had tried to eat her child.)

Even so, such stories of cruelty are easily exaggerated. It's almost certainly false that John forced a troublesome arch-deacon to wear a ceremonial cloak of lead so heavy that it crushed him to death. Likewise, there's a powerful tale that John extorted money from a Jewish man by pulling out a molar each day until the victim paid the ransom; it's unlikely to be true, but due to John's persecution of the Jews and his passion for extortion, it has that hint of veracity that fuels many a folktale.

So, who was the real John? He was, first and foremost, a king in a particular political fix. Whereas things had gone well for his forebears—Richard I and Henry II—John inherited a host of political problems through no real fault of his own. Inflation was rising dramatically, the crown's reserves were low, and a disastrous military campaign in 1204 led to the loss of all English lands in northern France. The loss of territory resulted in a host of disenfranchised barons at home, further compounding his political headaches. John was never destined for an easy ride.

Of course, the real test of one's character is how one copes when the going's tough, as opposed to how successfully one sails along when life is easy. John, however, could not be said to cope well under pressure. The king became obsessed with the desire to reclaim those lost lands in France but, lacking the financial might to do so, began to use every lever possible to pry, cajole, and downright extort money from his barons and the English population.

Some of his methods bordered on the ingenious. After a 1208 squabble with the pope, the prelate placed an interdiction upon England, preventing almost all religious services from taking place (the only exceptions to the rule were baptisms and funerals—essential ceremonies for the preservation of the soul). As a consequence, the church bells ceased to ring within England, and so John took the opportunity to confis-cate land and property from the clergy, which he later sold or leased back at a grossly increased price. Incensed, the pope excommunicated John in 1209; by all accounts, John took little heed and continued to merrily appropriate money from the Church.

Other methods were cruder. John levied vast taxes upon the Jews, took noble hostages and demanded ransom, hiked the

A contemporary image of King John.

golden jewelry, undoubtedly to the chagrin of those whom he had fleeced.

But the problem with John was not just his meanness, nor was it his cruelty (after all, Richard I and Henry II had similarly nasty streaks). Rather, it was his unpredictability and paranoia that set England on edge. He would fly into an intemperate rage with a baron about the smallest of issues and then demand an arbitrary payment to assuage his anger. He demanded men to swear fealty, but developed a system of codes and secret gestures to indicate to courtiers when he was lying to a vassal. He would demand debt payments with no notice and seize lands at will. He roamed around England at dizzying speed, doing exactly as he pleased, seemingly with utter impunity. In combination with his cruel, sniggering wit and hot flashes of temper, he was a thoroughly dislikable king.

It's no surprise, then, that John was vastly unpopular with the majority of landowners in England—the barons. The barons felt that the king was becoming overmighty, but their discomfort was not purely the consequence of John's rule. Over their lifetimes, the balance of power in Medieval England had slowly shifted. You see, shortly after the Norman Conquest, feudal government had given local barons real power and jurisdiction over local territories. However, over the last hundred years or so, baronial power had been slowly ceded to increasingly omnipotent monarchs. With the disaster in northern France, John had lost overseas territories that had belonged to a number of

equivalent of inheritance tax, and even increased the fees for widows who wished to remain single. It quite quickly appeared that he'd forgotten the point of even raising such revenues, as the royal vaults became so stuffed with coin that more had to be minted to maintain sufficient circulation. John also developed a penchant for hideously expensive

Note the rough, ragged state of the window frames—quite a contrast to the Great Keep of Dover Castle. Over the years, the weather has eroded away much of the stone. The process has been exacerbated by the fact that the castle is still roofless—chiefly because of a lack of finances for restoration.

barons, and his unpredictable, unaccountable ruling style put men ill at ease. The barons loathed him.

The gulf between John and his barons got worse as his reign wore on. Indeed, during early 1215, it even appeared that civil war could break out. The result was the Great Charter—or Magna Carta—effectively a peace agreement between John and the barons, which set out exactly what powers a king should—and shouldn't—have.

Many of the clauses related only to immediate political concerns. For instance, the assertion that "Earls and Barons should be fined only by their equals," and that "No 'scutage' or 'aid' [broad taxation] may be levied in our kingdom without its general consent . . ." are two clauses written with John's grasping hands in mind. Intentionally or unintentionally, however, other clauses readdressed the relationship between king and state. "No free man shall be seized or imprisoned, or stripped of his rights or possessions, or outlawed or exiled, or deprived of his standing in any other way . . . except by the lawful judgment of his equals or by the law of the land," says the clause later numbered 39. Clause 40 continues, "To no one will we sell, to no one deny or delay right or justice." These were deceptively revolutionary ideas. Many years later, during the American Revolution, the colonists asserted that they were entitled to the same rights as Englishmen, and so cited clauses from the Magna Carta to justify action against George III. These same rights became embedded into the laws of their states, and into the Constitution and Bill of Rights of the United States of America.

An image of the Magna Carta—albeit the 1297 version.

Although the Magna Carta provided a profound legal framework that is still of importance today, John proceeded to ignore it and continued exactly as he had been doing beforehand. The barons were incensed. Their one recourse was to use force. It marked the beginning of the First Baron's War, and Rochester Castle would be the setting for one of the greatest sieges to ever take place upon English soil.

Some sections of curtain wall (such as the section in the foreground) date to the 1100s, although much is the work of the 1370s.

The Great Siege of Rochester Castle

"Living memory does not recall a siege so fiercely pressed or so staunchly resisted." —The Barnwell Annalist

Baron William's men began by plundering every morsel of food they could find in Rochester. It was October 11, 1215, and morale was high following an early, symbolic victory: they had

A panorama of Rochester Castle poking out behind its curtain wall. The image was taken from its east side—that is to say, standing in front of the Cathedral.

already taken London in their name. It was a remarkable achievement, but it hadn't exactly been a hard-won battle—the Londoners hated John to such an extent that they simply flung open the city gates to the rebels.

Although Baron William's men were flushed with success, they understood that the war was far from over. King John was consolidating his own position, commanding a smattering of castles that included Norwich, Corfe, and Winchester. The rebellious barons sensed that this would be a war of attrition, fought from within castle walls, and so sought to capture their own strongholds to counter John's.

Rochester was near the top of their "most wanted" list. The castle commanded the main roads through the county of Kent and thus the artery between London and mainland France—a key strategic location. You see, every good medieval rebellion needed to coalesce around a powerful figure, and the barons had chosen Prince Louis of France as their patron. Louis could claim a tenuous connection to the English throne, and so, the barons had decided, he should be king in lieu of John. They strategized that securing Kent would allow Louis free passage from France to London and, in the capital, he could shore up military support and declare himself true king of England.

Rochester Castle and the adjacent Cathedral, taken from across the River Medway.

Another, more strategic reason made Rochester so desirable. The possession of London was crucial for either side, and the barons knew that John would fight long and hard to regain the city. If nothing else came by holding Rochester, it would distract John's attentions from the capital—giving them breathing space until Prince Louis's men rode to their rescue.

On October 11, the troop of rebels arrived in Rochester and immediately provisioned the castle for a grand siege—scouring the town for every morsel of food and every barrel of drink. The rebels consisted of around ninety-five knights and forty-five men-at-arms, and the troop was led by an enigmatic baron named William d'Albini—one of the twenty-five signatories upon the Magna Carta.

Baron William was a tremendous military commander, but remains a rather mysterious figure to this day. He owned significant swathes of land within the English Midlands and appeared entirely loyal to the king—as late as 1213, he audited northern tax

126

returns, ensuring nothing got lost on the way to John. However, when London first fell to the rebels, it appears that William had a sudden change of heart. It's unclear whether he sensed that the political climate was changing or if the vast debts he owed to King John had anything to do with the matter. Either way, he transformed from royal servant to military agitator and commanded the Rochester garrison throughout the siege.

The troops undoubtedly needed a strong commander. On their arrival in Rochester, the castle was ill-equipped for even the shortest siege; although a deep well was sited within the keep, there were no stores of food whatsoever. It's said that many men were ready to give up then and there, but Baron William rallied the troops, "extorting and continually animating the minds of his companions to deeds of valour," according to the chronicler Roger of Wendover.

They had little time to prepare themselves. Just two days later, King John arrived with an army that may have numbered one thousand men. The rebels realized that they would have to make do with what little food they'd found and so barricaded themselves in the castle, waiting for the storm to begin.

They didn't have long to wait. To break the siege as quickly as possible, John had invested in the latest medieval technology: an array of five mighty siege machines, which were ceremoniously wheeled to the top of Boley Hill, a mound positioned opposite the castle. It's thought today that these monstrous devices were trebuchets—effectively gigantic catapults that utilized a system of ropes and potential energy to hurl stones, in an overhand motion, at any unfortunate target.

These whirling beasts were put to good use. Roger of Wendover tells us that the trebuchets lobbed "incessant showers of stones and other weapons" directly at the walls of the castle, ostensibly with the purpose of wreaking as much damage as possible. But there was also an important psychological aspect to siege warfare. For Baron William and his men inside the fortress, the ceaseless noise and jeopardy would have lead to sleepless nights and short tempers. In combination with claustrophobia, debilitating hunger, and fear of reprisals should they lose, the siege would have tested the will of the strongest among them.

That's not to say that William's men were entirely outflanked by John's forces—indeed, they had some state-of-the-art kit of their own. Those inside the castle were equipped with the crossbow—a deadly evolution of the commonly used longbow. Whereas it took years of skill and training to become efficient at shooting with the longbow, the crossbow was a mechanized monster, requiring only brute strength to pull the bowstring to extreme tension, using a crank-like device. When the pent-up energy was released, often via a trigger, a small, thick projectile (named a bolt) would fly at any enemy with astounding force and speed. Its impact would be enough to penetrate a knight's armor—even at four hundred yards.

It's no wonder, then, that none of John's army were keen to get too close to the besieged castle. Indeed, a crossbow shot had finished off John's elder brother, King Richard

The green around the castle is nowadays used for community fairs and fetes.

"The Lionheart"—an agonizing death from a gangrenous wound to his left shoulder. The crossbow was a weapon so "hateful to God" that, in 1139, the pope tried to ban its use upon Christians, and the 1215 Magna Carta had tried to

127

Mark A Bond/Shutterstock

As in medieval times, the main entrance to the castle is above ground level, accessed by a flight of stairs. This would protect the main wooden doorway from attack with a battering ram.

outlaw "foreign crossbow men." (Despite such protestations, it was still in common use after 1215 and would remain so for centuries to come.)

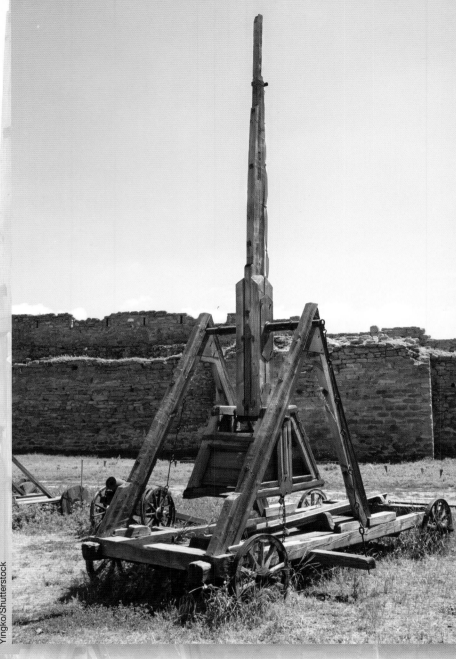

Yingko/Shutterstock

One of the many different designs of medieval trebuchet. Fundamentally, the trebuchet was capable of flinging vast rocks, overhand style, at an enemy; it's thought that King John brought five of these beasts to the siege of Rochester.

Quite clearly, then, King John would have had no desire to stray too close to the walls of Rochester Castle. However, he was a cunning man, adept at using other strategies to try and smoke

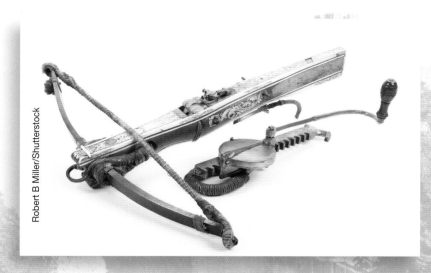

Robert B Miller/Shutterstock

A modern replica of a medieval crossbow. The crossbow could pierce armor at more than four hundred yards—it was a feared medieval weapon.

got as far as Dartford (about fifteen miles from Rochester) before they got cold feet and decided to return to the capital. It's not entirely clear why they hightailed it back so quickly. Some say that the men were plied with false rumors that John had Flemish reinforcements who were swiftly advancing toward them or perhaps they were put off by the stories of the burned bridges. Whatever happened, it was a rather ignominious end for a rescue party, and those in the castle would have been forever waiting, patient and puzzled, for reinforcements to arrive.

out the occupants. One of his most nefarious tricks was to burn the bridge that spanned the River Medway—thus making it extremely difficult for baronial reinforcements to reach those besieged within the castle. (By one account, just burning the bridge was a tricky proposition—only the second attempt was successful and involved a man in a boat sailing downstream with a rather large torch.) However, as the bridge rose in flames, those besieged within the castle must have felt their hearts sink—it was a message that aid would struggle to reach them.

Indeed, their fears would have proved correct. Some two weeks into the siege, around seven hundred men set out from London, ostensibly aiming to assist their allies within the castle. According to Roger of Wendover, these troops "had sworn on the holy gospels that if he [Baron William] should happen to be beseiged, they should all march to raise the siege." If William were expecting his friends to rout out John, however, he was to be sorely disappointed. The troops managed to leave London, but only

Despite such trials, Baron William's men in the castle remained resolute. It's hard to picture the true privations of a siege: the squalid sanitation, eked-out rations, and the terrible problem of what to do with the bodies of the sick, dead, or maimed still within the castle walls. But, despite such horrors, the men held on—for weeks more. Perhaps Baron William's leadership was superlative or the men were resolute to their cause. Either way, the twelve-foot-thick walls of Rochester withstood the constant bombardment from John's siege engines—and the siege continued.

Quite evidently, the length of any siege was dictated by the amount of food held by those in the castle. (Indeed, the etymology of the word *siege* comes from Latin, meaning "to sit.") But King John was impatient and wanted the affairs of Rochester to be dealt with as speedily as possible. If stones were unable to break down the walls, he reasoned, they'd need to force their way in through some other fashion. Thus, it was time to tunnel.

Undermining the castle was a common tactic within siege warfare (it was similarly used within Dover Castle—see

129

One of King John's first actions during the 1215 siege was to burn the bridges that crossed the Medway. Nowadays, the river is a frequent site for pleasure sailing, given its proximity to London.

Rochester Castle as seen from the other side of the tidal River Medway.

page 91). Providing the ground was favorable, a gaggle of unfortunate men would be forced to burrow down beneath the castle walls, supporting their tunnel with wooden props as they went. If their job was completed efficiently, the castle tower would be standing only upon flimsy wooden posts, rather than solid ground; introducing fire into the tunnel would burn the props and, if everything went to plan, cause the stone towers to fall. (In modern English, the verb *undermine* now has a figurative meaning.)

Tunneling would have been a horrendous, precarious occupation, with the miners ("sappers") at constant risk of collapse or asphyxiation. The spectacle would have been nearly as heartrending for those within the castle: it would generally have been self-evident as to what was going on, and there wasn't much that could be done about it (save for shooting crossbows into the ground in the hope of striking lucky, or tunneling out themselves to fight the sappers, hand to hand). The architects of later castles attempted to circumvent this defensive flaw by building on rock rather than upon earth, but it was a bit late for this in Rochester.

With the tunnels nearly completed, the siege of Rochester was to take an infamous, and somewhat surreal, turn. In mid-November, King John wrote to an ally, asking him to "send to us with all speed by day and night forty of the fattest pigs of the sort least good for eating." (Maybe misguidedly, I had thought any big pig was the best type for eating; perhaps John was particularly pernickety when it came to picking porcine.) The purpose of the pigs was primarily for their fat: the animals were slaughtered, and the flammable grease was used to baste the wooden props within the tunnels. Presumably, John's men ate barbequed sausages for some time afterward.

The Last Moments of the Siege

November 25, 1215, was the date of the big pig blast. After weeks of careful preparation, a lighted torch was taken to the freshly dug tunnels—and flames licked the wooden props. The triumph of John's men would have been mirrored by the sheer terror of Baron William's besieged forces. Fire ripped through the underground network, devouring everything within, and the earth would have trembled as the entire southeastern face of Rochester Castle crashed to the ground.

A contemporary image of medieval "sappers"—miners who dug beneath castle defenses.

Extensive curtain walls surround the castle, and if you couldn't get through them, you'd just have to burrow under them! Note that the walls you see today were broadly the work of refortification during the 1370s.

There can be no doubt that chaos followed. The air would have been thick with dust, the ground scorched by flames, and panicked yells would have resonated against the remaining, unstable castle walls. Yet somehow—either through tremendous planning and foresight or due to phenomenal discipline—Baron William's men eluded John. Although an entire face of the fortress had tumbled to the ground, William's troops managed

131

A panorama of Rochester Castle and Cathedral from across the River Medway.

to move swiftly through its rooms, scurrying to the opposite side of the castle, behind the massive internal wall that slices the keep in two. Using everything at hand, they blocked up the doors and windows of this dividing wall, ensconcing themselves in relative safety within the opposite side of the castle.

King John's fury would have been a sight to behold: Baron William's men still defied him. Conversely, upon Baron William's side, the forces undoubtedly fretted that their luck would soon run out—the wall separating themselves from John was tenuous, to say the very least. To make matters worse, their supplies of food were distressingly low; the one ray of light would have been that the fresh-water well, essential for survival, was situated within their side of the keep.

It was the beginning of the endgame of the siege of Rochester. Although the surviving crosswall protected the rebels from John's physical might, it didn't shield them from his cruel and cunning intellect. He chose to use a spot of psychological warfare to end the siege, likely encouraging his men to shout threats of torture and death through the wall. The ceaseless barrage of grim threats echoed the earlier, unyielding barrage of rocks and stones; the aim was to psychologically break Baron William's men.

Given the paucity of their resources, we shouldn't be surprised if Baron William's men were close to giving up. By this stage, it's said, the forces were starved and reduced to eating horse-meat. With supplies so low, William chose to release some of their weakest men—those least capable of fighting—in the hope of prolonging the supplies they did have.

Some, including the *Barnwell Chronicler*, wrote that King John received the refugees with cruel vengeance. Although he spared the men's lives, John chose to mutilate each of them—lopping off their hands and their feet as penance for the trouble they'd caused him. His actions conveyed an important message to those remaining: the king would not have clemency, and those inside should fear for their lives.

The End of the Siege (and its Hollywood Depiction)

The Great Siege of Rochester ended on November 30, 1215. The siege had lasted nigh on two months (one of the longest sieges ever to take place within Medieval England); had involved the efforts of more than a thousand men; and had cost, it's approxi-

The Eastern Mural Tower—one of the smaller towers within the string of curtain wall that wraps around the castle. This was built under King Edward III in the 1370s; it has now been converted into a cottage.

siege ended, concocting a particularly grisly demise using a knife, a trebuchet, and a brick wall—I'll leave the rest to your imagination. In reality, William survived the siege and was bundled to Corfe Castle where he was held a prisoner for about a year and a half (he died of natural causes around twenty years later). Ironically, to many modern readers, the historical reality

mated, between fifty and one hundred lives. By any accounts, it was one of the most dramatic sieges in English history, and so, in 2011, movie studios were inspired to make a film. The result was *Ironclad*—"an *Ironclad* turkey," quipped one critic.

There's much to dislike about *Ironclad* ("[its] historical credentials are made of mulch," grizzled the *Guardian, UK*), but its most bizarre deviation from English history is its incongruous happy ending. According to *Ironclad*, the rebels held out and King John was defeated: a mind-boggling reimagination, given that Baron William's men actually surrendered, resulting in a critical military victory for King John.

Another one of *Ironclad's* deviations from fact is its depiction of Baron William's death at the hands of King John. According to the Hollywood version, King John killed William before the

The castle is impressively lofty—113 feet in height, and the taller parts of the towers add another 12 feet.

seems less believable than the Hollywood fiction. King John was a cruel man, so why didn't he seek the bloody revenge he'd promised? The answer is that John almost certainly wanted to kill him ("In his anger," says the chronicler Roger of Wendover, John "ordered all the nobles to be hung"), but was counseled to leniency by one of his advisors. Clemency now, it was said, would protect John's own men in the future. This was the medieval code of chivalry—sparing the necks of other nobles so, if the tables were turned, the same might be done to you.

Indeed, all the men in the garrison were spared their lives—except one. King John focused all his rage and anger upon one of the young crossbow men; this youth, he claimed, had been raised as a ward in his own home and so his actions in the siege were tantamount to treason. The unfortunate adolescent was hanged in Rochester town, and so John shed some of the blood that he had so lusted after.

Epilogue: The Fate of John, and the Rebuilding of Rochester

Like any good story, the siege of Rochester Castle deserves an epilogue. What became of the ruined Rochester Castle? And what, exactly, happened to King John?

Evidently, Rochester Castle was in a poor state come December 1215. The entire southeastern aspect was reduced to rubble, meaning the castle required extensive rebuilding; the works started from 1221 onward. Today, it's plain to see exactly which parts of the castle were re-rendered, as the

second batch of stonemasons cared little for architectural consistency. Practicality (and speed) was almost certainly their primary consideration, and you'll notice that the reconstituted tower is curved, whereas the three originals are

At the front of the image, you'll see the Drum Tower, which was added to the curtain wall of the castle during the reign of King Henry III (the successor to King John). Note the profusion of arrow-slits: this was designed for defense!

134

square in shape. The overall aesthetic effect isn't exactly pleasing, but round towers were much trickier to undermine than square ones. Rochester was reloaded for future siege.

As for John—well, the flailing king would have been reinvigorated by his success at Rochester. It was a victory of quite considerable magnitude, and it set the tone for capturing a handful of other castles—including Framlingham and, most notably, Belvoir—which was the home of Baron William. In fact, the people of Belvoir had prepared the castle for an equally mighty siege, and William's son, Nicholas, was set to lead the garrison. King John, however, was in no mood for such antics and simply threatened to starve the imprisoned Baron William unless his son immediately surrendered. Nicholas was grudgingly forced into silent submission.

Later in 1216, however, the tide turned against John. The king still didn't hold control of London, and Prince Louis of France (the baron's ally from the continent) had landed in England, complete with army. Louis captured chunks of the country in the name of the rebels, and John increasingly looked like a king without authority: a dangerous position for any monarch.

As a result, John's efforts became desperate. He traversed the country at speed, trying to maintain a grip across his lands. In October 1216, with characteristic impatience, he encouraged his baggage train to cross the tidal Linconshire Wash while the water was rising; he lost most of his property to the water, including, stories say, the English crown jewels.

Alan Jeffery/Shutterstock

Look closely at the tower on the left of the picture, and the tower on the right. Spot the differences? The right sided tower was brought down in the 1215 siege, and was subsequently rebuilt in the 1220s. You can see that it's round rather than square, and the stonework is much rougher and more uneven—a bit of a medieval bodge-job.

A couple days after that disaster, John fell ill. Although the story's quite likely apocryphal, it's said that John gorged himself at a feast, wolfing down a "surfeit of peaches." Whether the peaches were the cause of the malady (perhaps

Newark Castle—where King John died in October 1216. Tradition says that the king died in the southwestern tower, his death due to a "surfit of peaches"—the truth is likely that he died of dysentery in a grand apartment within the gatehouse.

they were especially ill-washed), we do know that King John contracted dysentery.

Like any medieval illness, the progress of his disease would likely have been terrifying: from feasting king to a wretched, moribund skeleton of a man in a matter of days. The strange poignancy of such a sudden demise is captured in Shakespeare's history play *King John*. Upon John's death, Prince Henry rather poignantly remarks, "What

surety of the world, what hope, what stay / When this was now a king, and now is clay?"

With John's demise, the throne passed to his son Henry—a boy king, age nine. Henry inherited an England at war with itself: a country blighted by a rampaging French prince and a rebellious capital city. However, such chaos was to be short-lived. The cause of the baron's war was the behavior of John. With John gone, the rebels had little cause to continue fighting. Much of

England breathed a sigh of relief at the advent of peace; although, rather comically, Prince Louis seemed to be rather enjoying his conquest and had to be cajoled into leaving the country.

In retrospect, King John's unexpected death rendered the eight-week siege of Rochester Castle—with all its bloodshed and grueling hardships—into a mere footnote: an interesting but fundamentally insignificant blip in the thousands of years of a nation. John and his men may well have perceived their success at Rochester to be a defining moment of his reign; ironically, it was that abandoned and forgotten baronial peace deal (the so-called Magna Carta) that would turn out to be the most enduring aspect of all of King John's achievements.

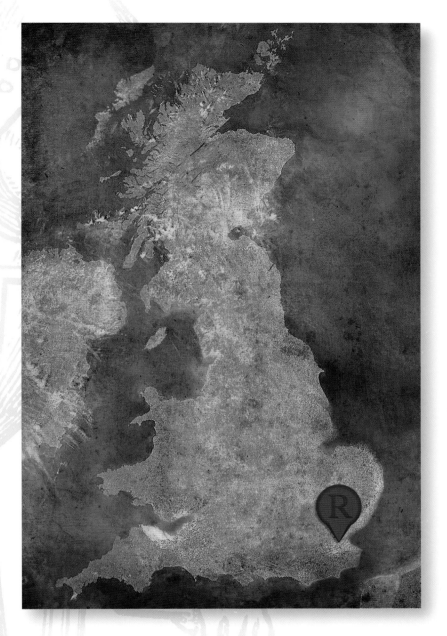

The location of Rochester Castle.

Rochester Castle

Rochester Town Centre
Kent, ME1 1SW
+44 (0)1634 335882
Managed by English Heritage
Official Website: **www.english-heritage.org.uk/daysout/properties/rochester-castle/**
My Website: **www.exploring-castles.com/rochester_castle.html**
Open year-round

Bodiam Castle and its surrounding spectacular, reflective moat.

The Puzzle at the Heart of Bodiam Castle

Bodiam Castle could have fallen from the pages of a fable. It's a perfectly shaped little fortress—a squat, square castle with a round tower at each corner. Crafted from gentle golden sandstone, its perfect symmetry is accentuated by the shimmering reflections from the surrounding moat, which wraps around the castle like a ribbon around a birthday gift.

To most visitors of England, Bodiam embodies everything they ever imagined of a medieval castle. It has round turrets and jagged-tooth crenellations, a moat and drawbridge, a deep green well, and a secure inner stronghold. The perfect appearance of the castle is exaggerated by its rather perfect backstory: the fortress was built in the late medieval times for a brave knight returning from a long war within continental Europe.

Bodiam Castle therefore fulfills every flight of imagination about what an English castle should look like. It marries the formidable appearance of a medieval stronghold with romantic ideas of medieval chivalry.

Unsurprisingly, then, the castle has become one of the most photographed fortresses in the whole of Europe. For more than 150 years, the image of Bodiam has been used to decorate postcards and picture books, chocolate boxes, and jigsaw puzzles. In fact, the image of Bodiam Castle is so pervasive around the world that it may have influenced people's imaginations as to what a castle should actually look like. Rather than just appearing like something from a fairytale, Bodiam may have inspired some of those fairytales.

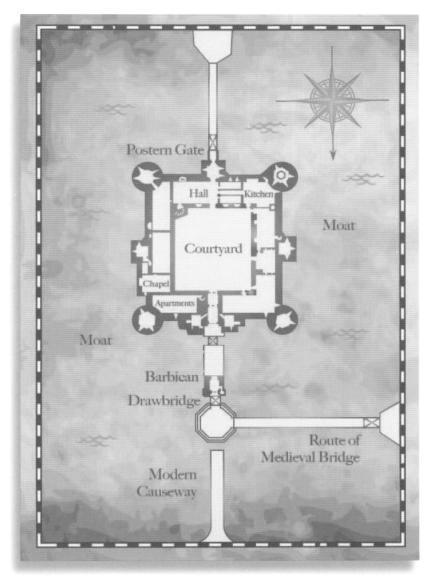

A floor plan of Bodiam Castle.

However, there's an intriguing puzzle at the heart of this beguiling fortress. Although Bodiam was built in medieval times, modern historians have wondered if its perfect appearance is just a bit too good to be true. Are the turrets a little too carefully formed, the crenellations a little overexaggerated, the arrow-slits too impractically large to have ever been used in war? Could England's most photogenic castle be

nothing but an elaborate medieval sham—a trick of architecture designed to aggrandize the knight who commissioned it?

To understand a little more about the true nature of Bodiam Castle, and solve the puzzle at the castle's heart, we need to learn more about the fortress itself—and the all-conquering knight, Edward Dalyngrigge, who commissioned the castle in the first place.

Sir Edward Dalyngrigge and the Hundred Years' War

Writing in 1860, a historian named Mark Antony Lower described Edward Dalyngrigge as being "born in the most flourishing period of English chivalry." It's a wonderful description. Edward was the son of Sir John Dalyngrigge

The inner courtyard. Despite the superlative condition of the exterior, little of the internal rooms or chambers survive.

and was born around 1346 into a high-ranking family. From his early years, Edward would have been made a squire and would have trained to become a knight. The young man would have been schooled in swords, horses, and in heavy armor, and, in 1367, he departed to take part in the Hundred Years' War—where the troops in England battled in the lands of modern France.

Edward undoubtedly earned respect during his exploits in France. He fought beneath the banner of the fearless Earl of Arundel and succeeded in battles in Vannes, Thouars, and Cressy. The Hundred Years' War was only just beginning, and, at that time, it appeared although the English forces had an upper hand (see page 157). Large chunks of northern France became power-vacuums, and such disorder provided an opportunity for ambitious, battle-hungry young knights to seize the spoils of war for themselves. These knights joined together to form *free companies*—an allegiance of roaming mercenaries who were independent of any government.

The free companies quickly became the scourge of lawless northern France. These nomadic tribes were comprised of a rag-tag of unlikely warriors—opportunistic troublemakers and battle-hungry knights joined forces with disenfranchised peasants who had fought in battle but felt unable to return to their past lives as herdsmen or bakers. These disparate men coalesced into groups of itinerant rebels who roamed the countryside looking for conflict—either to be paid by a lord to address a particular spot of trouble or to create it themselves after robbing and pillaging an attractive settlement.

Philippa Kendall/Thinkstock

Perhaps enticed by the independence and plundered riches that marked these free companies, Sir Edward left the side of the auspicious Earl of Arundel and instead allied himself to three infamous knights of the free company movement: Sir John Calveley, Sir John Hawkwood, and Sir Robert Knowles. Sir Robert Knowles was the most feared and fearless of the three men, and the one to whom Sir Edward held the greatest affection. Indeed, the Knowles crest can still be seen in Bodiam Castle today (more upon his life within "A Most Invincible Knight" on page 156). Under his guidance, Sir Edward would have plundered, ransomed, and gleaned a great deal of money (as well as military skills) from his time in Northern France. And, with his newfound wealth, he could set out to build a fortress in England.

The Beguiling Setting of Bodiam

Bodiam is a tiny village nestled upon the sweeping downlands of England's southern counties. It's a place of undulant downland, buffeted only by rolling winds and wholly untroubled by any threat from beyond the nearby English Channel. On infrequent occasions, a puffing, whistling, coal-powered steam train breaks the peace as it ferries tourists along a heritage railway track between the village and historic Tenterden, an idyllic town nearby.

This hamlet is a little more than twelve miles, as the crow flies, from the coastal town of Hastings and not more than seven

The License to Crenellate Bodiam Castle

Created on October 21, 1385, by King Richard II, in the ninth year of his reign. Translated from Latin.

"The King to all persons to whom &c. greeting.

Know that of our special grace we have granted and given licence on behalf of ourselves and our heirs, so much as in us lies, to our beloved and faithful Edward Dalyngrigge, Knight, that he may, with a wall of stone and lime, fortify and krenellate the manse of his manor house of Bodyham, near the sea, in the County of Sussex, and may construct and make thereby a castle for the defence of the adjacent country for resistance against our enemies, and may hold the aforesaid manse so fortified and krenellated, and the castle thereby so made for himself and his heirs for ever, without penalty or impediment from us or our heirs or our officers whosoever.

In witness whereof, &c- Witness the King at Westminster, on the 21st day of October."

miles from the Battle—the site of the 1066 conflict, which changed the course of England's history. Although the place may be sleepy today, it was evidently anything but tranquil during medieval times.

After the successful invasion of William the Conqueror, those in the southern counties of Medieval England were understandably perpetually jumpy about any potential threat from the channel. In the mid-1300s—when England was a much more stable place than in those centuries prior—the specter of invasion once again reared its head as a consequence of the Hundred Years' War, where England battled within France. The French troops upon the opposing side were restrained only by the choppy waters of the English Channel and, in 1377, their forces managed to cross the water and burned and sacked the nearby towns of Rye and Folkestone.

The construction of Bodiam Castle likely began about ten years later, during the tail end of the 1380s. In accordance with a number of other medieval castles, Sir Edward sought permission from the king to build such a castle, and this was granted in 1385.

Some historians have interpreted this license to crenellate, and the timing of construction of the castle, to indicate that Bodiam was built in response to a real French threat. Other historians have argued that the 1377 coastal raid was the final salvo from the French side and, by 1385, the threat of French invasion was entirely over. In addition, they argue that the license to crenellate was pure medieval pomp, and the document boasted had little real-world significance.

Whichever side you fall, there's no doubt that Bodiam was one of the very last castles to be built in England during the medieval period. The majority of fortresses were finished during the 1100s and 1200s. Dunstanburgh Castle (see page 188) was built at a comparatively late stage, but construction took place in the late 1320s—some sixty years before work on Bodiam began. Chronologically, Bodiam was probably the last castle to be built in Medieval England.

A License to Crenellate

Want to build a castle? Well, in the Middle Ages, you might have needed a license for that. Back in Medieval England, nobles wishing to construct a castle ostensibly had to apply to the king for a "license to crenellate," should they have wished to build a fortified castle or manor-house. *Crenellations*, if you're wondering, refer to the up-and-down notches that you'll often see along the top of a castle wall—they're also sometimes referred to as battlements.

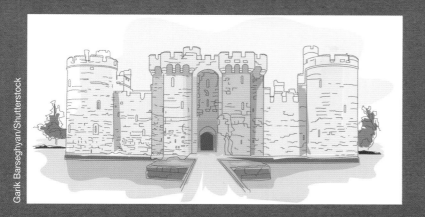

You might well wonder why the king of England would worry about such trivial matters—surely he had better things to be doing than approving architecture? Well, one theory to explain the need for these licenses was the decentralization of power in Medieval England. Although the king was at the top of the feudal tree, his power over his distant lands was rather more tenuous. If the monarch only granted selected permission to build castles, the theory goes, he would have prevented overmighty subjects from getting too powerful in their local areas.

Resultantly, about 480 of these "licenses to crenellate" were signed between 1200 and 1589, with the majority (around 150) agreed during the reign of Edward III (1312–1377). Curiously, most licenses related only to the fortification of manor-houses: only about one hundred of all licenses granted applied to castles.

The internal layout of the castle. As you can see, little exists beyond simple partitions—the entire second floor has long since eroded away.

In the past, historians believed that anyone building a castle without an appropriate license could have had their property confiscated by the king. On closer inspection, though, this theory doesn't really hold water. The majority of castles in England were built without ever obtaining licenses, and licenses were often granted retrospectively, too. Many people applied for licenses without actually building anything, and multiple licenses were often applied to the same building.

So, what exactly was the point of obtaining a license? The most convincing explanation was that a license was a rather grand expression of personal importance. In the same way that you can shop online today to buy a chunk of Scottish land and thus the title *Lord* or *Lady*, a license to crenellate was a medieval expression that you were going up in the world. Most of the recipients of such licenses, studies show, were the up-and-coming in society: knights, squires, and yeomen, who sought proof of their newfound positions in society.

In this context, it's somewhat easier to understand the glowing language within Edward Dalyngrigge's license to crenellate—the king, after all, refers to him as being "beloved and faithful." The license is less a legal document and more a seal of royal approval. In short, the license proclaimed to the world that Sir Edward had made it—and he could build a grand castle to demonstrate his status to any onlooker.

The Exterior Might of Bodiam Castle

Bodiam Castle is situated upon a small spur of sandstone, some three hundred yards from the banks of the gentle River Rother. From a distance—with its dramatic drum towers and jagged battlements—Bodiam certainly looks like a formidable medieval castle. The curtain wall is more than forty feet tall and around six and a half feet thick, and the castle is built of an imposing sandstone—a fine grained rock sourced from a local quarry. The close-jointed, carefully worked stone can be described as *ashlar*—a mark of the high quality of the castle's masonry.

This distinguished finish helps Bodiam to maintain an imposing air: perhaps heightened by the fact that the windows and doors are plain and unadorned by any stone carvings.

What's remarkable is that the present-day exterior of Bodiam Castle is essentially unchanged from medieval times. Many other castles in England were rebuilt and reimagined during the 1800s and 1900s: rescued from ruin and reconstructed with artistic license. Bodiam, by contrast, is enviably authentic, and the photographs upon these pages reflect how the fortress would have looked to Sir Edward in the late 1300s.

A direct bridge leads across to the octagonal platform, and then to the castle. Note the remains of what is thought to have been a barbican—the wall on the right side of the octagon.

145

As the photos illustrate so strikingly, the castle is an impressively symmetrical affair—a square shape with a vast, round drum tower positioned at each corner of the fortress, entirely surrounded by a deep green moat.

What does this moat tell us about Bodiam? Surely, you might think, a moat was a primarily defensive structure. A good moat would have made a castle much more difficult to besiege, preventing attackers from getting uncomfortably close to the walls with battering rams. The moat would also have prevented the scaling of the walls using makeshift ladders.

However, the jury's out if the Bodiam moat could ever have successfully protected the castle against assault. Archeologists have calculated that it would be temptingly easy to drain this moat, as it is, effectively, "raised." Rather than just filling in a ditch with water, those building the castle instead raised the ground where the castle would stand, and then built banks around fit for a moat. As a result, any attacker would be able to drain the moat by digging through a thin earthwork bank on one side. Some historians have a counterargument to such a belief: they believe the drained moat would have still been an obstacle protecting Bodiam, as the deep, sludgy clay would have made it difficult to reach the castle walls. Even so, there are plenty of medieval records showing how assailants traversed a drained, muddy moat using hay and gangplanks.

So, perhaps the moat might not have served Bodiam too effectively in times of siege. But how about the other water defenses—the drawbridge and gateways, the barbican and bridges? Well, there are two main entrances to the castle—the gatehouse and the Postern Gate. The castle crouches with its backside, the Postern Gate, facing today's entrance and parking lot. The Postern Gate functioned as a smaller doorway into the castle (likely a "tradesman's entrance" to the kitchens), and it would have been connected to the mainland via a bridge. Nowadays, this bridge is long gone, meaning that the only entrance to the castle is through the main gatehouse, which is sited on the opposite side of the fortress.

When you walk around the castle to reach the main gatehouse, you'll notice an unusual hexagonal platform that almost seems to float in the middle of the moat—like an oversized lily pad between castle and bank. In the 1400s, between this octagonal platform and the gatehouse, one would have encountered a

A panorama of the castle. Note the consistency of sandstone— Bodiam was built in one fell swoop in around 1385. It would have been one of the last castles built in Medieval England— and the fundamental question is whether it would ever have been capable of defending itself.

Chamomille/Shutterstock

rather large obstacle that's almost entirely missing today: a defensive barbican. Today, all that remains of the barbican is a stump of stone masonry, which pokes up toward the sky like a stele. We can only imagine the threats and defenses posed by the barbican: perhaps a portcullis or two, or a tremendous wooden door, which protected the entrance to the castle. In 1919, the castle moat was drained for cleaning, and a large cast-iron bombard was discovered within—leading some historians to theorize the item was pelted at the barbican (likely during the English Civil War), entirely destroying it. Whatever

Today, a modern bridge leads directly to the entrance of the castle, via the octagonal platform. Back in medieval times, the bridge would have been an "L" shape—running from the bank on the right side of the photo to the octagonal platform, and then crossing to the castle door.

happened to the barbican, its absence is a frustrating omission that makes it harder for us to understand if Bodiam was a true, defensive fortress or a rather cunning trick.

Nowadays, to reach the gatehouse from the shore, you cross the moat in a straight line—a bridge runs from the mainland to the octagonal platform, and a second bridge crosses the gap between the octagonal platform and the castle entranceway. This wouldn't have been the case in Sir Edward's day. Back then, a drawbridge system would have connected the octagonal platform to the gatehouse (via the barbican), and a curious, meandering bridge would have linked the platform to the shore.

The shape of this bridge is rather intriguing. Rather than cross the moat directly via the shortest path to from the northern bank, this bridge instead ran a much longer course across the moat from the western side. The arrangement of bridges and drawbridges resulted in an L-shaped or "dog's leg" pathway into the fortress, rather than the direct I-shaped pathway used today.

Why bother with such a complex arrangement? There are two possible reasons, and it's up to you to decide which is the most likely. Some have argued this convoluted pathway was a defensive masterstroke—any assailant would have been remarkably vulnerable to arrow-fire while traversing the narrow bridge, and the lengthy pathway would have given archers more time to pick off the intruder.

The opposing view, though, was that the lengthy bridge arrangement was just designed to create an even grander entrance to the castle. This view continues that if you had

wanted to ambush the medieval castle, you'd not have bothered with this convoluted pathway altogether and would have simply crossed the shorter, direct bridge to the effectively undefended Postern Gateway at the backside of the castle.

The Remaining Ruins of the Fortress

Most visitors are quite surprised at the innards of Bodiam Castle. Whereas the outside of the fortress is in a beautiful

Rose Smith/Shutterstock

The castle contained at least twenty-eight latrines and thirty-three fireplaces—three of which are quite clearly visible within this photograph.

condition, the buildings and chambers within the walls of the castle have been reduced to ruins. Little survives apart from the remnants of partition walls, hollowed-out fireplaces, and the dusty foundations of once-grand buildings. The grand exterior and ruined interior result in a disconcerting juxtaposition.

So, rather than dwell on the present-day disrepair, let's imagine that we're back in the 1400s and lucky enough to visit the fortress. What would we have found within its four walls?

Well, a lot of toilets, for a start. There's evidence for at least twenty-eight different guaderobes within the castle, all equipped with relatively sophisticated plumbing—the toilets would have "flushed" down flues into the moat, discharging just below the waterline. What's more, these toilets were even equipped with doors (or, at the very least, rails for curtains). Surprised? Well, privacy was an alien concept in Medieval England, and a door upon a toilet was a surprisingly radical idea!

In addition to this profusion of sanitary facilities, the remains of the castle include at least thirty-three different fireplaces. The largest of these would have been those in the rooms belonging to Sir Edward. The next grandest rooms in the castle were those positioned close to the lord's chambers; the farther away one's chambers were from the lord's apartments, the poorer quality the accommodation provided (and, generally, the smaller the fireplace within). The large towers would also have provided living accommodation, and each was split into three floors, with the best rooms usually located within the higher levels.

The organization of the castle means that most residential chambers connect, either directly or indirectly, to the Great Hall. This would have been a most impressive place to banquet. Here, we can suppose that Sir Edward would have dined upon a raised dais at the head of the hall, which measured some fifty feet by twenty-six feet. Grand windows, facing the outer court, would have allowed light to flood into the room, and an adjacent alcove was possibly used as a music gallery, where minstrels would have played fashionable music to delight those dining below.

With so many rooms, the castle could evidently have hosted a large number of people. Some historians have seen this as proof of Bodiam's military purpose—it could have housed a garrison of troops, ready to be deployed at a moment's notice. But it's rather easy to counter such an argument—you might as well say that the number of fireplaces, and the grandeur of the Great Hall, proves that the castle was more devoted to domestic duties and hosting other noble families. In the case of Bodiam, the contents of a castle give little clue to its purpose.

A Trick Worthy of Disney

Almost every visitor to Bodiam is taken back by the state of the ruinous interior compared to the neat exterior, and most are equally surprised at how small the fortress is inside. From the outside, Bodiam looks quite remarkably large, but, when viewed from the inner court, the castle feels quite tiny indeed.

In recent years, the castle has been reappraised by architects, who've studied the form of the fortress and come to conclusions

The chapel window, located on the western side of the castle. If you glance at the castle plan, you can see that the chapel pokes out of the curtain wall a little—it was probably a conscious compromise to provide sufficient space for family worship. The medieval piscina (stone sink to wash the holy vessels) is still visible today.

regarding its design. Their findings support the idea that Bodiam was built for show, not for defense. Based on measurements and reappraisals of the castle's form, they've established that there's an architectural trick at work in Bodiam's design, using a technique nowadays known as *forced perspective*.

Forced perspective is something that you might be aware of if you've ever visited Disneyland. In these theme parks, when you cross the gates and walk down Main Street, you might have remarked upon how huge the castle looks and how long Main Street appears. When walking back down Main Street at the end of the day, though, the distance on the way back feels half as long as you walked that morning. How ever did it shrink?

The answer lies in the sleight of an architect's hand. When we look at a building or landscape, we naturally interpret smaller things to be farther away, and cunning designers can engineer landscapes to manipulate our sense of depth and height. For instance, the towers of Cinderella's Castle in Disneyland are much smaller than they should be, and the castle tapers upward in a quite alarming fashion. As a bystander, we wrongly interpret the castle to be much taller than it actually is. The designers of Disneyland used similar tricks in the design and decor of the upper stories of the stores and buildings upon Main Street: standing at the beginning of the road and walking deeper into the theme park, these tricks make the street appear longer and the castle taller than either actually is.

Bodiam Castle perfected such tricks of the eye around 550 years before Walt Disney did. A profusion of chimneys and

The number of internal windows provides a wealth of interesting viewpoints upon the castle.

Markus Gann/Shutterstock

to be the same size—but, on closer inspection, these jagged markings actually vary in scale.

The battlements that crown the turrets are half the scale of those that line the drum towers, and the battlements that adorn the chimneys are teeny-tiny in real life. Similarly, the windows on the upper floors of the castle are quite deceptively small, and the visible doorways are minute (even by medieval standards!). This deliberate manipulation of perspective makes the castle look much taller than it actually is.

Evidently, such tricks of perspective will fall apart if viewed from the wrong angle. This could be another cunning reason for building a moat. The moat creates distance between us and the castle, exaggerating Bodiam's height. It also makes it hard for us to compare the height of the castle to the height of surrounding trees, which would otherwise give away the game.

The construction of the castle appears to have attempted to remove similar visual anchors that give bystanders a sense of perspective—the staircases that join the towers, for instance, are alarmingly small, but resultantly make the towers appear much broader than they actually are. The overall effect? Bodiam appears mighty and menacing from the outside—but its real dimensions can't be concealed from a visitor entering its four walls.

An Engineered Landscape

Modern excavations have unearthed other clues about the true purpose of Bodiam Castle—but some of these clues are evident to any visitor with a keen eye. Glancing around

turrets poke out from above the castle, and each of these is crowned with jagged battlements. Our eye is first drawn to the battlements upon the drum towers—then to the battlements on the taller turrets, and then to the battlements that crown the chimneys. We naturally interpret all the battlements

the immediate environs of the castle, it quickly becomes apparent that Bodiam is built on a flat patch of ground that is immediately overlooked by a rather sizable mound around 220 yards to the west. In fact, this neighboring mound is so tall that if you were firing a bow and arrow from the top of it, you'd be ten feet higher than the towers of the castle and forty feet above the level of the curtain wall.

Considering most other English castles were built upon the highest land possible, it seems like an unfortunate mistake that Bodiam was quite so overlooked. Such an opposing vantage point would have been a defensive disaster—a gift to any man with the cannons or trebuchets to bombard the fortress. Either someone made a terrible error in choosing the spot for the castle or there was a different purpose altogether to this mysterious mound.

Archeology can give us some clues as to its purpose. Modern excavations have shown that the castle was, rather unexpectedly, surrounded by six man-made pools—and the bank around the outside of the moat was actually a causeway. In medieval times, special significance was placed upon the shimmering, reflective potential of water—moats and lakes surrounded the grandest homes and castles and accentuated their size and aesthetic appeal.

Paul J Martin/Shutterstock

Within medieval times, Bodiam would have been surrounded by a series of six man-made pools in addition to the moat. It's thought that the shimmering reflections would have bedazzled important visitors to the castle.

An aerial view—there's no doubt that it's a truly spectacular sight. You'll notice an area of higher ground toward the top left corner of the photograph—it's thought that this would have been an intentional panoramic viewpoint for medieval visitors to the castle.

The shimmering moat accentuates the symmetrical appearance of Bodiam, but it may also have been designed to create distance between a spectator and the castle walls. This creates the illusion that the walls and towers are much taller than they actually are.

Bodiam would have therefore been surrounded by a profusion of peaceful pools, and each different aspect of the building would have been reflected at differing angles upon the surfaces of the water. Today, the moat alone provides an excellent setting for photography: imagine yourself as a medieval visitor admiring the reflections made from six different ponds. The castle and its surroundings would have been incomparably impressive.

Some modern academics even believe that the medieval pathway into Bodiam was deliberately tortuous. Do you remember when we discussed the odd arrangement of bridges into the castle—that "dog's leg" or L-shape, which took an unnecessarily convoluted path across the moat? Historians argue that this bridge was the final stage of an elaborate pathway that traversed the causeways around the six pools and finally looped in front of the castle to reach the gatehouse. The overall aim, they argue, was to provide a shimmering, fluctuant vision of the castle from every angle—an incomparable, evocative approach that would have impressed the most discerning of visitors.

This theory—of a deliberately contrived landscape—would help explain this mysterious mound next to the castle. Rather than being the Achilles heel of a defensive fortress, it was instead intended to be a point of panorama—a lookout across the castle and its reflective landscape, and the point where the symmetrical design of Bodiam could be most easily appreciated. Indeed, excavations suggest that the mound was once the site of medieval gardens and a viewing platform: the castle was to be shown off as an enviable aesthetic achievement.

A Trick of the Eye

On balance, then, it certainly seems like Bodiam Castle was designed for good looks rather than for any practical purpose of defense. There can be no doubt that the fortress was designed to look mighty, but the reality was that the castle would have been rendered impotent if actually held to siege.

Does this mean that Bodiam is any less impressive, or less important, than we once imagined? Of course not! The castle actually demonstrates to us a fascinating development in medieval warfare—the emergence of soft power. In more dangerous times past, a castle would have had to be able to defend itself from the mightiest of attacks. In the late fourteenth century, however, England was becoming a more peaceful place. Rather than brute strength, Bodiam exudes an inner confidence—its deceptively defensive appearance would have deterred attackers and also suggested the owner was an important man with status in society. And that's exactly what Sir Edward wished to prove: he was an up-and-coming knight in possession of "new money." He desperately wanted to gain societal acceptance for his new status.

The solution to our puzzle appears to be that Bodiam Castle was, essentially, a grand display of power and status—so-called "militant architecture" rather than "military architecture." Nonetheless, it's still a magnificent example of medieval design and ingenuity, made all the richer for this pearl of truth hidden within its oyster-shell exterior. When you visit the castle, be prepared to be bowled over by its dazzling symmetry and beguiling charm—and take satisfaction from your understanding of its deepest secrets.

A Most Invincible Knight

From the crest still visible within Bodiam Castle, we know that Sir Edward Dalyngrigge idolized his mentor, the infamous Sir Robert Knowles. Who exactly was this fearsome fellow?

Well, Sir Robert Knowles has been called "a most invincible Knight" and "the most famous English professional soldier of the Hundred Years' War." He was known by contemporary chroniclers as "the most able and skilful man of arms in all the [Free] Companies"

Note how turrets spring from above the main towers and are capped with their own little battlements. These decorative features are somewhat smaller than the eye might suggest, creating the optical illusion that the castle is taller than it actually is.

and gained infamy for defeating a force of 5,800 with just 600 men—slaughtering more than 500 of the opposition.

There can be no doubt that this short, stocky warrior possessed phenomenal strength in battle. He was, sources suggest, a man of "few words" and one of his greatest military successes occurred in 1359, leading a victorious two-month siege of the French city of Auxerre. But Sir Robert's lofty achievements were driven as much by personal greed as a desire to further the cause of the English crown. Sir Robert had chosen his target carefully—Auxerre was a rich city, and the knight extorted 40,000 mouton, plus a further 10,000 worth of pearls (around $16,000, or £10,000, in value) from the townspeople upon their surrender.

Such plunder was not unusual—Sir Knowles's strong-arm tactics were infamous throughout France. The man left a trail of destruction in his wake, and the smoldering gables of torched houses became known as "Knowles's mitres." He was a knight of questionable honor, burning abbeys and churches that lay upon his route through northern France, and his brutal efforts in war were captured quite magnificently by a medieval poet: "Robert Knowles, the stubborn souls, of Frenchmen well you check / Your mighty blade has largely preyed, and wounded many a neck." (These words have, of course, been rendered into modern English.)

Andrea Ricordi/Shutterstock

There can be no doubt that Sir Knowles would rather have enjoyed such a grand reputation. In 1358, he held a provocative banner during a raid into French territory. "*Qui Robert Canolle prendera,*" it read, "*Cent mille moutons gagnera.*" ("He who captures Robert Knowles will earn one hundred thousand moutons.") Unsurprisingly, no one was able to take him up on such a bargain.

Sir Edward Dayrigge's involvement with Sir Robert Knowles would have been quite a change of pace from his previous engagements in fighting the Hundred Years' War under the Earl of Arundel.

However, for both Sir Edward and for Sir Robert, there were amends to be made as the bulk of the French conflict drew to a close. Medieval England was—understandably—a God-fearing land, and both men would have needed to atone for the pillage and plunder of the Hundred Years' War. Before investing in Bodiam Castle, Sir Edward donated money to a good number of English churches, but Sir Knowles's contributions were dryly amusing. In return for a papal pardon for his efforts in war, Sir Knowles was forced to repay much of the forty thousand mouton he had extorted from the people of besieged Auxerre.

The spectacular curtain wall is more than forty feet tall and six feet thick. Although impressive, do remember that many other medieval castles boasted walls that were more than twelve feet thick.

The Hundred Years' War

The Hundred Years' War is rather deceptively named: it was a conflict lasting 116 years, between 1337 and 1453. In simplistic terms, it pitted England against France and was a series of rumbling conflicts rather than a perpetual state of war between the two countries.

Since 1066, the fate of England and France had been intertwined. William the Conqueror had arrived from across the channel, bringing with him the Old French language. England and France had coexisted as two squabbling feudal nations—England with umbilical ties to the French lands. In England, the peasantry spoke in Old English (using words such as *dog, ox, calf,* and *sheep* to describe their daily chores of animal husbandry); their noble rulers spoke in the Old French of the more prosperous mother country (using words such as *veal, mutton,* and *venison* to describe the richer meals they enjoyed).

The eastern face of the castle is on the left of the photograph, the entrance gatehouse to the right. Intriguingly, the gatehouse's original wooden portcullis survives to this day.

By the 1200s, however, the two nations were moving in separate directions. The French monarchy held impressive poewer over a nation of seventeen million; by contrast, England had just four million and had lost most of its claim to lands within the boundaries of modern France (with the exception of some rich, wine-producing regions in the south).

In 1328, Charles IV of France died without a natural heir. King Edward III of England was the nephew of Charles, whereas Philip of France (later crowned Philip VI) was his cousin. The French naturally claimed the Frenchman as their king. Edward felt he had the stronger claim—and was also worried about losing the fertile wine regions in the south of France. And so the war began.

Despite England's smaller size, it initially outflanked the French military—using spectacular new technology such as the Welsh-inspired longbow, which could fire a volley of twelve arrows a minute at an unsuspecting target. In the initial years of the war, the English claimed vast swathes of French lands and decimated French castles using siege tactics and the use of rudimentary gunpowder. Of course, there was a deft French resurgence, followed by a period of dramatic English counterfighting, led by the bellicose King Henry V from 1413 onward.

The final French victory, however, was inspired by a rather unlikely figure. In 1428, a young peasant girl,

The Postern Gate—positioned at the "back side" of the castle. It's likely that, during the medieval period, this gateway provided direct access to the kitchens.

Joan of Arc, entered the French court claiming to have received divine inspiration to lead the French forces to war. Despite her preposterous ideas, she was allowed to proceed with the French military and—seemingly by divine intervention—the French forces unexpectedly won the Siege of Orleans.

From then on, Joan became a rallying cry for the French forces. She was soon captured by the English, who proclaimed her a witch channeling demonic voices. Joan was burned at the stake in Rouen in 1431.

It was a propaganda disaster for the English. Joan became a figurehead of rebellion, and her image provided the stimulus to raise the forces to expel the hated English from French territories. In 1451, the French defeated the last English army upon their lands, and in 1453, the conflict was over.

The result? France and England became separated forever—two nation states determined to go in their own separate directions. The language of the two countries became a perfect demonstration of their separation. English—rather than being the tongue of the peasants— morphed slowly into becoming the tongue of the country. A separate sense of English national identity emerged. Poets such as Geoffrey Chaucer—"the father of modern English literature"—had traveled throughout France and participated in the Hundred Years War. Chaucer then returned to England and wrote in Middle English, a powerful demonstration of the birth of England as a nation.

The location of Bodiam Castle.

Bodiam Castle

Bodiam, Robertsbridge,
East Sussex, TN32 5UA
+44 (0)1580 830196
Managed by the National Trust
Official Website: **www.nationaltrust.org.uk/bodiam-castle/**
Official Facebook: **www.facebook.com/BodiamCastleNT**
My Website: **www.exploring-castles.com/bodiam_castle.html**
Open year-round

The Siege of Corfe Castle, and the Might of Lady Mary Bankes

A beautiful panorama of Corfe Castle.

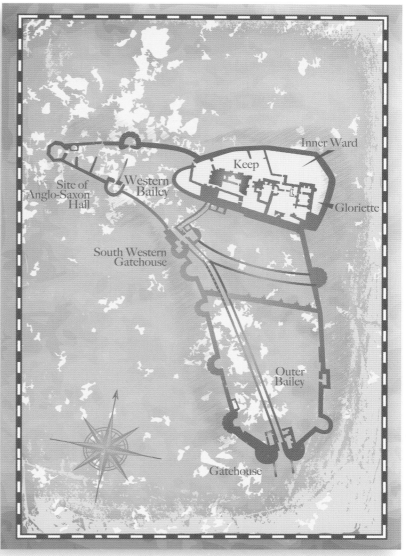

A floor plan of Corfe Castle.

Corfe Castle is reduced to ruins. Paradoxically, though, the crumbling remains of this vast fortress convey its strength more effectively than still-intact walls. Corfe was undoubtedly one of the greatest castles in England, with a checkered and sometimes bloody history that spans more than one thousand years.

Corfe was founded by the Anglo-Saxons, favored by William the Conqueror, and fortified by King John. However, the castle is most famous for its role in the English Civil War of the 1640s. Despite all odds, Corfe was held under sustained siege by the indomitable Lady Mary Bankes, a devout Royalist. Despite every privation, and the death of her husband, she denied the Parliamentarian forces from capturing her castle—until a devastating act of treachery delivered the fortress to the opposing side.

Once Lady Bankes lost the castle, the Parliamentarians wasted no time in plundering its contents and attempting to destroy its walls. Despite their best efforts—and untold barrels

Corfe Castle is a stop on the route of the Swanage Heritage Railway—a puffing, steam-powered railroad, sensationally popular with local tourists.

The Western Bailey is at the forefront of the image. You can see the line of hills that runs behind the castle—the name "Corfe" comes from the Anglo-Saxon "Ceorfan," which means a cutting within the hills.

of gunpowder—the romantic ruined remains of this feared fortress still fleck the Dorset hills and fascinate more than one hundred thousand visitors every year.

Exploring Corfe Castle Today

The word *Corfe* comes from the Old English word *ceorfan,* which means "gap" or "cutting," and the unusual name originates from the remarkable topography of the area. The meandering shoreline of this part of southern England sweeps into a small peninsula, which is commonly (but misleadingly) known as the Isle of Purbeck, despite its connection to the mainland. A series of evocatively named hills cross the narrow peninsula, with their passage broken only by a narrow gap at the midway point of the isle.

This pass was known as Corfegeat in Saxon times—a gateway through the peninsula. The potential to control the flow of

trade and money therefore made Corfegeat the perfect spot upon which to construct a castle. Indeed, the Anglo-Saxons built the first fortifications, some time before the Normans even arrived in England. The old Saxon hall of Corfe was the unfortunate backdrop for the cold-blooded murder of Edward the Martyr, an unlucky youth and brief king of England (see boxout, page 164). The foundations of the hall (later re-appropriated by the Normans) are visible to eagle-eyed modern visitors of the ruined West Bailey.

The Normans expended an unusual amount of energy in fortifying Corfe beyond this old hall. When creating other castles, their usual strategy was to render the first fortifications in wood and then return years later to rebuild in stone—providing the fortress had proved its worth. Significant chunks of Corfe were built from stone from the off, however, and Henry I commissioned the seventy-foot Great Keep to be completed in just eight years—finishing in 1105. It would have been a true medieval monolith—the tallest man-made structure hereto glimpsed within the southwest of England. From the early days, it appears that Corfe was one of the most important castles in the whole of England.

The scale of the Great Keep was matched by the size and ambition of the remainder of the castle. The Keep was the symbolic heart of the fortress, standing upon the highest patch of land. A thick curtain wall encircled this tower and its hilltop, with the space within forming the Inner Ward. During medieval times, treasures were added to this Inner Ward, including King John's 1203 Gloriette—a decadent palace, now sadly much destroyed, and likely filled with richly colored tapestries. The Inner Ward therefore housed much of the high-status accommodations of the medieval castle.

The Inner Ward is connected to a further, vast loop of external curtain wall, which drapes across the hillside like a giant lasso. The space within is designated as the Outer Bailey—a sizable enclosure that would once have been filled with the hubbub of market traders, blacksmiths, pigs, hounds, and muddy children: the hallmarks of everyday castle life. The western section is separated from the southern part by a dividing wall and internal gatehouse, which would have acted as a second layer of protection if the Outer Gatehouse was breached.

The grand Outer Gatehouse lies at the most southern tip of the loop of curtain wall and acted as a ceremonial entrance into the Outer Bailey—and thus into the castle itself. Access would have been gained via a connecting bridge, which traversed the rocky, defensive outer ditch, dug in about 1214. Today, the ruined towers of the Gatehouse stand at less than half their original height; they would once have been about two and a half stories high, and the whole structure would have been fortified with at least one portcullis and heavy oak doors.

The ruins of King John's Gloriette. Effectively a mini-palace, the Gloriette would have contained a number of state rooms, including the Long Chamber and King's Solar. It's likely all would have been decorated with luxurious tapestries.

The Murder of King Edward the Martyr at Corfe Castle

The ruins of the castle, viewed from the village graveyard below. As well as the obvious parallels, both the headstones and the castle are built from similar local sandstone.

"No worse deed than this was done to the Anglo-Saxon race, since they first came to Britain."

The story of Edward the Martyr delves back more than one thousand years to the turbulent years of the late 900s. The tricky-looking Old English names that stud this story—Ethelred, Elfrida, and so forth—are a linguistic clue that we're dealing with the Anglo-Saxon period, prior to the Norman conquest of England. (As an aside, although the name Edward sounds familiar to our ears, it's actually an unusual example of an Old English name, Eadweard, being exported to the European continent. The name evolved into Édouard in the romance languages, and, ironically, its modern use probably owes more to its continental appeal rather than its Old English roots.)

Anyway, I digress. The martyr at the heart of our story was a boy born around 962 and twelve or thirteen years old when he succeeded the English throne. From the first days of his reign, Edward was embroiled within an early English succession crisis. His father had been King Edgar, who had had two wives. Edward was the son of the king's first wife. His younger half-brother, Ethelred, was the son of his second wife—the wicked stepmother of our story, Queen Elfrida.

Edward legitimately inherited the crown from his father, but early England was left divided by King Edgar's earlier efforts to import Catholicism. Queen Elfrida understood the simmering discontent within the isle and saw an opportunity to foist her own son onto the throne in the place of unfortunate young Edward. Her machinations were not unnoticed by the young king: to draw her into his fold, he granted her lands and status in the county of Dorset. However, like a malevolent spirit, the queen chose to reside outside of the Royal Court and spent her days at Corfe Castle with her son, devising dark schemes to hand her boy the English crown.

It's at this point of our story that verifiable facts become hazy, and we stray into the realm of legends and tales that have been told and retold over the centuries. What we know for a fact is that Edward the Martyr died just two years after he came to the throne. His place of death was close to the Old Hall of Corfe Castle (a Norman hall built upon Anglo-Saxon foundations). The cause of his death, so many tell, was murder at the hands of Elfrida.

On March 18, 978, stories tell, Edward was part of a royal party hunting in the countryside of Dorset. As his half-brother lived in Corfe Castle—and because of his naive desire to build bridges with his stepmother—Edward paid a visit to the castle on his way back from the hunt.

At the castle, Edward was greeted with uncommon hospitality by Elfrida. She was warm, expansive, and welcoming to the boy and ushered the youth into her home. As a gesture of hospitality, she offered Edward a drink of wine. However, as Edward lifted the cup to his lips, he was stabbed in the back by one of her servants. Some tales even tell that Elfrida was the one who delivered the fatal blow, stabbing her stepson with her own

Doyle, James William Edmund (1864) "Edward the Martyr" in A Chronicle of England: B.C. 55—A.D. 1485, London: Longman, Green, Longman, Roberts & Green, pp. p. 72. Licensed under Public Domain via Wikimedia Commons.

A modern illustration of Elfrida offering the chalice to Edward.

dagger as he lifted up the heavy cup with his two young hands.

Some stories tell that Edward survived the wound and clambered onto his horse to escape, only to collapse within the woods, falling from his steed into the rotting leaves of the forest floor. Other tales say that the boy died immediately within Corfe. Either way, the tales assert that young Edward was quickly buried in secret in nearby Wareham, leaving his half-brother, Ethelred, to take the crown.

Edward's death certainly wasn't the end of the story. It's said that Elfrida was wracked with remorse for her actions, and, a year following the boy's death, arranged for his body to be disinterred to provide a more fitting burial and to atone for her sins.

There was a shock in store. When the body was exhumed and unwrapped from its shroud, onlookers gasped at its immaculate condition—it was miraculously preserved. It was, to Anglo-Saxons and to contemporary Catholics alike, a sign of sainthood.

Edward the Martyr is still, to this day, revered as a saint. His feast day is March 18—the anniversary of his death. The supposed position of the Old Hall, where the king died, is visible to anyone touring Corfe Castle today.

The Might of Lady Mary Bankes

When it comes to tales of bravery and persistence, few heroes or heroines can equal Lady Mary Bankes. If a surviving sculpture is true to life, Lady Mary was a tall, broad-shouldered woman, her sharp nose offset by a cascade of curled hair. Her epitaph—carved into a plaque within a quiet church chancel—describes the lady as having "borne . . . a noble proportion of the late calamities [referring to the English Civil War] . . . with a constancy and courage above her sex." In any civil war, of course,

"Mary Bankes-Hawtry by Henry Pierce Bone, after John Hoskins"; by Henry Pierce Bone. Licensed in the public domain via Wikimedia Commons.

A painting of Lady Mary Bankes, painted in 1837. Note the stylized keys of Corfe Castle in her hands and the castle in the far distance, to the left of the image.

heroes and villains necessarily spring from neighbors and cousins—but the persistence and bravery of Lady Bankes was quite remarkable.

Lady Bankes was married to Sir John Bankes—a rarefied couple who moved in the higher echelons of English society.

Sir John was an eminent English lawyer with an admirable reputation—knighted in 1634, later made attorney general, and awarded Doctor of Law at Oxford University in 1642.

The pair were married in 1618 and purchased Corfe Castle in 1635 as a grand family home, rather than as a fortress. It was, of

The Inner Ward contained the majority of the high-status accommodations of the castle, and was protected by that second ring of curtain wall.

Finely worked window frames, found in the Inner Ward of the castle. It's easy to imagine how this was a luxurious home for the Bankes family.

course, a sizable castle, but the Bankeses were a similarly sizable family, raising fourteen children between 1621 and 1644.

Of course, the late 1630s were a time of political turmoil within England, and the seeds of civil war were being sewn. Undoubtedly as a consequence of his knighthood and past service to the crown, Sir Bankes was a devout and uncompromising Royalist. As the opposing Parliamentarians tightened their grip on London, Sir Bankes was ordered away from his family home to attend the court of King Charles in the Royalist strongholds of York in 1642 and then in Oxford in 1644. As he rode to York in April 1642, he would have left his wife and children isolated within the walls of Corfe Castle, with only a handful of servants to keep them company.

During that year, Parliamentarian forces had been making steady progress along the southern English coastline, led by two notable commanders, Sir Walter Earle and Sir Thomas Trenchard. Neighboring castles—including Portland—had been taken for the Parliamentarian cause and Corfe was recognized as a significant fortress that, if seized, would bolster the Parliamentarian effort. It was widely known that Sir Bankes was away and that the castle was occupied only by the lady, her children, and a small retinue of servants. The Parliamentarians mistakenly assumed its capture would be a simple task.

Their first attempt to claim the fortress was to use cunning. On May 1 every year, the village of Corfe held the May Day Stag Hunt: a day of festivities, filled with the distractions of hunting, drinking, and dancing. The Parliamentarian plan of action was unsophisticated: they would gallop to the

168

Residential accommodation within the Inner Ward. The technical term for this is ashlar—*the stone is finely worked and closely jointed, demonstrating that this was a place for nobility.*

gates of the castle and would tell Lady Bankes they would spare her and her castle if she would agree to a peaceful inspection of the four remaining cannons still mounted on the northern wall. Their actual intention, however, was to seize the fortress once they had gained entrance—calculating that with so many local men engaged by the stag-hunt, their scheme would be unhindered.

This first Parliamentarian plot was entirely unsuccessful. Lady Bankes had many sympathizers in the town who got wind of these poorly concealed plans—and, luckily for her, these locals chose to come to her aid, rather than to continue hunting deer. In addition, the Parliamentarian troops were ill-disciplined. When they arrived at the barricaded castle doors, their ringleaders continued with the pretence of a peaceful inspection, but some of the younger, more impatient members of the party threatened to storm the castle.

Lady Bankes was under no misconception about their true motivations and barricaded the doors.

The Parliamentarians realized that, with little more than themselves and their horses, they were out-maneuvered. They retreated slowly from the locked wooden doors of the fortress, but their attentions were still focused upon those four cannons lining the walls. Some days later, a letter arrived at the castle from the army commissioners in Poole, requesting the cannons removed and surrendered to the Parliamentarian forces. With her token aplomb, Lady Bankes sent a speedy reply: she was, she wrote, alone in the castle without a husband, and she wished to keep these cannons for her own protection. The commander seemed to take pity. He sent a response and terms were agreed: Lady Mary could keep the cannons as long as she unmounted them from the castle walls. She acquiesced to their demands.

As a result, while war raged elsewhere in England, Lady Mary and the inhabitants of the castle were free to live in a temporary peace. Of course, this was just the beginning of a lengthy saga, and there was no doubt that Lady Mary's movements were being carefully watched by the opposing Parliamentarians.

A Siege of Forty Sailors

One chilly gray morning, some weeks after that first altercation with the Parliamentarians, Lady Mary was awoken by a thundering knocking upon the wooden castle door.

Rather than send a servant to establish the cause of the commotion, Lady Mary acted with real presence of mind, descending herself to the gate of the fortress. There she discovered an ominous party of around forty threatening sailors who had reached Corfe by boat. The demands of this gang of men were simple: they wished to enter the castle and made it clear that they would do so using any means necessary.

Lady Mary's first strategy was negotiation. She explained the previous terms agreed with the commissioner in Poole and the prior assurance that she would be left in peace. But the men had a trick up their sleeves and produced a warrant for immediate entry signed by one of the army commissioners. It's not clear if this warrant was signed by the commander who had previously agreed to leave Lady Mary in peace or by another man from the same command station. Nonetheless, it marked an unexpected U-turn by the Parliamentarian forces.

Lady Mary thought quickly. Within the castle that morning, she had her children, a handful of servants, and just five men. On the other side of the gatehouse, there were around forty armed sailors. A lesser mortal might have given up there and then—but Lady Mary possessed quite uncommon bravery. She refused the men entry, barricaded the doors of the castle, and sent the word to all inside that they must remount the cannons onto the wall of the fortress. In a frenzy of activity, the five men at her command managed to do so and fired one thunderous shot of the cannon at those outside the gates. Outflanked by such weaponry, the men scurried away—for now.

The Great Gatehouse is to the left of the image. Flanked by two massive drum towers, this is likely the place where Lady Bankes would have negotiated with the forty sailors who arrived at her home.

Time was still of the essence, as Lady Mary expected that the troops would return with reinforcements. Not sparing a second, she threw open the doors of the fortress while one of her servants beat out a rhythmic march on a mighty drum. The drumbeat was the call to Corfe village that the castle was endangered, and around fifty neighbors and tenants of her land rushed to her assistance, barricading themselves inside the castle with whatever provisions they had at hand.

The enemies, however, did not return with reinforcements. Instead, the Parliamentarian approach was much more subtle.

They stationed a small guard of men outside the castle, who ensured that no messenger could pass in or out of the stronghold. No food or provisions were allowed into the fortress, and those inside had to make do with what little they had taken with them.

The next stage of this understated conflict was propaganda. The Parliamentarians sent letters to those men who had joined Lady Bankes in her siege, threatening to burn their homes and hurt their families unless they withdrew their support. These same letters were distributed to the wives in the neighboring town—causing many to come to

The Gatehouse was built in around 1280, and was at least two stories tall—today, it's reduced to less than half its original height. It would have contained at least one portcullis, and it's likely that there were a series of machicolations.

Corfe Castle communicates directly with the village below it —the path through the Gatehouse connects directly to the heart of the small town below.

the castle walls to beg and remonstrate with their husbands, urging them to return home.

On this occasion, Lady Mary knew she was utterly outflanked. She lacked sufficient supplies to withstand a lengthy siege,

and her own supporters were growing nervous and restless, worried about the well-being of their families outside. This first siege had gone on for more than a week, and so Mary decided to negotiate a truce—offering her four cannons in exchange for the liberty of all those in the castle. For the second time, a peace deal was agreed, and those living in the fortress were allowed to remain so, provided they would do nothing to equip or fortify the castle for any future use.

Although both sides had reconciled, it was an uneasy peace. Local Parliamentarian sympathizers living in the community were covertly asked to keep an eye on Lady Bankes's movements and to report any efforts to fortify the castle with food, gunpowder, or other supplies for siege.

However, these spies were lazy, and Lady Bankes—in conjunction with a significant groundswell of local supporters—was cunning. Beneath the noses of the Parliamentarians, she smuggled in vast quantities of food

The remains of King John's Gloriette—the decadent medieval palace built adjacent to the Great Keep, within the Inner Ward of the castle.

171

A panorama of Corfe and the adjacent village, taking in the castle and many of the rolling hills that constitute the Isle of Purbeck.

and equipment, ready for the mighty siege, which she perceived was imminent. She also sent a messenger to nearby Royalist troops, explaining the importance of Corfe to their cause, encouraging them to come to her assistance and command the castle with her. The messenger returned with two commanders and a smattering of soldiers—a token gesture, but nowhere near enough to secure the fortress against future onslaught.

A Further Siege, and a Royalist Rally

On the misty morning of June 23, 1643, the Parliamentarians marched toward Corfe with an army of between five hundred

and six hundred men, a cannon, and siege machines. It was an unprecedented show of force, and it was motivated, in part, as retribution for the actions of Lady Bankes's husband.

Sir Bankes, you'll remember, was a lawyer loyal to King Charles. Some weeks prior, in Salisbury, he had denounced the behavior of some key Parliamentarians—including the Earl of Essex—to be treasonous. In return, Parliament declared him a traitor and ordered that all his lands and property be seized to finance their war efforts. As a result, an army of men commanded by Sir Walter Earle marched on Corfe Castle with incomparable ferocity. Earle, too, held a grudge against Lady Bankes, as he was one of those first commanders

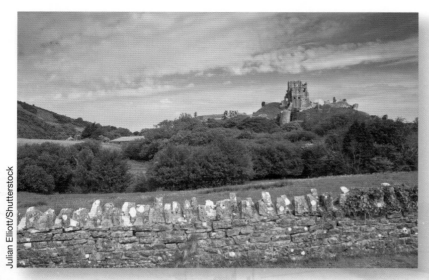
The castle from another perspective—this time taken from the north (often considered its "back").

The village of Corfe unfurls from beneath the foot of the castle.

who failed to trick his way into the castle some months ago. This time around, he approached Corfe with a firm resolution to capture the castle.

The troops were instructed to stop at nothing to claim the castle for their own. They were instructed to act without mercy, and to kill any man, woman, or child within the fortress, and their commanders told tall tales of vast riches and plunder within Corfe that would be granted to the men when successful. The forces were enviably armed with battering rams and cannons, and, with so many at their disposal, surrender looked inevitable.

They hadn't bargained upon the strength of the castle—and of Lady Bankes. The few soldiers stationed with her in the fortress used gunfire to inflict heavy wounds on those attacking the castle, and the strength of the walls foiled the efforts of the opposition's cannon and siege machines. In frustration at the poor progress, some

younger members of the army—lacking discipline—ransacked the church next to the castle and burned down many of the houses in the town, plundering as they went. Their actions lead to a hardening of popular, local support behind Lady Bankes's cause.

Understanding that the walls of the fortification were too thick to break down, the Parliamentarian commanders devised a change of tactic. They sent for reinforcements and asked for climbing equipment and so received 150 more men alongside a collection of ladders and ropes. If they couldn't go through the walls, they reasoned, they'd have to go over.

The Parliamentarian commanders also tried everything possible to psychologically propel their troops to success. They bribed and encouraged their soldiers, offering grand financial rewards for the first man to scale a ladder and enter the fortress, and plied their men with vast amounts of drink to give them the courage to undertake the task. Such invocations were doubtless

173

required, as the first man climbing a ladder into a besieged fortress was effectively undertaking a suicide mission. Sure enough, those men scaling the Lower Ward of the fortress were greeted with the musket shots of the resident Royalist soldiers, and those climbing to the Upper Ward were met by the redoubtable efforts of Lady Bankes and her young family, who threw any implements on hand—including burning embers and heavy stones—onto the heads of all those attempting to enter.

During the course of the siege, the Parliamentarian forces sustained significant losses—more than one hundred men and vast amounts of ammunition and supplies. By contrast, although those defending the castle had consumed equal supplies, only two on their side were killed. On August 4, 1643, some six weeks after this siege had begun, word arrived that the Royalist forces were to descend to Corfe to finish off the Parliamentarian army and would strengthen the castle further. These opposing troops had been foiled yet again—and bid a hasty retreat.

This minor Royalist victory mirrored the present state of Civil War in England. The western counties, including Dorset, had always leaned toward the king's side, and a recent series of battle victories had secured Charles's supremacy over the territory. Some weeks later, therefore, Sir Bankes would have been guaranteed safe passage to travel through this part of the country and so rode back to his family home to be reunited with his wife and children. It was, sadly, the last time he would ever see them.

The curtain walls are, in the main, more than twelve feet thick; this ruined section gives an excellent sense of their previous might.

"Floating" windows within the stonework give us some idea of where different rooms and chambers may once have been.

One can only imagine Sir Bankes's shock as he rode into Corfe. The village, by all counts, was utterly devastated—a maelstrom of ruined buildings and blackened timbers. The church, just outside the castle walls, was similarly ransacked—with its gold plate and cloth purloined by the opposing troops. As Sir Bankes rode closer to his castle, however, he would have been reassured that the outer walls of his home, although damaged, were still serviceable. On his arrival, cantering into the Inner Ward of the castle, he would have been greeted by a gaggle of his breathless children, all excitedly retelling the tales of the past months. For a few precious weeks, at least, Corfe Castle was a family home again.

The Parliamentarian Return

In the same way that the tide eddies along the Purbeck Coast, the flow of the Civil War changed dramatically during the course of 1644. Whereas the Royalists had appeared to be holding the upper hand within the West, a string of defeats and the strengthening of the opposition meant that past victories were being swallowed by the advancing Parliamentarian army. Sir Bankes was called from his family home back to the side of the king, and Lady Bankes was left again in the castle, helpless to prevent a terrifying string of Parliamentarian victories as the Civil War advanced toward her doorstep. In June, the nearby town of Weymouth fell, and this blow was quickly followed by the surrender of Lyme, Poole, and neighboring Wareham. The progress appeared unstoppable and, very soon, Corfe Castle was the only place held for the king's name anywhere in the 150-mile stretch between London and Exeter.

The days, however, were to get even blacker. On December 28, 1644, Sir John Bankes died in the city of Oxford, struck down by a sudden illness. This monumental blow to Lady Mary was compounded by the financial demands made by the emboldened

If you look carefully at the curtain wall on the right side of the picture, you'll notice a family standing alongside the ruins; the scale of Corfe is quite phenomenal.

The village of Corfe is exceptionally pretty—a very English tourist town of cream teas and lopsided cottages. The castle has always had a close relationship to the town, exemplified in the locals' efforts of aid Lady Mary during her siege.

One of the Parliamentarian strategies to curtail Lady Mary's resistance was to raid and plunder food and crops from the land surrounding the castle.

Statue of the Parliamentarian leader Oliver Cromwell in St. Ives, Cambridgeshire.

Parliament, who branded her family as a group of loyalist discontents deserving of punitive taxation. It was only through a sustained campaign of letter writing that Lady Mary avoided being dragged to London and placed in court for a failure to pay her dues. This minor episode of resistance was nonetheless symbolic of Lady Mary's character: she possessed dogged persistence—borne, perhaps, from a sense of upper-class entitlement or perhaps from a long-held belief in propriety and fair play.

Nonetheless, her Royalist fortress was a thorn in the side of the Parliamentarians. They decided to partially blockade the entrance to the castle and embarked on miniature raids of farms and property surrounding the outpost, intending to destroy the infrastructure that supported Lady Mary's resilience. Such a strategy negated the need for another expensive siege, and, although Lady Mary stood strong, the emotional and physical toll would have been incredible.

An Act of Bravery . . .

Although Lady Mary was trapped within the walls of Corfe, her story had, by this time, spread around the whole of England. This tale of the trapped but formidable widow became a cause célèbre, cheering every down-trodden Royalist, and Lady Mary's plight even found sympathy in some unexpected quarters. Her tale caught the imagination of an impressionable commander on the Parliamentarian side, a young man named Cromwell (of no relation to the Parliamentarian leader of the same name).

Cromwell appears to have had black-and-white beliefs of justice and ill-play, and, with chivalrous intentions, set out to free the woman and children who he felt had been unjustly captured. He therefore marched his small troop of Parliamentarians from Oxford to the castle, and, on arrival, attempted to storm the castle to free Lady Mary and her family. Despite such fine intentions, Lady Mary declined to go anywhere, but, in the little skirmish, those defending the castle managed to capture a few prisoners before Cromwell's efforts were stopped by others on the Parliamentarian side.

. . . And One of Treachery

By 1646, the Parliamentarians would have held the upper hand across most of England. Isolated within a castle, it's difficult to know how much Lady Mary would have understood about the broader political situation. We can't be sure whether she remained resolute while knowing of Parliamentarian success or chose to ignore the impending disaster.

Towers that once studded the curtain wall have now fallen or subsided into odd or impossible angles, adding to the charm of this mighty ruin.

Each side of the Keep was supported by four to five strip-buttresses (vertical reinforcements); many of these are still visible today.

Her strength of spirit was, sadly, not matched by all who shared the confines of the fortress. Earlier in the conflict, when the Parliamentarian troops had been on the back foot, their side had suffered from ill-discipline in the ranks. Now, with the outlook grim, some Royalist soldiers inside the castle began to lose their nerve. In the dead of night, probably in January 1646, two men escaped from Corfe to join the opposing side—a monumental blow to the morale of all remaining.

However, it was an act of unexpected treachery that would bring Lady Bankes's siege to an ignoble end. A lieutenant named Thomas Pitman, a relative junior in the ranks,

understood only too well that he was on the losing side. He feared for his career prospects, or even for his life, and so devised a cunning plan to deliver the castle to the Parliamentarians and so save himself from reprisal.

His plot was complex and hinged upon the Parliamentarian prisoners held within the castle. One of these men had a Royalist brother, also captured by the opposing side.

Pitman told Lady Bankes he would facilitate an exchange of the two prisoners—a mutually beneficial proposition. To do this, he said, he'd need to leave the castle. He explained to

Lady Bankes that when he was outside the confines of the fortress he would secretly send word to obtain more Royalist troops and convinced Lady Mary that he'd bring in reinforcements right underneath the Parliamentarian's noses.

This was a bluff. As soon as he left the castle, he made haste to parley with the opposing side, and instead of fetching 100 Royalist troops, he recruited an army of 140 Parliamentarians. The next part of his plan was even more devious. So as not to arouse suspicions, he had all men disguise themselves as Royalist soldiers and marched them to the castle entrance under the cover of darkness. They reached the barricaded door of the fortress, and, seeing their familiar uniforms, the gatekeeper let the men stream through into the garrison. Unbeknownst to Lady Bankes, her siege had been infiltrated.

It was a breathtaking act of duplicity, but some of the blame for the disaster should be apportioned to the castle

A selection of antique cannon balls, discovered in another castle but likely similar to those used in the English Civil War.

gatekeeper. After letting fifty men through the doors, he then grew suspicious and prevented the passage of the remainder. His concern came too late. The imposters distributed themselves throughout the castle, and, when a secret signal was given, troops outside the walls moved to besiege the fortress.

Those inside made speedy efforts to defend Corfe, rallying the new arrivals. To their horror, though, they realized that the men they had thought to be colleagues were actually imposters—with no intention of assisting them. These new recruits simply focused their efforts on aiding the men below. With mounting dread for their lives, those inside the castle realized they had been tricked. Corfe had fallen to the Parliamentarians, and Lady Bankes had been defeated.

It was, to be honest, an ignoble end to an episode of exceptional bravery. But there were still honorable men involved in the conflict. The commander of the Parliamentarian siege was Colonel Bingham, a wise leader who understood that the Royalists were desperately trapped in a corner—and desperate men make poor decisions. He realized that the capture of the castle could turn into a bloody slaughter of both sides, and two indiscriminate shots by Royalist defenders augured bloodshed to come. As a result, he immediately entered the fortress and commanded every man to lay down his arms—allowing the Royalists to leave with the promise of their lives if they left in peace.

Thanks to his noble actions, only a small handful of men lost their lives in the siege. His benevolence extended, too, to the defeated Lady Bankes. Whereas other Parliamentarians had

The Keep still stands more than ninety feet tall, and would have once stood forty-three by forty-eight feet at its base. When Lady Mary was finally defeated, it was extensively slighted by the Parliamentarians.

pledged death to the family upon their defeat, he recognized the widow for her outstanding bravery and courage. The Parliamentarians would take the castle and all items within, but the Bankeses could walk free with their lives. The family withdrew to property elsewhere in Dorset, rather than watch the Parliamentarians ransack all their possessions—and destroy Corfe.

Indeed, Parliament's warrant for the destruction of the castle was filed just days after the capture of the fortress, and, after everything of value had been plundered, troops set to work on destroying the remnants of the fortress with gunpowder and machinery. Their intention was to slight the castle—rendering it ineffective in the event of any further siege—but the stones of Corfe proved remarkably resilient, taking many men months to bring some of the walls and towers to the ground. Eventually, they just gave up. Vast chunks of the fortress remain today, some four hundred years later, illustrating the strength of this mighty castle.

Our indomitable Lady Bankes possessed similar fortitude. Having lost so many heirlooms and valuables in the plunder of her castle, she doggedly chose to petition Parliament for their return—engaging in a letter-writing campaign of characteristic persistence. Unfortunately, nothing of any real value was returned to her family—even her letters and diaries had been destroyed by the plundering troops.

Despite this, Lady Bankes was granted one sentimental memento of the castle. In respect of her bravery and persistence, Colonel Bingham collected all the keys to the castle and presented them to Lady Bankes as a token of esteem.

David Evison/Shutterstock

Over the years, the lime mortar between the stones has eroded away, necessitating large-scale restoration projects to keep the castle safe for visitors.

Some of the keys are vast, more than a hand's span in width, and some are tiny. All hang in the stately home of Kingston Lacy in Dorset, which later became the family home of the Bankes family. Today, the property is held by the National Trust of England and is open to the public.

The castle in late summer, viewed across the dark-yellow gorse.

Castles and the English Civil War

Historians have unearthed stomach-churning details of the horrors of the English Civil War. The tranquil and everyday became twisted and grotesque: a Royalist commander was beaten to death with his own wooden leg, and the Lady Jordan of Cirencester was so traumatized she regressed to a mute girlhood, interested only in playing with dolls. It was a conflict that brought unimagined brutality to quiet England—the 1644 battle of Marston Moor claimed four thousand lives from the king's side alone and was the largest ever fought upon English soil. Indeed, by the time the conflict ceased, one in four men in the country had been forced to bear arms.

This bloodshed spilled over into civilian life. Already-surrendered towns were ransacked, and men of the cloth were burned alive inside their own churches. Indeed, it's estimated a total of around two hundred thousand died as a consequence of war, disease, and famine; a similar proportion of the British population died during World War I.

The term *English Civil War* is itself misleading: although the conflict related to English politics, it was fought across the British Isles, with some of the bloodiest battles waged within Ireland and Scotland. In addition, the term refers not to one discrete battle;

it was a series of bitter, self-perpetuating conflicts waged between King and Parliament.

The central dispute centered upon the role of the king in seventeenth-century England. King James, and then King Charles, shared an unwise passion for largesse alongside a weak grip of the nuances of English politics. Ostensibly, England had a Parliament to keep the power of the monarch in check. King and Parliament, however, were rather like chalk and cheese: Parliament tended to be made of rapidly rising merchants who had strong Puritan tendencies. The king and his sympathizers tended to be part of the older, landed gentry. The more James, and then Charles, pushed Parliament to heed his will, the more they resisted. Both sides became entrenched in their positions, and Charles became more absolutist as time wore on.

If these political and economic squabbles were the kindling for an armed conflict, religion was the lighted flame. Charles was Catholic, Parliament was strongly Puritan, and very soon both sides began to conceive war in black-and-white terms of good versus evil. When the slaughter began in 1642, the more agricultural and conservative west of England sided with Charles, whereas the mercantile ports and trading belts of the southeast fell toward the Parliamentarians. Charles's supporters were commonly known as the Cavaliers;

For many years prior to the conflict, castles had lain dormant across the English countryside. They had been the sleeping dragons of medieval warfare—regarded as being hopelessly outmoded in comparison to the early modern innovations of gunpowder, cannons, and musket fire. In the Civil War, however, these forgotten fortifications took on a new lease of life.

Castles were generally held by Royalist-sympathizing landowners and rose again as mighty strongholds sympathetic to Charles I. It was a testament to medieval engineering that so many castles withstood siege, even with much more sophisticated weaponry; Corfe and Pontefract were structurally close to impregnable, and it took

Oliver Cromwell (1599–1658). Engraved by E.Scriven and published in The Gallery Of Portraits with Memoirs Encyclopaedia, United Kingdom, 1837.

the more plainly-spoken Puritans of the Parliamentarian side were dubbed the Roundheads, in part due to their simpler, shorter haircuts.

England's bloodshed quickly drew its neighbors into the conflict. The pastoral lands of Wales sided with the king, and Charles pulled in the Catholic people of Ireland. By contrast, Oliver Cromwell—devout Puritan and devastatingly effective leader of the Parliamentarians—recruited Scotland to his cause, meaning no citizen, from city to country backwater, was exempt from the brutalities of war.

The distinctive "Roundhead" helmet of the English Civil War, typically associated with the Parliamentarian side. Evidently, this costume is worn by a modern reenactor.

a monster mortar named Roaring Meg to force those in Goodrich Castle to give up their siege (See page 64).

Nonetheless, the Parliamentarians won the war: the emotionless efficiency of Cromwell's New Model Army scored a decisive string of victories that lead to the beheading of Charles I in 1649. (His execution took place on a cold morning, and so, it's said, the fallen monarch chose to wear two cotton shirts, lest the spectators should think he was shivering from fear, rather than the cold.)

The Parliamentarians approached the problem of still-surviving castles with similar methodical brutality. Many castles had posed a real headache to Cromwell during the conflict—requiring endless supplies of men and gunpowder to curtail the resilient sieges. To prevent any future trouble, he sought to have these fortresses destroyed for good.

Despite the efforts of innumerable men and thousands of kegs of gunpowder, however, the majority of castles still stood remarkably firm. As a result, the ever-pragmatic Parliamentarians simply scaled back their plans. Rather than destroy all walls of a castle, they sought only to "slight" its defenses—destroying just enough to render the fortress unusable in siege. In fact, over the next two hundred years, many local residents would finish the job for them—plundering the bricks and stones from the ruins to use in their own building projects.

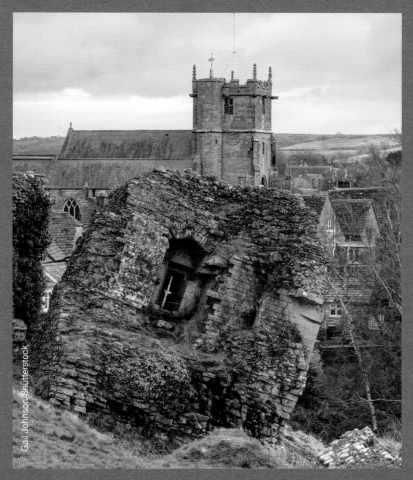

Gail Johnson/Shutterstock

This ruined section gives some idea of the depth and might of the old castle walls. It's no wonder why it took so many months for the Parliamentarians to slight the castle, even once they had won the siege.

Of course, although the Civil War may have marked the end of many English castles, it by no means marked the end of the English monarchy. The Puritanism of Lord Protector Oliver Cromwell jarred with moderate English society—although Cromwell was more liberal than his Parliament, the celebration of Christmas was disallowed, theatrical performances were curtailed, and even working on a Sunday could be punished.

Upon the unexpected death of the Lord Protector in 1658, power was supposed to transfer to his son, Richard—but the efforts faltered, and the Restoration of the English Monarchy took place some twenty months later. The new king was named as Charles II—later nicknamed the "Merry Monarch" due to his acknowledgement of at least a dozen illegitimate children from seven different mistresses. Charles was inarguably a flawed candidate for any public office, but newly wrought checks and balances meant that royal power had been dramatically curtailed. These same regulations have meant that a monarchy—albeit a constitutional one—has endured to until today.

The location of Corfe Castle.

Corfe Castle

The Square, Corfe, Wareham, Dorset, BH20 5EZ
+44 (0)1929 481294
Managed by the National Trust
Official Website: **www.nationaltrust.org.uk/corfe-castle/**
Official Facebook: **www.facebook.com/NTCorfeCastle**
My Website: **www.exploring-castles.com/corfe_castle.html**
Open year-round

Oliver Cromwell statue, in front of the Palace of Westminster, London.

A panorama of Dunstanburgh Castle on a calm day. As well as owning extensive lands in the North, Earl Thomas owned properties throughout the rest of England, making him the richest earl in the Kingdom.

The Fall of Earl Thomas, and the Ruin of Dunstanburgh Castle

The northeastern coast of England is a chilly, rugged place. The freezing waves of the North Sea crash upon gnarled crags and uneven cliffs, and the sharp wind whips along the steep slopes and through the tall grasses.

There's abundant beauty here, too. The coastline sweeps into frequent, sheltered, golden-sand bays, and, in the spring and summer, a plethora of delicately colored wildflower bloom along the meandering public pathways. Indeed, the coast has been designated as an English "Area of Outstanding Natural Beauty" and forms a protected habitat for gray seals, a feeding ground for thousands of wading birds, and a winter home to the diminutive Purple Sandpiper.

Perched above the shoreline you'll encounter the remains of Dunstanburgh Castle—an equal mix of rugged might and strange beauty. Simultaneously vast and vulnerable, the once-formidable great gatehouse of the castle is now reduced to a teetering tower of stone, possibly one of the most dramatic ruins in the whole of England.

The Lilburn Tower peeks out above the encircling curtain wall.

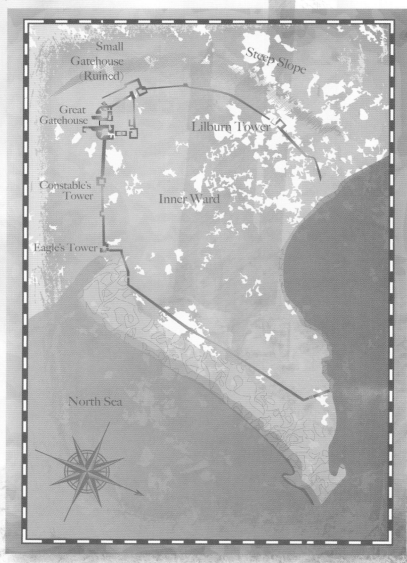

A floor plan of Dunstanburgh Castle.

Small
Gatehouse
(Ruined)

Steep Slope

Great
Gatehouse

Lilburn Tower

Constable's
Tower

Inner Ward

Eagle's Tower

North Sea

DPanglossian/Shutterstock

The castle is positioned on a naturally defensive plateau—there are sheer cliffs to the North and the East, and, as you can see, the western side is a steep slope.

The story behind Dunstanburgh Castle is also the tale of its creator: Thomas, Earl of Lancaster. Earl Thomas was a lanky, sallow fellow with limited charisma. Some would go as far as to say that the man had never felt human empathy. During the 1300s, the earl would become a thorn in the side of the troubled English King Edward II. Their mutual struggle resulted in their mutual downfall, and Dunstanburgh Castle would become the backdrop to this rather tragic tale.

An Overmighty Castle for an Overmighty Earl

You'll struggle to find any twentieth-century historian with a positive opinion of Earl Thomas of Lancaster. Writing in 2011, the historian Seymour Phillips described his deficits in simple terms: "[his] character won him enemies." Harold Hutchinson, writing in 1971, was somewhat less circumspect, describing the earl as "vicious and idle . . . he died without a friend." Nonetheless, Thomas was surprisingly powerful and popular in his day—described by one chronicler as a "gentle earl," and, incredibly, posthumously revered as a saint. Whatever else might be said of the man, there's no doubt he provokes strong opinions.

Thomas was born in 1277, the nephew of King Edward I (and thus the cousin of Edward II, who was born seven years later). As soon as Thomas came of age, he assisted his uncle in his military campaigns within Scotland, and violent Edward was deeply impressed with the equally vicious nature of his protégée. It's said by some that King Edward I preferred Thomas to his own son, but there's been a lot of baseless innuendo over the years about King Edward II's evidenceless "effeminacy," so I wouldn't trust that story too far. Indeed, the two young men appear to

The seal of Thomas of Lancaster, taken by an unknown photographer. Published in Howard de Walden, Lord, Some Feudal Lords and their Seals 1301, published 1904.

have been firm friends up until Edward II's coronation, dampening those salacious rumors that the old king had a "favorite."

It was just a couple of years into Edward II's reign that Thomas, as Earl of Lancaster, would start causing problems. Edward II was a weak king with an uncanny knack for surrounding himself with the very worst people—and his first obsession was with the deeply dislikable Piers Gaveston. Although there's no doubt that Gaveston was rude and overmighty, Lancaster summarily executed the man—an act of wild, overreaching insubordination to the king. Out of sheer political necessity, Edward pardoned the earl some months later, but he would never forgive Thomas for the murder of his favorite. And—mark these words— Edward would have his revenge.

The Earl, the Favorite, and the Murder: The Tale of Earl Thomas and Piers Gaveston

Carsthets/Shutterstock

Unlike many other English castles, which were destroyed by concerted human efforts, it's been the sea that has eroded away the structure of Dunstanburgh.

Things began to go badly at the coronation. It was 1308, and Edward II had just been crowned king of England. The post-coronation banquet should have been a joyful occasion—it boasted marble tables and a fountain of wine—but tempers were already simmering. As the day unfolded, Edward II had demonstrated an intractable, undistractable obsession with his favorite courtier, Piers Gaveston. Indeed, he devoted so much attention to the young man that the uncles of his new wife, Queen Isabella,

stormed out of the banquet in a huff. It augured ill, a taste of the problems that would blight Edward's reign.

Edward II was born in 1284. Piers Gaveston, we think, was born during the same year. Edward was the son of the mighty and terrifying Edward I, and Gaveston was the son of one of Edward I's most loyal lords. As a result, Piers became co-opted into the English royal household at the age of about sixteen, and he and Edward became extremely close. In his letters, Edward always speaks of Gaveston as an honorary brother; throughout the years, there's been much speculation if the pair had a long-term gay relationship. Whether that's true (and the stories of Edward II's proclivities have become all the more salacious as the years have passed), Edward and Gaveston were pretty much inseparable, to the detriment of the king's better judgment.

You see, Gaveston was petulant, proud, and promoted far beyond his station by the adoring Edward II. The king lavished his favorite with gifts, much to the chagrin of his other courtiers: lands and the Earldom of Cornwall, a politically expedient marriage; and even his hand-me-down wedding gifts (an ill-guarded secret that served to offend virtually everyone who'd given him something).

Gaveston was quickly elevated to the highest levels of English politics despite a complete lack of diplomatic skill; he treated every noble he met with ill-hidden disdain and provided the king with disastrously misguided advice. He also entertained ideas far above his station. Instead of wearing the gold-colored robes that befit a courtier, Gaveston chose to wear the purple silk dress of a king ("he more resembled the god Mars than an ordinary mortal,"

wrote one chronicler). But instead of slapping him down for gross insubordination, the king seemed to relish Gaveston's insouciance. Edward even chose to use some of the disparaging nicknames Gaveston had invented for his enemies: the Earl of Warwick was "black dog," Lincoln "burst belly," and Earl Thomas (the creator of Dunstanburgh Castle) "churl."

Unsurprisingly, Gaveston attracted almost universal opprobrium—an unlikable upstart with no political nous. As a result, the English barons tried to force him into exile, seeking to extricate naive King Edward from his disastrous

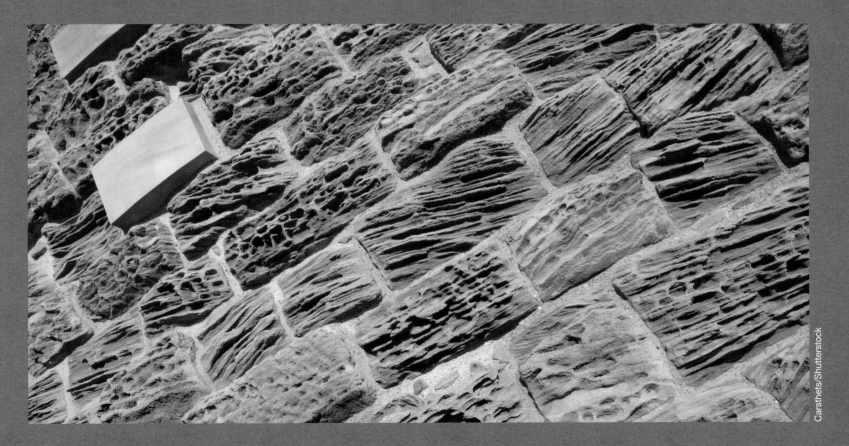

The sand and harsh sea winds have eroded these unusual patterns into the soft stone face of the castle.

orbit. Gaveston was first sent to Ireland in 1308, but returned the very next year and, exasperated by his presence, the English barons then produced a demand for his permanent exile from August 1311. Edward was distraught, and Gaveston returned illegally in January 1312. Empowered by his return, Edward then decreed the previous motion to exile Gaveston to have been illegal and returned all confiscated properties to his courtly favorite.

It was a provocative act that would almost spark a civil war. Gaveston came to symbolize Edward's every political problem and isolated the king from those powerful lords who should have been natural allies. Left to their own devices, the barons therefore decided that if they couldn't exile Gaveston, the next best thing would be to try and imprison him. As a result, some months into 1312, the young man was captured from Scarborough Castle. It was here things began to unravel.

Whereas the Earl of Pembroke pleaded caution with their prisoner, two other barons were far more bloodthirsty. The Earl of Warwick (the man previously nicknamed the "black dog") seized Gaveston from Pembroke's safekeeping and escorted him down to Warwick Castle. It was here the Earl Thomas decided that their prisoner's time was up. After a show trial, Earl Thomas's men dragged Gaveston to a nearby hill, where the young man was executed: first sliced through with a sword, and then beheaded.

"Gaveston's Head Shown to the Earl of Lancaster" by James William Edmund Doyle (1864) "Edward II" in A Chronicle of England: BC 55 – AD 1485, London: Longman, Green, Longman, Roberts & Green, pp. p. 280. Licensed under

An 1864 image of Piers Gaveston's head being showed to Earl Thomas, who stands alongside the Earls of Hereford and Arundel.

The execution was probably intended to solve England's political problems, but it inevitably made everything much worse. The English nobility became divided, with a significant proportion reacting in horror to the death. Earl Thomas, they muttered, was dangerous, bellicose, and overmighty. How could an earl ever think to kill a fellow earl?

Understanding things could get a little tricky, Thomas chose to momentarily remove himself from the political limelight. He chose to squirrel himself away in his most remote lands, the farthest he could be from London, in the county of Northumberland.

The Wealth and Power of Earl Thomas

From previous inheritance and acquisitiveness, Earl Thomas was one of the richest men in England, possessing significant lands and resources. In 1311, his estates brought in around $17,700 (£11,000) a year, which was more than double the income of the next richest earl. As a consequence of this financial clout and extensive land ownership (the north was just one part of his holdings), Thomas managed to attract substantial numbers of personal supporters, including a significant retinue of knights. It seemed not to matter that many of these knights had an exceedingly questionable moral compass: one, named Sir John de Lilburn, had once attempted to murder a royal judge and later robbed and kidnapped two traveling cardinals. Thomas would turn a blind eye to such indiscretions: he was a power-hungry pragmatist and saw the need to shore up all possible support.

From his northern power base, Thomas then sought to do everything he could to make King Edward II's life a headache. He plotted, griped, and pulled every lever to destabilize the monarch: squabbling over the most minor lands and titles, shirking his responsibilities at court, and—most devastatingly—refusing to participate in the great battle against Scotland at Bannockburn. This bickering was probably due to simple jealousy. The earl was a man with vast delusions of grandeur, and he almost certainly conceived himself to be politically more important than the king—or, at least, more suited to the role. As an expression of his perceived power, Thomas therefore decided to use his not-insignificant wealth to build himself a castle as overmighty as his own personality. In 1313, the fortress of Dunstanburgh was born.

Sea winds have wrought unusual patterns upon the face of the castle. You can see that the weathering is worse upon the left side of the tower—the side most exposed to the prevailing winds.

An Isolated and Exaggerated Fortress

As its name might well suggest, Northumberland is the last English county before Scotland. Indeed, Dunstanburgh Castle is less than ninety miles from Edinburgh, crouched upon a moody, rocky coastline and surrounded by acres of tall grasses that bend and bow to the brusque winds. Today, access to the castle is strictly limited to those visiting on foot so as to minimize disturbance to the rare sea birds that nest in this carefully protected environment.

Given its proximity to the northern border, and considering that England and Scotland spent much of the reigns of Edward I and Edward II at war, historians have naturally assumed that Dunstanburgh once played some role in the historic conflict. Although it's a logical assumption, we can be pretty sure this wasn't actually

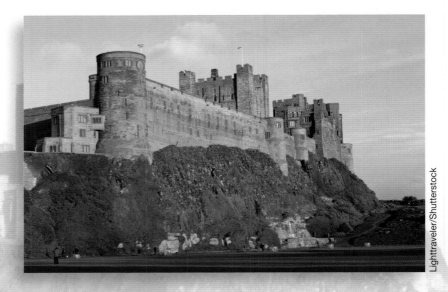

Until 1610, Bamburgh Castle was the property of the reigning English monarch. The inner core of the castle is Norman in origin; evidently, it was greatly fortified over subsequent years.

the case. Earl Thomas probably plumped for this spot partly due to its distance from London and partly out of a pigheaded desire to antagonize King Edward. You see, Bamburgh Castle, a royal possession, lies about twelve miles north upon the same coastline; on a clear day, it's possible to see one castle from the other. Earl Thomas's Dunstanburgh was a very obvious exercise in one-upmanship on the king, and so the silhouette of his fortress is bigger, bolder, and brasher than its comparator.

The Domineering Gatehouse of Dunstanburgh

Almost all the might of Dunstanburgh is derived from its phenomenal gatehouse—the defining feature of the castle—and is the most obvious place to start any tour. If anything, its present, ruinous state makes it all the more impressive to the

Bamburgh Castle, which lies upon the shoreline some twelve miles north of Dunstanburgh. On clear days, one can see between the two fortresses: Earl Thomas appears to have wanted the upper hand, and the grander castle.

modern eye: the once-mighty drum towers taper into teetering piles of masonry, which almost seem to defy the pull of gravity. (It's been the weather, rather than warfare, that's chiefly responsible for the ruinous state; the Northumberland coast is a cruel spot for a medieval relic.) Nonetheless, the sheer scale and ambition of the gatehouse makes it remarkable—it dwarfs

Peresanz/Shutterstock

This is the gatehouse of Harlech Castle, Wales, as viewed from the inner courtyard. Built to secure Edward I's conquest of Wales, the gatehouse absolutely dominates the fortress; its upper levels would have been used for residential chambers.

John Braid/Shutterstock

Construction of the gatehouse began in 1313: the year after Earl Thomas audaciously killed Piers Gaveston, the favorite of the king.

any comparable structure in England. Despite this, it's not entirely without precedent within the isle of Great Britain.

If you were to travel across the border to northern Wales, you'll discover a smattering of mighty gatehouses within Edward I's "iron ring" of indomitable fortresses. Edward I—Earl Thomas's mentor, don't forget—had commissioned the construction of these castles around thirty years previous, and all bristle with the very latest medieval designs and state-of-the-art building techniques. Arguably the most formidable of all was Harlech Castle, boasting a gigantic gatehouse measuring eighty feet by fifty-four feet—to that moment, the mightiest castle in the British Isles. (Unlike ruinous Dunstanburgh, Harlech survives today in remarkable shape: its intact gatehouse is useful for our understanding of comparator castles, and the entire fortress is reason enough to book an immediate trip to North Wales.)

The exterior view of the mighty gatehouse of Harlech Castle.

Although the Dunstanburgh gatehouse shares many similarities with Harlech's, it was clearly built to outshine its predecessor—and, by association, the old king of England. It is a work of unparalleled ambition, measuring approximately 110ft by 40ft;

The passageway through the gatehouse, which would have been protected by a portcullis. The foundations just visible in front of the building (foreground, right) are likely to have been a defensive barbican.

at its tallest points, it is two stories higher than its counterpart. This additional height was uniquely achieved by crowning the upper story with two tall, thin, rectangular turrets.

The front facade of Dunstanburgh also appears to have taken some inspiration from its Welsh relative. It boasts two vast, D-shaped drum towers, which flank a projecting ("salient") entrance passageway through the heart of the building. The passageway would have been barricaded against intruders, but it appears that Dunstanburgh may have only included one portcullis, whereas the evidence is that Harlech had at least three. What it lacked in defensive might, however, the Dunstanburgh gatehouse made up for in aesthetic design: its entrance passageway is studded with five long-eroded, decorative stone corbels. Using your imagination, you might be able to pick out a lion, a fleur de lys, and two scallop shells; the fifth and final image is indecipherable.

These decorations illustrate the dual purpose of Dunstanburgh's gatehouse: it combined residential and defensive functions. On the ground level, one would have been amongst the guard rooms; the upper stories contained the castle's grandest Hall and also the Earl's Chambers. This mixed use wasn't necessarily unusual—Harlech's gatehouse also contains a grand suite, perhaps fit for a king—but this represented an interesting divergence in the design of late-medieval castles. For more on this, see "The Emergence of the Late Medieval Gatehouse Keep," page 210.

To allow guests to pass between the different floors of each gatehouse, it would have evidently been necessary to build spiral stairwells—and this is one area in which Dunstanburgh

The gatehouse would once have spanned three floors; nowadays, the top floor is virtually entirely missing. Records suggest that it contained a hall and great chamber; access between the levels was via two spiral staircases.

demonstrates a much greater level of architectural sophistication. Here, the stairwells are built into the stone fabric of each drum tower, whereas, within Harlech, the two spiral staircases are stuck, crudely, on to the facade at the back. Indeed, the overall construction of Dunstanburgh suggests a much greater level of architectural skill, whereas the innards of Harlech are sliced through by internal walls that serve to support the outer towers. In Dunstanburgh, all external walls are self-supporting. The result is that the internal chambers are sizable, open-plan, and relatively light and airy.

As a result of all these factors, Dunstanburgh's gatehouse surpassed Edward I's finest fortress in size, skill, and sheer ambition. It was a bombastic expression of Earl Thomas's personality. But there was a further facet to its impressive appearance: its surroundings.

A Touch of Theater

England's greatest castles are rendered most impressive by their natural context: the relentless seas surrounding Tintagel or the rolling green countryside of Goodrich. In the same vein, Dunstanburgh leverages its environment to achieve the greatest possible aesthetic appeal.

Although most traces are lost today, the medieval castle would have been surrounded by a network of three connecting man-made meres (lakes, of a similar form to those that once encircled the castles of Kenilworth and Bodiam). Despite the adjacent ocean, evidence shows that the lakes were freshwater, connected to a nearby spring via a complex arrangement of channels and causeways. The largest of these meres probably measured 330 feet in length by 80 feet at its widest point; the

Sheep graze where the mere would once have stood. These freshwater lakes were man-made, formed by digging water-channels from nearby springs.

199

depth of water was generally around the five-foot mark, although there were a couple of points that were eighteen feet deep. (By contrast, you'd generally have been able to wade through the other two lakes, as their average depth was about two feet.)

Evidently, there were practical benefits to a series of freshwater lakes: although their defensive potential was limited, they'd have been an excellent place to breed fish and attract wildfowl (indeed, there's evidence for three small fishpools adjacent to the middle lake). But the predominant purpose of these meres was aesthetic impact. There appears to have been a particularly tortuous pathway around these pools, connecting the mainland to castle entrance (exactly as we've seen within Bodiam Castle, see page 138). The obstinate indirectness of this route suggests it was designed to maximize the visual impact of the castle for anyone arriving by road: one would have ridden past a succession of mirror-like sheets of water and have seen the phenomenal bulk of the castle reflected at many differing, breathtaking angles.

Of course, not all visitors would arrive by road; the noblest might arrive by sea. As a consequence, historians have recently theorized that the gatehouse may have been purposefully oriented to face the shoreline. The theory goes that, logically, a gatehouse would look toward the roads and pathways arriving from nearby settlements; at Dunstanburgh, however, the building faces onto a man-made quay and disembarkation point.

Was it intentionally angled to impress these seafaring visitors? We'll never know for sure, but, nonetheless, arriving by boat would have been a spectacular experience. The topography of the coast would have concealed the scale and breadth of the gatehouse until the last possible moment, creating a breathtaking impression when visitors finally disembarked from their vessels.

As modern tourists, we're presently limited to approaching the castle by foot, but there's still an interesting optical trick on walking toward the remnants of the castle gatehouse. Approaching from a certain angle, you'll see the Lilburn Tower perfectly framed through the arched entrance passageway.

Although it's a pleasing little quirk, this surprise is almost certainly more to do with luck than with design. In medieval times, a fortified barbican would have protected the entranceway and likely obscured the sight line, and the position of both buildings was dictated more by the lay of the land rather than

Ron Ellis/Shutterstock

The front face of the castle. The small tower far in the foreground, on the right, is the "Eagle's Tower."

The Strange Emptiness Within

For its mighty gatehouse and magnificent approach, the innards of Dunstanburgh are strangely barren. The castle's mighty curtain walls—measuring more than 1,700 feet in length—surround a vast inner bailey of more than four hectares (c. 430,000 square feet) in area. Nowadays, there's little inside the enclosure— it's empty, except for the wind that whips through the long grass.

You might be surprised to discover that, even in medieval times, this vast enclosure never really contained anything. Save for one sea-sprayed barn, there's no particular evidence for any buildings—residential or otherwise—within these walls, and there's equally little proof that the enclosure was filled with the traders, hawkers, and merchants of everyday medieval life.

Kevin Tate/Shutterstock

The castle is situated upon a rough, rugged coastline; if you were brave enough to arrive by medieval boat, you'd have been dropped off in this quay in front of the gatehouse.

the architect's decision. Nonetheless, it's a detail that delights modern visitors and exemplifies the sort of aesthetic impact for which Earl Thomas's castle was designed.

Gail Johnson/Shutterstock

Look closely and you can see the Lilburn Tower framed through the castle gatehouse. It's a cute illusion, but it's likely more a happy accident than a deliberate plan.

Patjo/Shutterstock

The mighty curtain walls of Dunstanburgh measure more than 1,700 feet in length—and the inner bailey spans more than 430,000 square feet.

201

Should the people of the neighboring villages have come under threat (such as during the 1350s, when the Scots were on the rampage), they were entitled to seek shelter inside the broad walls of the lord's home, but, otherwise, it appears that the castle of Dunstanburgh had little connection with the communities surrounding it.

Given the emptiness of the inner bailey, you might then wonder why it was built at such scale. Undoubtedly, like everything to do with the castle, there was an element of pretension and overreaching ambition: after all, few other English castles could boast a four hectare bailey, so that alone may have been reason to attempt it. However, it's likely that topography also dictated the scale of

The Lilburn Tower, as viewed from further down the coastline. The Tower is thought to have been named after the "bad knight" Sir John de Lilburn—a servant of Earl Thomas who had once robbed and kidnapped two traveling cardinals.

A panorama of the castle. The gatehouse is immediately obvious toward the left of the photograph. Working toward the right, along the curtain wall you can see the Constable's Tower; the next along is the Eagle's Tower.

these walls: with sheer cliffs to the north and east and a steep slope to the west, the size of the enclosure was partially dictated by the natural environment. The curtain wall was therefore built to run alongside these natural defenses, and the resulting compromise was that the bailey became unnecessarily large.

Although the purpose of the curtain wall was predominantly defensive, three significant towers do emerge from its flanks: on its southern face, fifty feet from the great gatehouse, you'll encounter the Constable's Tower and then the Eagle's Tower; far along the western wall, quite isolated from the rest of the castle, lies the Lilburn Tower. The Lilburn Tower stands on one of the highest patches of land and directly overlooks Edward II's Bamburgh Castle from across the bay, perhaps a direct challenge to the king's authority.

Although the Lilburn Tower boasts quite a view, it's unlikely that it, or any of the two other towers, would have been used as lookout posts. Their purpose appears primarily residential: slightly lower status rooms for guardians or custodians of the castle (the Lilburn Tower is, of course, named after the ill-behaved knight we mentioned before, Sir John de Lilburn). All in all, aside from the vast gatehouse, Dunstanburgh Castle appears to have been rather empty, a grand facade with little behind it. In that sense, it was wrought in the image of its creator, Earl Thomas.

The Inexorable Decline of Earl Thomas

For all the efforts of building such a mighty fortress, there's scant evidence that Earl Thomas spent any significant time in the castle. From historical records, it's a fair assumption that in August 1319, the earl stayed here on his way to the join the disastrous siege of Berwick on Tweed, Scotland. Aside from this, however, Thomas seemed to prefer spending time in his other properties, most notably another northern castle, Pontefract. (As an interesting aside, Pontefract was once one of the greatest and most feared castles in the whole of Medieval England, but it's long since been razed to the ground.)

Charitably, though, we should perhaps forgive Earl Thomas's seeming disinterest in Dunstanburgh. In the late 1310s, the earl was rapidly sinking within the political quicksands of Edward II's struggling reign. The king was bankrupt and increasingly rudderless, surrounded by a cabal of crooked advisors—including the repugnant father and son duo of the Despensers. The Despensers probably rank as two of the most disgusting characters in the history of Medieval England: a sadistic pair who casually used every conceivable form of violence to further their means and who famously extorted a juicy bribe from any other courtier who sought to speak to the king.

The Despensers were almost universally hated throughout England, and, as a consequence of his allegiance, King Edward grew increasingly isolated—and Earl Thomas increasingly disenfranchised. But rather than attend court and try and lance the boil of the Despensers himself, Earl Thomas preferred to lurk and to grumble within his northern lands,

Back in the time of Earl Thomas, the castle would have been surrounded by a grand array of reflective, man-made meres. Today, small sections of these ponds have been reinstated as wildlife refuges.

Darren Turner/Shutterstock

filled with discontent but unwilling to make any positive political contribution. On occasions, rather like a sulky child, the earl used destructive techniques to try and grab the attention of the king: he snatched a series of castles from under other nobles' noses and, most sensationally, formed a whispered alliance with the enemy in Scotland. Nevertheless, his efforts to engage Edward resulted in little more than frustration.

In addition to these aggravations, the earl's personal life was a bit of a mess. In 1317, his wife, Alice de Lacy, was "kidnapped" by the Earl of Surrey—almost certainly a deliberately provocative act to make Thomas appear a courtly fool. On the other side of the arrangement, Alice was probably delighted at this enforced separation from her husband: their marriage was childless, universally said to be loveless, and the chronicler Higden had described Thomas to be a man of particularly unpleasant sexual tastes, having "defouled a greet multitude of wommen and of gentil wenches."

On some occasions, Earl Thomas did decide to take some constructive role in the governance of the realm—for example, he participated in the disastrous siege upon Scotland of 1319.

Throughout, however, he remained aloof and disengaged, insisting that any army that fought with him would be paid for by him, not the king (thus rendering himself outside of royal control). In any case, his squabbling with the other English earls

The view from the Lilburn Tower, which gazes across the shoreline toward (rival) Bamburgh Castle.

Another perspective of the Lilburn Tower. In 1797, Turner painted the Tower at sunrise from more or less exactly this angle—ruined castles were a favored motif of the Romantic movement.

before the battle led to an embarrassing rout by the Scottish; his involvement was not exactly an asset to King Edward.

Around 1320, however, matters finally came to a head. The vile Despensers had wound their tentacles around Edward and, with king distracted, were mounting a vast power grab of lands in Wales—seemingly with utter impunity. Understandably, the barons of the Welsh environs were horrified, but Royal redress would not be forthcoming. Those endangered nobles decided their only option was to rebel—and Earl Thomas, as England's second greatest landowner, was a logical choice to lead the insurrection and overthrow the king and his cruel companions.

If there are ever any "rights" and "wrongs" in history, Thomas was now probably on the "right" side: there's no doubt the Despensers were acting outrageously and, if King Edward wasn't keen to curb their excesses, someone else certainly

When Earl Thomas's 1322 rebellion failed, he attempted to gallop up to his stronghold of Dunstanburgh, hiding from the king. He was, however, captured en route.

needed to. However, the earl proved a questionable rebel leader. While a motley crew of barons pillaged the Despensers' seized lands, Thomas vacillated, indecisive, holed up within his northern territories. More scandalously, when the king's men besieged an allied earl in his castle, Thomas remembered an old grudge and refused to assist. A similar act of calculating cruelty occurred later in the conflict when the king's forces encircled a group of rebels, adjacent to the Welsh border; rather than assist, Thomas decided he couldn't afford to send any more men.

Quite rightly, all those rebels who had coalesced around the earl began to seriously doubt their allegiance. What use was it fighting for a leader who showed such little loyalty to those beneath him? Naturally, supporters drifted from the cause, and the rebellion fell into terminal decline. Its downfall was cemented upon March 10, 1322, when one of the earl's closest allies and henchmen—Robert Holland—treacherously decided to desert to the enemy. Realizing the game was up, Earl Thomas rallied the few men still in his command and galloped northward, seeking to barricade himself in the safety of Dunstanburgh Castle. Their little troop never made it: Earl Thomas and his men were intercepted and captured at Boroughbridge, near York, on March 16, 1322.

The Death of Thomas, Earl of Lancaster

Edward II devised a particularly bitter death for Earl Thomas. The sweetest form of revenge, the king decided, would be to execute Thomas in exactly the same fashion that

Thomas had killed Piers Gaveston. Duly, the earl was subjected to a show trial held within Pontefract Castle (his old home, now repossessed) and, found guilty of treason, was bundled onto the back of a haggard old mule and led to a nearby grassy hill. In an exact parallel to that horrible death in 1312, Thomas was first sliced through by sword and then beheaded.

This next part is incomprehensible—well, to a modern audience at least. You see, Earl Thomas quickly became revered as a popular *saint*. Six weeks after his death, miracles were said to have taken place at his tomb, and a riot took place in 1323 as the devout jostled to pray and make offerings at the site of his execution. His hat and belt were held for many years in Pontefract: the items, it was said, would help cure headaches and were a good omen for childbirth.

The upper stories of the Lilburn Tower would have boasted grand, light rooms, and there's even evidence of a built-in latrine.

An 1864 image of Earl Thomas being led to his execution.

How on Earth did such a monster command such popular adoration? The answer was that Edward II was regarded as cruel and tyrannical, particularly due to his collusion with the Despensers, and Earl Thomas was one of few who'd stood up to him in recent years. No one seemed to acknowledge that Thomas's insubordination was entirely due to sulky self-interest rather than any form of ideological conviction; instead, the egregious earl was held up as a hero who had defied the dastardly Edward II. The historian Harold Hutchinson, in 1971, summed up the whole situation neatly: "It is a sad commentary on vulgar credulity," he wrote, "that the absentee from Bannockburn, the deserter of his own allies, the traitor to his king, was soon hailed as a saint by the populace."

Edward II: An Epilogue

King Edward II would briefly enjoy some of the spoils of war. Two days after Earl Thomas's death, he took possession of Dunstanburgh Castle and chose to further fortify and garrison the stronghold, perceiving it to be potentially important in the event of a Scottish invasion. (As things turned out, Dunstanburgh was in too remote a position to ever be involved in the border wars.) This accomplished, Edward hobbled onward through his disastrous reign, still supported by those terrible Despensers. The duo was to prove a poor choice of ally as, just five years later, the king would meet his own sticky end.

Edward II of England (1284–1327). Engraved by Bocquet and published in the Catalogue of the Royal and Noble Authors, United Kingdom, 1806.

You see, some years earlier, Edward's wife, Isabella, had fled to France. It's said that she left England due to her husband's allegiance with the hated Despensers (in fact, there's one historical theory that says that she was raped by a Despenser—an example of the casual brutality the two men meted out upon their enemies). Upon the continent, she bided her time and gathered her forces, and, in 1327, she sailed to England with her eyes set on revenge.

Isabella was remarkably successful: Edward and his cronies were so despised that most of England flocked to her anti-monarchical rebellion. In no time at all, the king's entire power base collapsed, and ailing Edward was seized and imprisoned in Berkeley Castle. The Despensers were equally quickly captured, and Isabella wasted no time in organizing a "trial" of both the older and younger man. To popular delight, the detested pair were hung, drawn, and quartered in front of vast audiences.

The remains of the Lilburn Tower, with the crashing sea below. The tower extended to three stories, with a single room on each level; it appears to have been used for midstatus accommodations.

Berkeley Castle, Gloucestershire, where Edward II died in September 1327. The castle contains a "cell" that was supposedly the place of his murder; in reality, there's not enough evidence to know exactly what happened, and where.

As for King Edward? Well, to that point, there was no real precedent as to how England could depose an unwanted monarch. As a consequence, Edward II died a mysterious, rather convenient death in the prison of Berkeley Castle on September 21, 1327. Of course, we can be pretty sure the man was murdered, but his demise allowed for the constitutional succession of King Edward III, his son, around two months later. The English, it appeared, would readily tolerate clandestine violence over any form of constitutional impropriety.

The Emergence of the Late Medieval Gatehouse Keep

The two drum towers of the gatehouse were crowned with two square turrets, positioned to flank the passageway through the building. The remnant of the left tower is easily seen on this photograph—it teeters upward above the drum tower on that side.

Visiting Dunstanburgh today, you won't be able to miss the great gatehouse. However, on closer approach, you might be surprised to spot a second, ruined gatehouse, nestling against the western face of the big one. Why on earth did a castle need two? Well, it's a convoluted story, so bear with me!

Dunstanburgh's great gatehouse has been dubbed a "gatehouse keep," as it combined residential rooms with military might. This wasn't an uncommon design in the late-medieval period; you'll note a similar use of space in Harlech Castle.

In itself, this was a strange example of history repeating itself. The very earliest Norman castles—places like Rochester or the Great Keep in Dover—similarly combined domestic and military functions and packed both into one great tower. Later castles, like Goodrich, separated residential buildings and defensive fortifications within one castle complex. Now, in the late-medieval period, the pendulum swung back toward fulfilling two purposes all within one grand building. (Unlike the early Norman castles that existed as solitary towers, however, these new gatehouses still communicated with other buildings inside a larger complex.)

So why did late-medieval builders turn back toward mixed-use buildings? The reasons aren't entirely clear and are likely castle dependent. In Harlech Castle, Wales, there's very limited space, and it probably made most sense to put the best rooms in the gatehouse because it was already the largest part of the castle.

Conversely, in Dunstanburgh, there's heaps of room: the most convincing theory is that the gatehouse was the grandest, most high-status building, and was therefore befitting of the most high-status chambers.

Interestingly, though, the Dunstanburgh gatehouse underwent a further reversal some sixty-five years after its first completion. In around 1383, the gatehouse portcullis was removed and the entrance passageway blocked. We might assume that those living upstairs were disturbed by the incessant clanking chains and banging doors of a true gatehouse, and so the building was converted to serve a residential purpose only. (Nonetheless, I wouldn't envy the person allocated the dark, drafty ground-floor chambers of the converted

Gail Johnson/Shutterstock

The gatehouse once contained residential chambers on its upper stories and guardrooms within its lower levels. In about 1383, the passageway through the gatehouse was blocked up to convert the building into a residential space alone. Nowadays, the passage has been reopened.

guards' rooms.) With this entrance to the castle blocked, a new gateway needed to be built, and so a diminutive new gatehouse was constructed upon the western side of the old one, finished in the mid-1380s. This small new building served only to protect the passage into the castle.

Today, however, the passageway through the original great gatehouse has been unblocked and partially restored. This means unknowing visitors are generally perplexed by the spectacle of two grossly mismatched gatehouses—Little and Large—standing adjacent to each other.

The story of the gatehouse is a long and rather twisting tale, but there's one simple message at its heart: castle design and construction was a dynamic process, responding to fluctuating social and political demands. A fortress was a product of evolution and not a snapshot of a moment in medieval history.

The location of Dunstanburgh Castle.

Dunstanburgh Castle

Dunstanburgh Road, Craster, Alnwick, Northumberland, NE66 3TT
+44 (0) 1665 576231
Managed by English Heritage in conjunction with the National Trust
Official Website: **www.english-heritage.org.uk/ daysout/properties/dunstanburgh-castle/**
My Website: **www.exploring-castles.com/dunstan- burgh_castle.html**
Open every day in spring and summer; closed most weekdays during winter—check before you travel

A sideview of the gatehouse. Much more than a mighty facade, the building was large enough to host grand rooms and residential chambers.

A view of Framlingham Castle, taken from across the adjacent mere.

Framlingham Castle, and the Tale of England's First Queen

Mary Tudor foresaw the death of her brother, King Edward VI, and fled London because of it. She escaped from the city—galloping from property to property in eastern England until she reached the grandest of all her possessions: Framlingham Castle, in Suffolk.

ary had good reason to flee. Although her blood ties to Edward made her, in principle at least, the first queen of England, she was a wanted woman. The cunning Duke of Northumberland—one of Edward's closest advisors—had devised a plan to prevent her from becoming the next monarch. The duke needed Mary captured and imprisoned for his plan to succeed.

And so begins the story of one of the most sensational royal successions to ever take place upon English soil. It involves a dastardly plot, a struggle for power, a desperate chase, and a very daring proclamation. It is a story that pitted the sheer ambition and bravery of Mary Tudor against the cunning of the Duke of Northumberland, and the final scenes of this real-life drama were played out in the equally sensational setting of Framlingham Castle, one of the mightiest and noblest castles in the whole of eastern England.

A Fortress of Golden Flint Built Upon a Gentle Green Mound

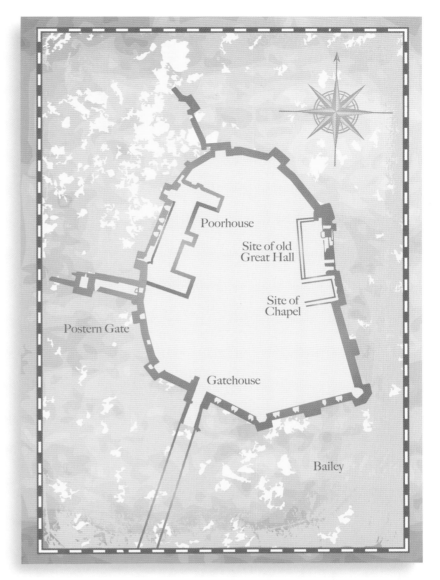

A floor plan of Framlingham Castle.

First of all, let's explore the setting of our story. Framlingham Castle is situated within the town of Framlingham—an affluent and attractive little spot in Suffolk, southeastern England. Framlingham boasts all the accoutrements of an idyllic English village: at its heart lies The Crown, a traditional pub established in 1553 as a coaching inn (it still hosts guests within antique-furnished rooms). The Crown fronts onto a cobbled market square, where two grand fetes, one at Michaelmas and one at Whitsun, have been annual occurrences for hundreds of years. A little up the cobbled road toward the castle you'll encounter a diminutive ducking pond, which is happily no longer used to torment suspected witches. A few steps further and you'll find a well-tended bowling green, which enjoys a stunning backdrop of the castle walls.

The present-day external appearance of Framlingham Castle is virtually unchanged from how the castle would have looked to Mary Tudor, some 440 years ago. Now, as then, Framlingham is a handsome fortress, built of golden flint and positioned on top of a gentle green mound, overlooking the lake and wetlands of the adjacent mere.

The castle is formed of thirteen mighty towers, each consecutively connected by an 8.2-foot-thick curtain wall, forming a loop shaped like a signet ring. The towers and the tops of the curtain walls have a distinct sawtoothed pattern of crenellation and are studded with arrow-loops for archers—marking out Framlingham Castle as a place of military might.

Eagle-eyed observers may, however, notice that many of the mighty towers are topped with slender red chimneys—a curious and incongruous addition, and one you can discover more about within the boxout "The Curious Chimney Pots of Framlingham." These chimneys were a late addition to the castle—built in the early 1500s, whereas the vast majority of Framlingham was constructed from about 1190 onward. They exemplify the castle's transition from a medieval stronghold into an extravagant palace.

The town sign of idyllic Framlingham, featuring its beautiful castle, church, and quaint duck pond.

The castle is a ring of thirteen tall towers, all connected by a thick curtain wall. Each medieval tower was later crowned—rather incongruously—by a red-brick Tudor chimney.

The Curious Chimney Pots of Framingham

The towers of Framlingham Castle are crowned with delicate, red-brick chimney pots. These tall ochre turrets, each one unique in design and detail, form striking contrast to the gray stone walls below. Mark Robinson, the head of the neighboring Framlingham College, described the chimneys as being "a Tudor addition, rather impertinently perched on top of the ancient mural towers."

It's quite clear to any visitor that these grand flues were added some time after the castle was originally built—indeed, they were added some 350 years after the castle walls were finished. What you may not appreciate from just gazing upward, though, is that most of the chimneys are blind ending: built for show, with never a fireplace below them. So, what on earth is the purpose of them?

Well, quite simply, their purpose was to keep up appearances. The red-brick chimneys were a mid-1500s confection, built on top of the thirteen towers as an ostentatious display of Tudor wealth. Nowadays, of course, a chimney isn't quite a status symbol—but, back in the early 1500s, most homes

One of the many distinctive chimney pots that crown Framlingham Castle.

had little more than a hole in the ceiling through which smoke could escape. (If this sounds surprisingly primitive, it bears saying that in medieval times, the concept of a fireplace and a flue hadn't yet been invented—meaning that stale smoke would have just swirled through the rooms of a residence.)

If a hole for a chimney was a modern luxury to Tudor people, a decorative chimney pot would have been a vision of modern decadence. Indeed, Hampton Court Palace, in London (undoubtedly the most fashionable building in the whole of Tudor England) was crowned with 241 red-brick chimneys, each with a subtly different design made of swirling red brickwork.

The selection of chimneys on top of Framlingham undoubtedly took a good deal of inspiration from those at Hampton Court—each has a unique finish and design, and there's a good deal of stylistic similarity between those in Suffolk and those that crown Henry VIII's palace. However, it's worth noting that none of the 241 chimneys in Hampton Court are original Tudor pieces—all were either rebuilt or re-created by Victorian builders in the 1800s. By contrast, the grand flues upon Framlingham Castle are authentically Tudor and date back to the 1500s.

These chimneys were the height of luxury.

The Short, Unhappy Life of King Edward VI

To discover just how Framlingham Castle came into the hands of Mary Tudor—and to comprehend the plots hatched against her—we must first understand a little more about the short, unhappy life of her poor half-brother, Edward.

Edward VI died at age fifteen. Despite his young age, it was a death that was not unexpected. Edward died of a lung infection, but modern scholars disagree over the course of his illness: the traditional view is that Edward was a perpetually sickly soul, troubled by tuberculosis since early childhood. The revisionist view, however, is that Edward suddenly developed a particularly nasty bout of bronchitis that developed into blood poisoning. The poor king's death, however, was a protracted affair, undoubtedly made all the more unbearable by the frantic efforts of Tudor physicians to "cure" him. Edward was whisked between palaces in London, ostensibly in search of cleaner air, and endured all manner of experimental medications, ranging from arsenic to leeches. John Banister was a trainee surgeon attached to the physicians caring for Edward, and he spoke of the poor adolescent's "black, fetid sputum" and foul-smelling, gangrenous feet.

As these months of ill-health passed by, there could have been no doubt the king's illness was terminal—a contemporary writer poignantly described his inexplicable ill-health to be an "invincible malignity." Wracked with fevers and pain, dutiful Edward became obsessed with the importance of safeguarding the English succession after his demise. "I desire . . ." the sick young man uttered, "to prevent my death from providing our beloved country with an occasion or proffered opportunity for civil war."

Unfortunately, despite Edward's best intentions, he was surrounded by a cabal of dodgy advisors. As a young king, he had always relied upon these powerful men to provide shrewd political advice and, as he lay on his deathbed, he needed ever more support. However, led by the Duke of Northumberland, the nobles who assisted him were motivated less by national duty and more by their own grasping ambitions.

The title of Duke of Northumberland belonged to John Dudley, an imposing and diligent public servant with an impressive

A portrait of Edward VI (1537–1553).

record of service in the Royal Navy. Although it doesn't appear that he was a particularly religious man, Northumberland did subscribe to the Protestant faith and had enjoyed a particularly impressive military record against the Scottish. Given his skills and successes, he became the regent for the country when nine-year-old Edward VI was crowned king of England.

There has never been any doubt that Northumberland was skilled at government, but, even during Tudor times, he was nicknamed the "evil Duke." His ambition was known throughout the country, and he drew popular ire for the fact that during any confrontation between the poorest and the land-owning classes, he would always side with the wealthier party.

The Duke of Northumberland did not like Mary Tudor. Mary was a Catholic in a country rapidly converting to Protestantism, and her devout faith had done little to engender her to any of Edward's cabal of Puritan advisors. But she and Northumberland had a particular animosity, on account of old courtly rifts. The duke knew she would have him immediately expelled from the Royal Court should she become queen. As a result, he plotted to remove her from the succession—and install someone much more favorable to his cause.

To this end, he uncovered an inexperienced youth who would be receptive to his political guidance: Lady Jane Grey. The fifteen-year-old girl was the great-granddaughter of Henry VII, granting her tenuous blood connections to the royal line. By many accounts, she was a conscientious scholar, but her malleable nature, coupled with her devout Protestant beliefs, made her an attractive choice for Northumberland's plan for succession. To cement his control over young Jane, Northumberland also orchestrated a marriage between herself and his son, Guildford. Should Jane have become the queen of England, there could have been no doubt that Northumberland would have become the most powerful man in the entire country.

With his candidate found, Northumberland plotted how best to remove Mary from the line of English succession. We can be sure he tormented Edward with predictions of Civil War should Catholic Mary become queen of Protestant England. To a young, ill man, obsessed with leaving his people in a state of tranquility, these cunning words undoubtedly had a potent political impact. Edward created the first draft of his will in March 1553, and the document disinherited his half-sister, Mary, in favor of Lady Jane Grey.

Although this was a dramatic example of filial betrayal, Mary's claim to the throne had been disputed for quite some time. In 1533, her own father, Henry VIII, had used the first Act of Succession to rule her illegitimate and thus ineligible to be queen. Although this act had been repealed in 1544, some eleven years prior, it meant that Edward's will was not entirely without precedent.

A Twist of Good Fortune

During Edward's last months, financial affairs were never far from the young king's mind. To put it quite bluntly, the English crown was broke. Northumberland and his team therefore orchestrated a money-making wheeze. It was a cunning plan: they sought to reclaim the most desirable assets from the wider royal family and would then sell these attractive properties on the open market to earn cash for the crown.

Georgios Kollidas/Shutterstock/Engraved by H.T.Ryall and published in Lodge's British Portraits encyclopedia, United Kingdom, 1823.

A portrait of Mary I of England (1516–1558).

Of course, they realized that no one was going to give up their property voluntarily. Instead, they painted their scheme as a form of obligatory exchange, reclaiming valuable lands from each royal in turn and granting a string of lesser properties as recompense—giving just enough back to keep each person quiet.

Mary Tudor was forced to opt in to the scheme. She was made to surrender fourteen of her manors and five of her

Paul Wishart/Shutterstock

The castle is shaped like a perfect hoop, perched upon a spot of high ground on the outskirts of Framlingham village.

parks, but was granted a series of properties in the east of England. On paper, these new properties were worth much less than those that had been taken away from her. However, this series of trades had an unforeseen consequence: they had accidentally concentrated all of Mary's existing assets into one area and made her the greatest single landowner (and, arguably, the most powerful figure) in the whole of East Anglia.

Among all these properties, King Edward chose to give Mary a special gift: majestic Framlingham Castle. It was worth much more than the other properties, and we can only speculate why Edward did this. Perhaps the king was a particularly conscientious young soul who wished to do something kind after disinheriting his half-sister.

When Edward's will was completed in early 1553, Mary's agreement to take the castle was widely interpreted as her acquiescence to her disinheritance. In June 1553, satisfied that his scheme was working, Northumberland then disclosed the plan for Lady Jane Grey's succession to a select number of nobles (for good reason, the arrangement was concealed from the English public at large).

Despite such careful plotting, however, it appeared that Northumberland hadn't entirely thought things through. Although Mary had been written out of the English succession, she had unexpectedly gained enough land in eastern England to render her a formidable force in English politics. She had also never made any *formal* agreement that she would not seek the crown of England—and, being in peacetime, the duke had no pretext to detain her. The stage was set for her dramatic grasp at power, just one month later.

The Death of Edward: And the Beginnings of the Chase across England

Edward VI died July 6, 1553, just before the clock struck nine in the evening. By contemporary records, the evening was marked by ferocious thunderstorms and sudden flooding, and, while the rain beat down, those at his bedside grieved briefly for the fifteen-year-old before setting their own devious schemes to work. According to their well-wrought plans, Edward's death would be concealed from England until their own strategy for his succession had fallen entirely into place. In the meantime, Mary—their main obstacle to success—needed to be

Imposing but also homely, Framlingham Castle possessed the strength and elegance to support Mary's claim for the crown.

The curtain wall of Framlingham Castle is around 8.2 feet thick. A Tudor writer called the fortress "the strongest castle in Suffolk."

captured and dealt with. Northumberland quickly dispatched three hundred men to find Mary and throw her into the Tower of London. From there, Northumberland knew, it would be impossible for her to make any claim to the English throne.

Mary, however, had agents of her own. Although Edward's death was known only to his closest courtiers, the news permeated through the crevices of the royal household, reaching ears sympathetic to her cause. Resultantly, an undercover messenger scurried to Mary's household in Hunsdon, near London, on the very night of Edward's demise. But canny Mary had a sixth sense: she had begun her journey to eastern England some two days earlier.

Mary, like most of the Tudor lineage, was a tenacious soul, equipped with guile to match the Duke of Northumberland. Mary's father was, of course, Henry VIII, and her mother was

Catherine of Aragon—Henry's first wife. Like any adolescent, Mary was deeply affected by her parent's drawn-out divorce and became a rather withdrawn character as a result of it. Mary was stubborn to the point of being dogged and held an unshakable belief in the Catholic faith, even as England transitioned to Protestantism around her.

Prior to Edward's death, Mary's friends and advisors—more cool-tempered souls—had encouraged her to abandon any claim to the English crown and to exile herself to Europe. They sensed that Northumberland would prefer to have her killed rather than risk his plans for succession to go awry. However, Mary was an ambitious woman. Her devout Catholicism, newly accumulated lands, and blood ties to Edward encouraged her to make a dramatic attempt to become the first queen of England. Her political strategy was simple: she needed to escape the Duke of Northumberland for as long as possible. She would hide out in her eastern lands and would cultivate the popular support necessary to make a claim for the throne. If she failed in her quest, she reasoned, her proximity to the English Channel would mean that she could easily flee the country and shelter in Catholic, continental Europe.

As a result, Mary's success depended upon putting distance between her and the Duke of Northumberland. She therefore rode quickly from her home in Hunsdon, with her first stop being Sawston Hall in Cambridgeshire. Sawston was a noble Tudor manor house owned by John Huddleston, a kindly gentleman who hosted Mary for one night. Although Mary sped onward that very next morning, the Duke of Northumberland was hot on her tail. When he arrived at Sawston some days later, he flew into a rage and burned the building to the ground as retribution for her stay. (All was not lost, however. When Mary became queen, she knighted John Huddleston and granted him stone from the ruined Cambridge Castle to rebuild his home. Nowadays, Sawston Hall is a stunningly beautiful Tudor mansion, held in private ownership. Folklore says the Hall is haunted by the smiling figure of Queen Mary, who is eternally grateful for the hospitality offered to her upon this genteel spot.)

After her brief stay at Sawston, Mary traveled quickly across her lands to Kenninghall Manor, a small property in Norfolk. From her wooden writing desk, in consultation with her closest friends and allies, she drafted her initial proclamation to be the rightful queen of England. She addressed her words to members of the Privy Council and invoked the Divine Right of her blood lineage to give her legitimacy to rule. This proclamation was a sensational salvo in a battle for succession that could conceivably have lead to Civil War.

Framlingham is a rural spot—a perfect distance from London, where Mary I would have been able to bide her time and build her forces.

This proclamation was sent posthaste to London, carried by a brave messenger, Thomas Hungate. Hungate was one of Mary's most loyal servants—an elderly man who was "second to none in obedience and diligence"—and his mission was surprisingly dangerous. In Tudor times, messengers were frequently killed for bringing unwelcome news, and the Duke of Northumberland indeed had Hungate thrown into the Tower of London as punishment for carrying such ill tidings.

It's likely that Mary's proclamation came as something of a shock to Northumberland; it was a bold move, and, from where he was, her position would have appeared weak. Her actions would have galvanized his desire to have her immediately captured for, as long as she was free, she would become a focus for popular discontent.

Mary therefore knew that she must act decisively. She dispatched numerous other proclamations of her status, sending messengers to the neighboring towns of Ipswich and Norwich in an attempt to rally the public to her cause. Her strategy was successful, and she found the English people extremely sympathetic. This might have been because of her standing as a local landlord, but the public seemed to regard her blood ties to Edward VI as a more legitimate claim to the throne than any Lady Jane Grey could manage. Emboldened by such a favorable reception, Mary decided to march her domestic household, troops, and supporters on from Kenninghall toward Framlingham Castle—the jewel of her estates.

Framlingham Castle was a perfect location to mount her campaign to become queen. It was, of course, founded as a

225

Each of the red-brick chimney pots sports a subtly different design; they represent the height of Tudor luxury and affluence. The status of Framlingham Castle helped to lend legitimacy to Mary's campaign.

mighty medieval fortress—see "The Foundations and Defenses of Framlingham" on page 229—and its grand walls, tall towers, and surrounding ditch afforded the same defensive potential in 1553 as when the castle was first designed and constructed in 1190. Indeed, one Tudor writer described Framlingham as "the strongest castle in Suffolk." In the back of Mary's mind, she must have been formulating strategies to hold back Northumberland's troops—and the strength of Framlingham would have enabled her to resist a dramatic siege, if only for a short while.

However, Framlingham Castle was fortuitous not just for its brute strength. During the Tudor years, the castle had been transformed into one of the most luxurious and fashionable palaces in the whole of eastern England. Filled with modern residential suites, beautiful tapestries, and crowned with those delicate red-brick chimneys, the castle was an awe-inspiring

226

display of Tudor affluence. Symbolically, this mattered a great deal to Mary's bid for power. It would be hard to proclaim oneself queen of England from a dingy manor-house. The grandeur of Framlingham gave legitimacy to her bid and helped draw local people to her cause. It helped build people's confidence in her social status and reinforced her connection to the wealth of England.

In fact, when she arrived at Framlingham Castle at eight o'clock on July 12, Mary was greeted by an impressive array of support—a volunteer army of more than one thousand participants. In addition to this "great crowd of country folk," the Earl of Sussex and the Earl of Bath were there to mark her arrival—although some historians would argue that their arms had been twisted to ensure their attendance. In addition to these men, Mary was greeted with a substantial sum of cold, hard cash. A regional tax collector, "laden with money," collected in the name of King Edward, presented himself at the castle with the

The castle walls are approximately 36 feet tall, and a wall walk (with dramatic views) spans the top of them.

intention of granting her every tithe he had thus far gathered in her half-brother's name. We can only imagine how relieved Mary would have felt as a result of such enthusiasm.

Indeed, the tide appeared to be turning against Northumberland. Although he had previously dispatched three hundred men to arrest Mary, not one had managed to capture her—and her position appeared to be strengthening, rather than weakening. Sensing his plan was unraveling, Northumberland rapidly rounded up fifteen hundred more to his cause, and dispatched all to eastern England. Despite their vast numbers, however, the troops were poorly disciplined, and many deserted enroute. Northumberland was also uncharacteristically indecisive in directing his men. Although he was greatly skilled in battle, he originally thought it more important for him to remain in London and for other nobles to lead the troops.

Mary, conversely, was to enjoy a tremendous stroke of luck. It just so happened that mutiny was brewing on five royal ships docked in Ipswich harbor—a river estuary not twenty miles from Framlingham Castle. These ships had been sent to the area to prevent Mary from escaping by sea; however, the sailors onboard were deeply unhappy, preoccupied with long-term grumbles related to poor pay and terrible working conditions. Mary's supporters manipulated the discontent of the five crews and persuaded all to mutiny in her name. It was a dramatic and provocative statement, illustrating that Lady Jane and Northumberland no longer had control of the Royal Navy.

By July 16, the tide was turning in favor of Mary, and Northumberland saw that he had to act. He marched with his remaining men in the direction of Cambridge. It was almost certainly too

The ruin in the foreground may be the ruins of an old Prison Tower. Although it sounds dramatic, it wasn't quite the dark dungeon of modern imaginations: it was used only to hold local poachers and ne'er-do-wells.

late. By that time, Mary's support had swollen throughout the entire east of England, leading to wild rumors that she had more than ten thousand men at her disposal—resulting in even more of Northumberland's troops deserted in fear. As the next two days passed, other English counties declared for Mary, too. More dangerously, now that Northumberland was out of London, his own supporters in the capital were beginning to get jittery, sensing that popular opinion was no longer on their side.

Although Northumberland himself was a thoroughly dislikable man, the events that took place in London on July 19 illustrated that the duke had surrounded himself with vipers. The people of the capital—and, indeed, the entire country—appeared to be decisively turning for Mary, and those nobles who had plotted to place Lady Jane Grey on the throne were now fearing for their own lives. As a result, in Northumberland's absence from London, his once-allies made a spectacular series of U-turns.

The oily Earl of Arundel, once one of the duke's keenest supporters, was the first to put the boot in. At a meeting of the Privy Council, he dared to stand and proclaim Northumberland to have a character of "perverse wickedness" and claimed that the duke really wished to "enslave a free Kingdom." The earl then declared that he supported the claims of Mary to become queen and condemned Northumberland to be a traitor and sole architect of the plan to place Lady Jane Grey upon the throne. The earl was persuasive. Over the next twelve hours, he succeeded in convincing the remaining members of the Privy Council that Mary should be declared queen. On July 20, the news of Mary's accession to the throne was announced throughout London, it is said, to much rejoicing.

Of course, such news would take time to reach Mary in Framlingham Castle. That morning, Mary had awoken determined to send her troops to take London by force—for she believed that the city was still held by Northumberland in the name of Lady Jane Grey. That afternoon, her troops were called to assemble on the flat ground just outside Framlingham Castle—adjacent to the mere—and "the standards were unfurled . . . the infantry made ready their pikes . . . and Mary rode out from Framlingham Castle at about four o'clock to muster and inspect this most splendid and loyal army."

She did not, of course, need to fight. Some hours later, the first messenger arrived from London, carrying the news from the previous day. He would have galloped into Framlingham Castle—racing through the grand wooden door and pounding up the steps to the red-brick residential chambers where he would have declared the news that his mistress, Mary Tudor, was the true queen of England.

Epilogue: The Demise of Northumberland

Mary, now the first queen of England, made a leisurely journey back to London from Framlingham Castle, visiting a number of the towns and villages to pay thanks for their support during her quest. She eventually arrived in London on August 3, 1553, riding alongside her half-sister, Elizabeth. Mary was accompanied by a vast retinue of troops and well-wishers and wore glorious ceremonial gowns of purple velvet accompanied by gold and pearl jewelry. Although the remaining years of her rule would be fraught with controversy, she enjoyed, for this brief moment, the unequivocal support of the whole of England—supported by those of both Catholic and of Protestant faith.

The situation for Northumberland, however, was much grimmer. On July 20—the day that Mary was announced queen—the news of his failure reached him as he stood in the marketplace of the city of Cambridge. Reports tell that he "laughed so that the tears ran down his cheeks for grief," and the duke was brought to the Tower of London on July 25. It is said that a crowd of onlookers booed and jeered him as he was dragged into the prison—the entire country, it seemed, had sided against him.

Northumberland, however, was an opportunistic soul. Despite his previous Protestant beliefs, he made a last ditch conversion to Catholicism—presumably in an attempt to persuade Mary to spare his life. He was not to be so lucky. He was beheaded in late August in front of an audience of ten thousand people—an ignoble end to a disastrous plot.

The death of Northumberland, however, did not spell the end of the pretensions to power of his wider family. His son—Robert Dudley—was to have a rather interesting relationship with Queen Elizabeth I. The setting for their romantic liaison was to be Kenilworth Castle—and you can discover more about this beguiling romance in the next chapter of this book.

The Foundations and Defenses of Framlingham Castle

Our first records of Framlingham village date to 1086. Back then, Framlingham was not much more than a settlement—a few grand manors and country houses scattered across the green, fertile lands of eastern England. However, these records tell us something more about the political state of the area: they demonstrate to us that this part of England was entirely controlled by the Normans, twenty years after the 1066 conquest.

King Henry I therefore granted the lands of Framlingham to one of his most loyal Norman subjects, Roger Bigod I. From there, the Bigod family built a rudimentary wooden fortress overlooking the lake and boggy marshland of Framlingham Mere. That original wooden fortress has, of course, become lost to the passage of time; however, the first stone buildings of the modern-day castle were laid by Roger Bigod II in around 1190. Owing to the natural geology of the area, Bigod was forced to build his castle of flint and septarian stones, giving the walls an unusual rough-hewn finish—and a gentle golden color.

Paul Wishart/Shutterstock

The thirteen towers are topped with tall battlements, which would have granted an excellent viewpoint across the surrounding countryside.

Roger Bigod II's design of Framlingham Castle is quite notable for a number of reasons. As described before, the castle was structured rather like a ring—comprising a grand outer curtain wall that wrapped around thirteen towers of varying sizes. Perhaps owing to the width and breadth of the curtain wall (it's around eight feet thick), it's the only defensive structure protecting the innards of the fortress from the outside world. Most other early medieval castles concealed a central stronghold (a great tower or keep) behind the outer wall, resulting in two layers of defense—this wasn't the case in Framlingham.

This certainly doesn't mean the castle was ill-protected in the event of battle. Each of the thirteen towers was studded with arrow-loops, designed to give archers an unparalleled field of vision across the surrounding plains. A protected "wall walk" (still accessible today, with dramatic, windswept views) traversed the top of the curtain wall, connecting each tower and granting a lookout an unparalleled vista to spot any approaching enemy.

There was a sting in the tail of this wall walk, too. Architects realized that, should an intruder gain access to these upper levels, he'd have an excellent vantage point to shoot arrows down at those still defending the castle. They therefore engineered a neat trick. Whereas the majority of the wall walk was constructed of stone, some sections were formed of temporary wooden planks, balanced across a sheer drop. Should an intruder have accessed the wall walk, he would have been lured to a stone section between two wooden planks, and then the planks would have been kicked away, leaving him stranded, thirty-six feet off the ground. From such a vulnerable position, he could have been easily picked off by any archer still defending the castle.

There were other subtly defensive tricks of design. Surrounding the walls of the fortress, one encounters a

David Harding/Thinkstock

A deep ditch surrounds the curtain walls of the castle, forming an additional line of defense.

deep ditch, which you'd be forgiven for assuming was once a moat. In actual fact, that was never the case. The primary purpose of the ditch was to deter any attacker from burrowing beneath the castle's external walls.

Despite this, the original architects of the castle did consider the use of water to defend the fortress. The adjacent mere—an area of boggy marshlands and lake—would have made it very tricky for any assailant to approach the castle from a northwestern direction—instead forcing them to make an approach via the eastern side, which was more strongly fortified. Nowadays, however, the mirrored surface of the adjacent lake produces a stunning reflection of the castle—and an attractive place to stroll after exploring the fortress and grounds.

The Rooms and Residences of Framlingham Castle

During early modern times, the inner court of Framlingham Castle would have filled with noise and activity—crowded with grand residences and a banqueting hall, a buttery, and stables. Nowadays, although the mighty outer curtain wall remains intact, barely any buildings remain standing inside it. All we can see is a smattering of windows and fireplaces studded along the eastern aspect of the curtain wall, which, without the rooms that once surrounded them, almost appear to float in midair.

Although it may be tricky to imagine now, Framlingham Castle was always blessed with luxurious accommodations. In the earliest medieval times, following the completion of the grand curtain walls, the builders would have set to work upon a grand block of residential chambers. By the standards of the Middle Ages, these would have been exceptionally beautiful rooms, as the sturdy outer curtain wall (which the chamber block backed onto) was able to support vast windows, permitting an uncommon amount of sunlight.

Adjacent to the residential block, one would have found a grand chapel, which would have been the heart of the castle during the medieval period. As the years wore on—and as we enter the Tudor period, just before Mary's arrival—the chapel became filled with two or three extravagant tapestries and a beautiful gold plate.

Many other decadent additions were made to Framlingham Castle during the 1500s. In the early Tudor

The internal rooms of the castle have long since disappeared. Nowadays, fireplaces appear to hang in midair; we can't be entirely sure where Mary Tudor's chambers would once have been.

The swirling shape of one of the red-brick Tudor chimneys.

The old Framlingham Poor House, which was built within the walls of the castle. Nowadays, part of the old Poor House is the castle museum; part is a private residence.

period, numerous residential buildings were added or rebuilt in expensive red brick, transforming the fortress into a grand palace. Prior to Mary's arrival in 1553, there would have been a Great Hall, a Great Chamber, and an extended chapel; a new set of stables; a grand buttery; a wine cellar; and even an armory, filled with more than one hundred suits of armor.

We don't know exactly where in the castle it was that Mary received the news that she had become queen. Popular belief is that she received the news within the modernized eastern chambers, which were decorated with diverse and extravagant tapestries. In any case, the castle had become a palace, and it teemed with handsome red-brick buildings and every luxurious item that could have been procured during Tudor times.

The location of Framlingham Castle.

Unfortunately, nowadays, there's little visible evidence of such Tudor luxury. Although the grand curtain wall has remained intact, the inside of the castle slowly fell into disrepair during the 1600s. As a result, in 1729, the medieval foundations of the Great Hall were reappropriated for a new purpose altogether: they formed the base of the new Framlingham Poor House, which was built on top of it. From hosting some of the richest in England, Framlingham Castle was now home to some of the poorest and most destitute.

The Poor House was a very British institution: partly responsible for removing and "confining" the poorest from common view, but partly responsible for sheltering, educating, and caring for society's most vulnerable. In return for their board, inmates were delegated to busy programs of work and labor, alongside moral and social improvement drives. In the days of the Framlingham Poor House, the inner boundaries of the castle were converted into a small farming operation, nurturing sows, hogs, and simple crops.

Nowadays, the Poor House is the only building to survive within the walls of Framlingham Castle, and part of the structure has been converted into the castle museum and gift shop. The remainder of the building has, however, been commandeered for a unique purpose. During the early twentieth century, this section was converted into a three-bedroom home, intended for use by the castle caretakers. Nowadays, this residence—the Red House—is available to rent on the open market. The property was last offered to the public in 2011, at the cost of $1,500 (£850) per month. Every evening, after the day-trippers depart, the modern tenants have the run of what must feel like their very own fortress.

Framlingham Castle

Church Street, Framlingham, Suffolk, IP13 9BP
+44 (0)1728 724922
Managed by English Heritage
Official Website: **www.english-heritage.org.uk/daysout/properties/framlingham-castle/**
Official Facebook: **www.facebook.com/framlinghamcastle**
My Website: **www.exploring-castles.com/framlingham_castle.html**
Open every day in spring and summer; closed most weekdays during winter—check before you travel

Sunrise over Kenilworth Castle on a cold and frosty Warwickshire morning.

Kenilworth Castle, and a Very Elizabethan Love Story

Time stood still during Queen Elizabeth I's visit to Kenilworth Castle. In 1575, "Good Queen Bess" spent an unprecedented nineteen days at the castle and was plied with every luxury imaginable within Tudor England. The queen dined at a banquet of three hundred rare delicacies ranging from whale's vomit to pig's bladders, was entertained by a singing deity who rode the castle moat upon a papier-mâché dolphin, and was dazzled by firework displays of unparalleled grandeur.

On the queen's arrival at Kenilworth on July 9, 1575, courtiers symbolically stopped the castle clock as it struck 2:00 p.m. They chose not to restart time until the queen suddenly departed from this dream-like world on July 27, 1575.

Every aspect of Elizabeth's extravagant visit was organized by Robert Dudley, Earl of Leicester—"a male favorite to a Virgin Queen" and a tall and ambitious Puritan who sought to secure Elizabeth's hand in marriage. English society was held agog at Dudley's attempts to woo the queen during her stay at his castle, and no extravagance was too wild, and no flight of imagination too fanciful, for Dudley's frantic efforts of seduction.

Kenilworth Castle itself was a potent symbol of Elizabeth and Dudley's relationship. Earlier in her reign, Elizabeth had bequeathed to Dudley this old medieval fortress, and Dudley lavished money on converting its war-worn walls into a beguiling Tudor palace. His deep finances allowed him to satisfy every decadent desire: from glass-windowed state apartments to an ornate pleasure garden, a water fountain, and an aviary filled with a rainbow of exotic birds.

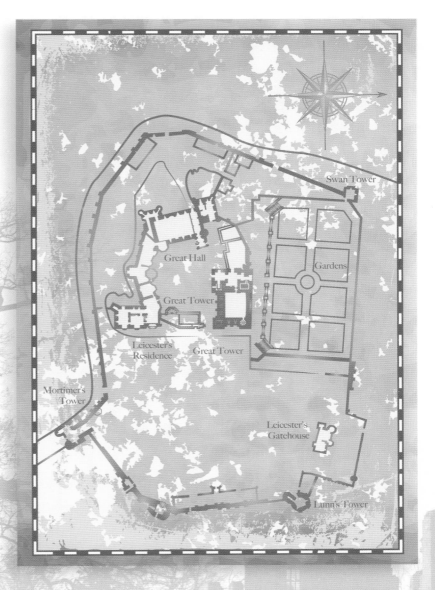

A floor plan of Kenilworth Castle.

Despite Dudley's concerted attempts at self-aggrandizement, his chances of taking Elizabeth's hand in marriage were hampered by his comparatively low status and his rather shady past. A miasma of scandal swirled around the earl, following the unusual death— or, as some would have it, murder—of an old lover. In fact, most inhabitants of Tudor England regarded Robert Dudley as a man with blood on his hands.

237

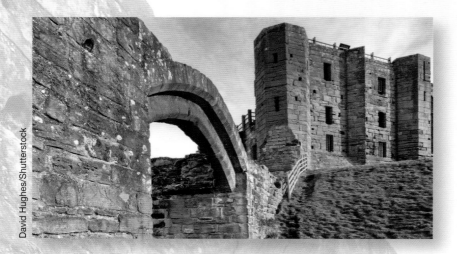

Certain parts of Kenilworth survive in remarkable condition, such as this archway connecting the outer court to the Elizabethan Garden.

Could the Virgin Queen of England ever marry such a questionable character? If she could, would the luxuries and extravagances of her seductive nineteen days at Kenilworth Castle convince her to take his hand in matrimony? Or were the earl's advances an impudent display of a power-hungry young political upstart, who had rather overreached himself?

Our story leads to the hot July of 1575 by way of a political plot, an imprisonment in the Tower, a mysterious death, and a grand pilgrimage. But first, we must focus on Kenilworth Castle itself, and its beautiful environs within the English countryside.

Red Sandstone Ruins in Deepest Warwickshire

Kenilworth Castle is, as one Tudor author put it, "at the navel of England." The fortress lies around one hundred miles from London, nestled in the rolling green farmlands of Warwickshire—a county of verdant fields, gentle hills, and pleasant views.

Warwickshire is bisected by the horseshoe curves of the River Avon, and, if you should care to venture along the river, you'll encounter Stratford—the birthplace of Shakespeare. Further downstream, you'll chance upon Royal Leamington Spa, famous in Victorian times for the health-giving properties of its water.

In 1564, Queen Elizabeth gifted Kenilworth Castle to her favorite young courtier—the ambitious Robert Dudley, a tall young man with a striking, "princely" appearance, a talent for languages, and a remarkable Puritan zeal. Robert had been the queen's favorite from early in her reign, and, in the early days of her rule, the pair would go on daily hunting expeditions together.

Elizabeth's gift to her "sweet Robyn" was one of tremendous generosity. It bestowed a vast honor on young Robert, blessing him with some of the grandest lands in England.

Delicate planting within the Elizabethan Gardens. The plants used today were chosen from books and engravings recorded during the Tudor period.

This was a gift with a practical purpose, too. Although Robert was hardly from poor stock, his family connections were, at best, dubious. The Dudley family was a relative upstart in English society, without the prestigious lands or social connections of true Elizabethan gentry. To make matters even worse, Robert's own father and brother had recently been executed, following an ill-thought plot against Mary Tudor. Their disastrous exploits had blackened the family name further still.

If Robert were to have any hope of marrying the queen of England, he needed to raise his social status by quite a few notches. Elizabeth's gift of one of the noblest castles in England—which he could adapt, reconstruct, and aggrandize in his own vision—would help him to achieve the status he required.

And so, when Robert Dudley rode into Kenilworth Castle for the first time in 1564, we can only imagine his sense of achievement at his new possession, alongside his optimism for his own future. Indeed, even to the modern visitor, Kenilworth's initial appearance is nothing less than spectacular. The stunning ochre-red sandstone of the castle walls complements the dark blues (or, more commonly, dark grays) of the English sky with a quite devastating effect.

In modern times, one enters the castle along a lengthy raised causeway; in Dudley's time, this would have been wide enough to host jousting tournaments and would have crossed one of the largest man-made moats in England. The reflective surface of the water would have mirrored and amplified the colors of the castle walls and sky, creating an incredible sense of scale and prosperity. We can only imagine how ambitious young Robert must have felt when entering his new property for the first time.

Indeed, to a man more humble than Dudley, this rapid turnaround in fate—from a condemned soul in the Tower of London to the owner of one of the grandest castles in England—may

One of the ruined towers of the castle curtain wall, built under King John in around 1210.

Kenilworth once housed "the finest sweep of semi-royal apartments of the later middle ages," but, today, much of the castle is reduced to mere facades of once-grand buildings.

239

have given cause to pause and reflect upon his good fortune. However, Dudley may have been rather too ambitious, and rather too self-centered, to truly appreciate his dizzying rise in English society.

The Remarkable Rise of Robert Dudley

Robert was born in the early 1530s and was one of thirteen children raised in Dudley Castle—a rather modest fortress, some thirty miles from Kenilworth Castle. By all accounts,

A portrait of John Dudley (1504–1553).

Robert had a noble stature, a talent for languages, and a remarkable Puritan zeal.

Robert's ambition was inherited from his overreaching family, whose dalliances with power would lead to an array of untimely deaths —and Robert's own imprisonment in the Tower of London.

In the 1550s, during the reign of sickly Edward VI, Robert's father had ridden a swelling tide to become lord president of the Privy Council. John Dudley knew that King Edward was soon to die and attempted to tinker with the line of succession for his own benefit. Rather than allow the crown to pass to Edward's half-sister, Mary Tudor, John Dudley contrived to position young Lady Jane Grey to be the rightful heir. To cement his grip on power, John Dudley even organized a marriage between Lady Jane and his own son Guildford (Dudley's brother, if the family relationships are getting confusing).

To say John Dudley's plans backfired would underplay the true misfortune of the situation. Mary Tudor convinced England to rally to her cause, and she was soon proclaimed the rightful queen. Mary's success led to the imprisonment of Jane ("the nine days Queen of England") alongside her husband, her father, and Robert Dudley, too. All were bundled into the Tower of London to await a grim fate. You can read much more about this whole episode within the chapter on Framlingham Castle (page 214).

Perhaps rightfully, Mary beheaded John Dudley in 1553. However, the execution of poor Lady Jane Grey and

Guildford Dudley in 1554 was a tragic consequence of the whole sorry affair: aged seventeen and nineteen, the pair were guilty of little more than being in the wrong place at the wrong time.

The curtain wall, which surrounds Kenilworth Castle, was built during the thirteenth century and protected the fortress during the Great Siege of 1266.

Robert Hackett/Shutterstock

Robert Dudley, by contrast, was spared the death penalty, and his stay in the Tower was remarkably short. His mother used her own political connections with Spanish royalty to achieve his release and, in December 1554, he was reinstated as a free man. Interestingly, his internment in the Tower coincided with the imprisonment of an old childhood acquaintance—the half-sister of Queen Mary, young Elizabeth Tudor.

It was not the first connection between Dudley and Elizabeth. During their childhood, both were privately tutored at Hatfield House, a mansion in North London. However, by a rather strange twist of fate, both Dudley and Elizabeth were present at Hatfield House some years later—on November 18, 1558. It was here that the pair received the news of Queen Mary's death and Elizabeth's ascendancy to the throne.

It necessitates explaining exactly how Robert Dudley came to be at Hatfield on such an auspicious day. The Spanish king, Phillip II, had grown fond of Dudley, and, as a result, his reputation had been somewhat rehabilitated. The young man was consequently invited to mix with some of the highest echelons of English society. Robert also inherited his father's political sixth sense and foresaw the death of Queen Mary and the consequences for her half-sister, Elizabeth.

So, whether by fate or intuition, he was at Hatfield House on the day that the Royal Seal passed to Elizabeth—and was one of the very first men to bow to the newly anointed queen of England. Perhaps because of his good looks, his skills in

241

Engraving of Elizabeth I of England, published after the queen's death in 1603.

Elizabeth I (1533–1603). Engraved by W. Holl and published in The Gallery of Portraits with Memoirs Encyclopaedia, United Kingdom, 1837.

battle, or lingering childhood affection, Elizabeth made him her master of the horse that very same day.

From that moment, Robert Dudley's star began to rise. Elizabeth and Dudley became an inseparable pair who rode out to hunt together every day. He moved into accommodations adjacent to hers, and the queen would have fits of jealousy when he was away from her side.

The Spanish ambassador wrote that "she will marry none but the favored Robert," and Elizabeth made no secret of Dudley being her favorite. She quickly promoted him to knight of the garter and bestowed him with lands in Denbigh (North Wales) and the title of the Earl of Leicester. When she fell sick with smallpox in 1562, she designated Dudley the protector of the realm in case she should die. In 1564, when fully recovered, she granted Kenilworth Castle and grounds to her closest mortal ally.

242

A Palace of Potential: Dudley's First Visit to Kenilworth

Kenilworth Castle was founded in 1120, and so was around 450 years old when Robert Dudley took possession. When he

The castle is built from a spectacular red sandstone. Much of Kenilworth was conceived and built in the age of John of Gaunt as one unified structure.

SIA/Shutterstock

first rode into the castle in 1564, Kenilworth would have assumed a surprisingly similar shape to the castle that we can see today—albeit it would have been a complete and habitable residence, rather than in its modern state of ruin.

Robert's attentions would have likely first focused upon the Great Tower—the heart, both symbolically and literally, of the castle complex. The building was started in 1120 and is very clearly the work of Norman architects. Back in the 1100s, it would have stood alone as a little fortress, most notable for its squat, square appearance with narrow arched windows. Architecturally, it has a great deal in common with other Norman castle keeps, such as the White Tower in the Tower of London.

Robert could not fail to have been impressed with the Great Tower, but his attentions are likely to have been drawn toward the complex of newer buildings surrounding it. The most magnificent of these was the Great Hall, a decadent banqueting hall constructed by a previous owner of the castle, John of Gaunt, in the 1370s. The Great Hall was an unmatched example of medieval largesse, with vast bay windows and six ornate fireplaces. It also boasted the widest vaulted roof of any hall in Medieval England (well, outside of Westminster, at least). Dudley would have been delighted with this part of his acquisition, as the Great Hall embodied the regal grandeur that he was so desperately seeking.

Strolling around the exterior of the Great Hall, Dudley would have noted a cluster of adjoining domestic buildings, which

243

The Great Tower—the stocky Norman construction at the heart of the Kenilworth Castle complex. It was completed in the twelfth century.

To enter the castle, there were two gateways through the curtain wall. The main entrance—Mortimer's Tower—was at the southern-most point. To enter this gatehouse—as we know Dudley would have when he first visited—one would have to traverse a wide causeway across the reflective Kenilworth mere. The mere was a huge, man-made moat, measuring more than a half mile in length and quarter mile in width. It's said that the waters were filled with tasty fish—including a delectable breed of carp—which made it an attractive spot for angling.

The vast mere and mighty curtain walls belied the faded military might of Kenilworth Castle. By the 1560s—and, to be honest, by as long ago as in the 1300s—Kenilworth had transformed from formidable medieval fortress into a noble English palace. However, some years earlier, the castle had been the site of the greatest siege to ever occur on English soil.

The six-month Siege of Kenilworth began in 1266 and pitched rebellious barons against Royalist forces. Those attacking the castle used every medieval technology to try and gain entrance. Some of their weapons—most notably the trebuchets, which were huge, stone-hurling catapults—had never been sighted before on British soil. One contemporary chronicler described these beasts as "previously unheard-of machines," and it's said that their power invoked awe among those who saw them.

Their might is still impressive today. During recent excavations of the drained castle moat, archaeologists have discovered vast round boulders, which were hurled by the trebuchets. Today's visitors can run their hands over the rough surface of

Remains of the windows within the Great Hall, built by John of Gaunt in the 1370s. The hall would have been a place of unprecedented luxury, boasting six separate fireplaces.

compromised the accommodation and domestic functions of the castle. Beside these, there would have been a large clearing with stables, and the entire perimeter of the castle was enclosed with a mighty curtain wall.

David Hughes/Shutterstock

Looking toward the Great Tower over the foundations of the old kitchens. The kitchens would have joined onto the Great Hall, and their significant size would have facilitated the preparation of huge feasts.

David Hughes/Shutterstock

Mortimer's Tower—which acted, in the main, as the gatehouse to Kenilworth. In Queen Elizabeth's time, the area to the left of the picture would have been submerged—it formed the Great Mere.

these otherworldly weapons—a little smaller than a wrecking ball, but still able to crush a man with little effort.

The 1266 Siege of Kenilworth would have been well-known to Dudley. The significance of Kenilworth in the history of Medieval England—combined with the glamour and prestige of its surviving buildings—provided him with an instant historical connection to some of the most glorious moments of English history.

Tom Blackie; Creative Commons BY-SA-2.0; with photographers acknowledgement. Cropped to focus upon bear motif.

Leciester's emblem (and indeed the emblem of Warwickshire): the bear with the ragged staff. This photograph was taken from the Lord Leycester Hospital in Warwick, England—Dudley visited the town while staying in Kenilworth Castle and decided to set up a home and hospital for retired soldiers. The spectacular medieval building exists to this day.

The bear with the ragged staff: the coat of arms of Dudley.

Dudley's next exercise in self-aggrandizement was to rebrand his tarnished family name through Kenilworth Castle's local connections. He cunningly chose to reappropriate the emblem of the country of Warwickshire—a bear clutching a ragged staff—to become his family motif. (The bear image is still used today and can be seen throughout the county by any modern traveler.)

When Dudley developed and extended his castle in preparation for Queen Elizabeth's visit, he instructed that the motif should be emblazoned upon all new additions to the castle. As a consequence, the emblem is stamped upon Dudley's reconstructed entrance to the Great Tower, and a large white

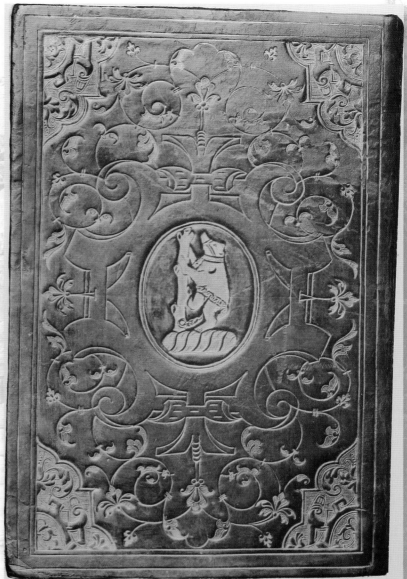

In Elizabethan times, some nobles chose to demonstrate their wealth by decorating books from their own personal libraries with ornamental bindings. These bindings often bore their own designs or coat of arms; this binding evidently belonged to Dudley.

statue of the bear was the focal point of his new pleasure garden. Not one for understatement, Dudley also slept in a four-poster bed with a bear statue supporting each corner.

As a result of Dudley's efforts to reinvent his name and his family connections, his status in English society did improve somewhat. Nonetheless, many still treated him with a fair degree of suspicion. Popular dislike of Dudley may have stemmed from his devout Puritanism, or his jealousy-inducing relationship with the queen. However, the most damaging rumors hinted at his involvement in a mysterious death that rather resembled a murder.

Looking onto the remains of Kenilworth, from the east. The visible ruined buildings include the Great Hall and the adjacent Strong Tower.

A Tudor Murder Mystery: The Death of Lady Amy Dudley

Robert Dudley's name was besmirched by the mysterious death of his wife, Lady Amy Dudley. Our sad story begins in 1550, when both were eighteen.

The marriage of Amy and Robert was organized by Robert's father and, although we know a good deal about the appearance and character of our groom, our bride is much more mysterious. Our knowledge is restricted to later years, where

248

Amy's letters suggest she was uncommonly fond of ornate dresses and expensive fabrics. We can suppose that she had patience and fortitude, as she showed unshakable dedication to Robert while he was imprisoned in the Tower of London—holding her head high while her own reputation was tarnished by association.

Of course, like many marriages during Tudor times, Amy and Robert's marriage appears more driven by social and political needs than motivated by true affection. Only modern conjecture has inferred that their marriage was unhappy. We do know that the pair had no children, but it's hard to draw much from that fact alone.

After Robert ascended to significance in Elizabeth's court, the young pair began to live increasingly separate lives. Robert spent most of his days at the side of jealous Elizabeth, whereas Amy retreated to her more permanent home in Hertfordshire. Amy, it appeared, was out of sight—but not entirely out of mind. Robert and Amy still wrote to each other, and surviving letters attest further to Amy's fondness for fine wools and velveteen clothes.

Amy's existence, however, made it impossible for Robert Dudley to come close to marrying Queen Elizabeth. Even so, it was inarguable that the queen was rather besotted with this married man. The Spanish ambassador wrote—either in jest or with rather unnerving foresight—that Dudley should like to have his wife poisoned to remove any obstacle to marrying the queen.

Our story takes a further disquieting turn in 1560. Earlier that year, Amy had moved to Cumnor Palace in Berkshire and, on

David Hughes/Shutterstock

One of the many alluring features of Kenilworth is its position in the rolling green English countryside. In Elizabethan times, the castle would have been surrounded by the shimmering waters of the grand meres.

the morning of Sunday, September 8, Lady Amy encouraged her entire retinue of servants to visit the fair in Abingdon while she remained home alone. It was a command that, in retrospect, does appear rather curious.

Later that day, when the servants returned full of holiday cheer, they were greeted with a most terrible surprise. Lady Amy's crumpled body lay at the foot of the palace stairs; it appeared she had tripped, fallen, and broken her neck.

Almost instantaneously, wild rumors began to circulate the country. Popular gossip said that Robert Dudley, in his ambition to marry Elizabeth, had arranged for his wife to be killed—and concealed the dastardly deed as an accident. Indeed, a clergyman writing nine days after Amy's death spoke of the "grievous, dangerous suspicion and muttering" surrounding her mysterious demise. Further to this, in the 1580s, an incendiary pamphlet claimed that Amy's body had been found at the base of the stairs with her headdress "undisturbed" upon her head. Foul play, it insinuated, had led to her death.

So, was it really cold-blooded murder—designed to further Dudley's own political chances? Modern-day scholars don't

David Hughes/Shutterstock

The castle ruins are spectacularly evocative—these teetering remains almost appear to defy gravity.

have any definite answers to the mystery—but most modern academics have steered away from the suspicion that Robert Dudley orchestrated his wife's death. (It should be noted that most writers from earlier in the century unquestionably believed that Dudley was guilty.)

There simply isn't enough evidence to reach a definitive conclusion, and the remaining clues—including a rather ambiguous inquest report noting two wounds to Amy's head—are of little use in forming a definitive answer. Most contemporary explanations posit suicide, misadventure, or underlying malignancy as the cause for Amy's demise.

The ultimate outcome, whether by sad accident or foul play, was that Robert Dudley was now a single man. This sorry episode removed the biggest hurdle in his quest to marry Elizabeth. And, in 1575, he had the perfect opportunity to woo the queen—as she proposed a lengthy visit to his Kenilworth Castle.

The Elizabethan Garden is a riot of carefully tended color. The garden bursts into bloom each July—to coincide with the month of Queen Elizabeth's visit.

250

Elizabethan Pomp and Progress

During each year of her glorious forty-four-year reign of England, Elizabeth I engaged in a series of "Royal Progresses"—an annual tour of southern England, visiting the grand castles and noble homes of her most loyal courtiers.

Her progresses were a quite remarkable example of Elizabethan ambition. Each tour lasted for a number of months during the summer—when the heat and stench of London made the capital truly inhospitable. These journeys permitted the queen, accompanied by a vast retinue of courtiers, horsemen, and servants, to travel to the furthest reaches of her lands and to capture the imagination and respect of her subjects in doing so. It was an exercise of image creation—perhaps responsible for the adoring images of Elizabeth I that live on in our imaginations.

The logistics of organizing an itinerant royal household would have been quite unbelievable. Elizabeth's retinue may, on occasion, have numbered up to three hundred men and women, and the slow pace of riding horseback upon the pot-holed English roads would have necessitated numerous stops in villages and hamlets for accommodation each night. (As an aside, modern tourists to Britain might be unduly sceptical of the innumerable hoteliers' claims that "Queen Elizabeth I stayed here." The truth is that Queen Bess stayed in so many places in southern England that this frequent boast is probably quite truthful.)

The unceasing demand for local accommodation meant that numerous nobles would have had the dubious distinction of being able to host their queen for a night in their property.

What sounds like an incredible honor may, paradoxically, have felt rather like an albatross being hung around the neck: modernizing their homes to a standard befitting a queen could prove financially ruinous. The queen was also a picky guest. She brought furniture, bedding, and even tableware with her on her many journeys; if the standard of accommodation was not up to scratch, her long-suffering courtiers would have to replace all the furniture in a local dwelling, if only for one night.

Despite the headache-inducing complexity of organizing a progress, the impact upon the English people would have been electric. The scale, pageantry, and ceremony of the occasion would have cemented Elizabeth in the public imagination, and the progresses also enabled her to keep abreast of very-local political problems and concerns. It also gave nobles the opportunity to petition Elizabeth upon their local political problems, resulting in a give-and-take of power that helped consolidate Elizabeth's lengthy rule of England.

In 1575, the annual progress was set to tour eastern Anglia and the southern counties. However, there was one stop en route that created tongue-wagging gossip throughout early modern England—a nineteen-day stay at Robert Dudley's Kenilworth.

It was not the first time that Queen Elizabeth had stayed at Kenilworth Castle—in the early 1570s, she had spent a couple of nights in the palace en route to other destinations. However, her 1575 progress promised an extended stay—the longest she had ever spent with any courtier, in fact. It was an opportunity for Dudley to pull out every stop to impress the queen.

These two arbors are connected by a raised terrace along one side of the Elizabethan Garden. This would have granted a beautiful view of the planned garden that stretched below.

The remains of Leicester's Residence are to the right of the image. Unlike Leicester's Gatehouse, this building—also constructed for Queen Elizabeth—is almost entirely ruinous.

251

Elizabeth in Kenilworth: Feasts, Fireworks, and Otherworldly Theater

Elizabeth's visit to Kenilworth Castle was an occasion of wild decadence. Dudley pulled together a program of hunting, dancing, and elaborate feasting, and skillfully combined such earthly pursuits with plays, poetry, and theatrical interruptions. His aim was to recast Kenilworth as a place of myth and of Arthurian legend: a little bubble of extravagant fantasy in the heart of Tudor England. This, he hoped, would elevate him to take the hand of a queen.

No surprise or extravagance was enough for Dudley. As Queen Elizabeth made her royal entrance to the castle on July 9, 1575, she was greeted by an actress playing the mythical figure of Sybilla. This divine figure addressed the queen in flowered verse and welcomed her to this land of fantasy—setting the stage for the next nineteen days of otherworldly pleasure. Next, as she proceeded forward, Elizabeth was serenaded by a retinue of magical trumpeteers—standing upon stilts to appear eight feet tall.

Elizabeth's visit was chiefly dedicated to country pursuits, with many days spent hunting in the dense forests surrounding the fortress. It's said that the forests were particularly rich in game, such as red deer and pheasants—we might assume that some of these were rather strategically released for the queen's enjoyment.

In the evenings, on account of both Elizabeth and Dudley's uncommon fondness for dancing, the pair attended increasingly elaborate balls and dances. On two of the darkest

Leicester's Gatehouse was built in 1571, as part of Dudley's efforts to woo Queen Elizabeth. It was to act as a grand new entrance to the castle; should you wish today, it's possible to stage your own wedding in the building.

SIA/Shutterstock

nights, the festivities climaxed with grand firework displays. The firework display on the Sunday after Elizabeth's arrival was "strange and well executed," wrote a contemporary source, "[and] would rise and mount out of the water again, and burn very furiously until . . . utterly consumed."

Dudley had spared no expense in making Kenilworth Castle suitable for a queen, and three of his grand projects merit special attention. The first of these was Leicester's Gatehouse—a new entrance so grand that it extended beyond the boundary of the fortress, meaning that the exterior curtain wall had to be rebuilt. (The gatehouse survives today in quite remarkable condition; you can hold your own wedding here, if you should wish.)

The second of his great projects was a grand residential tower, built specifically to accommodate the queen. Leicester's

Leicester's Gatehouse, built during his efforts to seduce Queen Elizabeth. From the 1600s, the Gatehouse came to be used as a residence; today, it houses many artifacts from the Tudor period, including a grand fireplace carved with the initials of Robert Leicester (that is to say, Dudley).

Residence was built to the most modern Tudor specifications and was notable for its vast array of glass windows, which were a quite remarkable luxury. Indeed, one contemporary writer described the residence as "glittering by glass" in the daytime sunlight and remarked upon the "continual brightness of candle, fire and torchlight" that flickered through these "lightsome windows" during the night.

The innards of the residence were just as grand as the exterior. Elizabeth would have enjoyed a suite of residential rooms, adorned with grand marble fireplaces and breathtaking views across the adjacent mere and pleasure garden. On the uppermost level, there would have been a large, wooden-floored chamber, most suitable for Elizabeth and Dudley's passion for dancing.

This panorama gives an excellent idea of the plan of the Elizabethan Garden. The aviary (the brown building at the back of the garden) would have housed exotic species of birds.

The third of Dudley's great projects was the sizable pleasure garden—nowadays called the Elizabethan Garden—fashioned

adjacent to the new gatehouse. Pleasure gardens were particularly in vogue in Tudor times and consisted of rows of neatly planted fragrant flowers and herbs, crisscrossed with gravel pathways. The gardens were an attractive locale for an evening promenade—and an intriguing location to discuss politics and to do business.

Many gardens—such as Dudley's in Kenilworth—were adorned with handsome statues of Greek and Roman gods, evoking visions of mythological piety. As well as the colorful flowers and tantalizing fragrances, the designers sought to incorporate a further sense into the garden—that of sound. The trickling of the water fountains, and the gentle squawking of the menagerie of birds in the garden aviary, was intended to create an otherworldly feeling of separation and relaxation.

The gardens at Kenilworth were intended for the exclusive use of Elizabeth and her closest courtiers, and it's said that the queen enjoyed the view of surrounding hunts from a sheltered patch under one of the vine-wrapped arbors.

To impress Elizabeth still further, Dudley had one more trick up his sleeve: theater. Throughout Elizabeth's stay, players dressed as mythological figures and appeared in her path, at various points, to recite poetry and verse. For example, on returning from hunting, a "wild man" appeared from the undergrowth and spoke in lengthy verse, explaining his eternal exile by Jupiter and the rumors he had heard of a "Queen of heaven" visiting this wilderness.

At one moment, when crossing the bridge into the mere, Elizabeth was accosted by the character of Triton, riding upon a

David Hughes/Shutterstock

mermaid, who regaled her with stories of the mythological dwellers of the lake. Proceeding further across the lake, she was then greeted by the Lady of the Lake, who was attended to by two nymphs riding a flotilla of bullrushes. A few steps later, it was Proteus's turn to sing to her—while riding upon the back of a papier-mâché dolphin, with an orchestra secreted in its belly.

It seems that Elizabeth grew rather tired of these theatrical performances. It's said that, rather than watch a play by the Men of Kenilworth from the window of her residence, she turned instead to watch the dancing inside the building, ignoring the show below.

The eighteen-foot water fountain at the heart of the Elizabethan Garden. The modern fountain is made from Tuscan white marble, and its octagonal base depicts scenes from Ovid's Metamorphoses.

In the Middle Ages, Kenilworth Castle would have been surrounded by four thousand acres of tended parks, filled with game and opportunities for hunting.

There may have been another reason for Elizabeth's frustrations at these "impromptu" pieces of theater: there was a none-too-subtle message running throughout. In initial interactions, the message was approached rather more circumstantially—the wild man appearing in the forest tangentially spoke of Robert Dudley as being "a worthy gift to be received, and so

The Elizabethan Garden is split into four quadrants, with a seventeen-foot-tall pierced obelisk positioned at the center of each.

I trust it shall." However, in later performances, the invocations were none too subtle. Dudley wanted to take Elizabeth's hand in marriage and was going to drop heavy hints to that effect.

Most notably, the very final performance of Elizabeth's stay was to be a masque titled Zabeta, named after the protagonist of the play. As the title might suggest, the piece had the subtlety of a sledgehammer—it told the story of goddess Zabeta, who had fallen to Earth. Zabeta had spent the last seventeen years—the same duration as Elizabeth's reign—captured by Diana, who was the goddess of chastity. Despite the entreaties of Juno (the god of marriage), Zabeta remained resolute in her intentions to remain single.

It would seem that no one could possibly miss Dudley's message, but if the point were not abundantly clear enough, the final lines of the masque were entirely unambiguous. "O Queen, O worthy Queen," runs the closing speech, "Yet never wight felt perfect bliss / but such as wedded been."

There can be no doubt that Elizabeth was truly fond of Dudley. She would forever treasure one of his letters to her, placing it in a special casket alongside her bed, where it remained until her own death. However, his planned performance of Zabeta bordered on insolence. Although officially the play was canceled due to poor weather, it's certain it was actually pulled by Elizabeth's courtiers, who deemed it wholly unacceptable.

Indeed, in light of Dudley's not-too-subtle invocations, Elizabeth curtailed her visit to Kenilworth—leaving with very little notice a couple of days before her stay was officially due to end. Looking

Note the delicate detailed stonework above these internal arches. Kenilworth Castle was always a place of luxury, constructed with admirable care.

back at at the whole sorry episode, it appears that Dudley had overreached himself: his invocations were inappropriate, and the queen simply had little inclination to marry. Nonetheless, it was a devastating blow—and a resounding rejection.

Poignantly—illustrating Dudley's tenacity—he made one last desperate effort to woo the queen. As she galloped from the castle, he asked his actors to follow her on horseback: as they rode, one extemporized to her upon the theme of deep desire and of duty, using everything on hand—including a holly bush—as a prop for the dramatic endeavors. Elizabeth was nonplussed. She left Kenilworth Castle without accepting the advances of Robert Dudley; implicitly, their courtship was now over.

Epilogue: A Ruined Romance

With the rapid exit of Queen Elizabeth, Robert Dudley's hopes of marriage were suddenly extinguished. We can

Rose Smith/Shutterstock

Queen Elizabeth, of course, remained the Virgin Queen of England and never married. By contrast, Dudley chose to lick his wounds and marry in secret, some three years after his rejection in Kenilworth. He wed Lettice Knollys, countess of Essex, ostensibly to produce an heir; when Queen Elizabeth eventually found out about the arrangement, it is said that she was furious. Speaking to an ambassador, Elizabeth described Lettice as a "she-wolf" with a "cuckold" husband; she proceeded to ignore Dudley at court for quite some time.

The queen's cruelty did little to dampen Dudley's lingering affections. After Elizabeth's departure from Kenilworth, he ordered his aides to preserve the castle forevermore in the same state as during Elizabeth's visit. After issuing those orders, he seldom returned to Kenilworth. Symbolically, Dudley had decided to prevent time from passing within the castle—in the same way that the clock had been stopped on Elizabeth's arrival, back in that hot July of 1575.

Of course, nothing can be preserved forever. Dudley died unexpectedly in 1588, and, on his death bed, he penned a final letter to Elizabeth. It was this letter that Elizabeth kept safe in the casket at her bedside, preserved until she, too, passed away.

Time continued to pass within Kenilworth Castle, too. Some sixty-four years after Dudley's death, the English Civil War broke out—and, in 1650, the castle was dragged into these bitter struggles.

Like many other fortresses in England, Kenilworth was originally held by the Royalist forces, who lost to the opposing Parliamentarians. Despite this, the castle narrowly escaped a

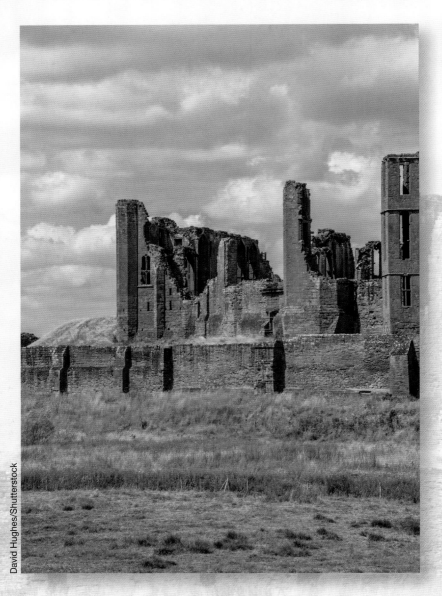

The castle fell into ruin in the late 1600s, following the English Civil War. The remnants give a tantalizing glimpse of the past luxury.

imagine him pacing Kenilworth after Elizabeth's departure, contemplating every luxury he had arranged and wondering where, exactly, things had gone wrong. Until this point, Robert must have felt that his rise in society was unstoppable; this very public rejection would have been a heavy blow indeed.

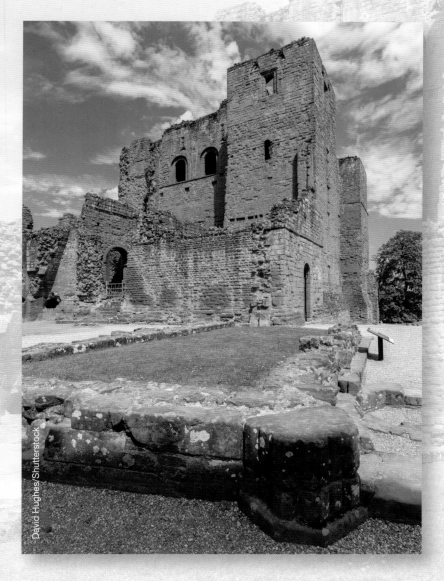
David Hughes/Shutterstock

The old kitchens and strong tower of the castle formed the fictional home of Amy Robsart in Sir Walter Scott's romantic novel, Kenilworth.

disastrous bout of slighting from the Parliamentarian militia. Slighting is the terrible technique of intentionally destroying a castle to prevent it from being used again in battle. Interestingly enough, the quality of the residential suites in Kenilworth meant that military commanders spared much of the castle to save these grand rooms for themselves.

That is not to say that the Kenilworth Castle remained unscathed—far from it. Although many of the great chambers were divvied up between army chiefs, the remainder of the castle was plundered and dismantled to provide stones, glass, and equipment to renovate the other buildings. Many of Kenilworth's grandest features—including the majestic Great Hall—became mere shells of their former glory, worn away by attrition. By the end of the 1600s, the castle was reduced to the jagged red ruins that one can see today: windowless and roofless, but standing proud against the English countryside.

Of course, the human stories of Kenilworth have kept the castle alive in the English imagination—even if the stone ruins were slowly consumed by ivy. Sir Walter Scott, the famous English novelist, visited the ruinous palace in the early 1800s and spent many hours in quiet contemplation, wandering through the decaying remains of a once-spectacular fortress. Inspired by the air of romance that still lingers around the castle, he wrote his masterpiece, *Kenilworth: A Love Story*, fictionalizing the ill-fated affair between Queen Elizabeth and Robert Dudley.

His novel was a Victorian publishing sensation and is still in print today. Of course, like any good story, Scott's work takes a few detours from the tale I've just told. His novel includes an unexpected twist in which Amy Robsart survives her fall, but smuggles herself into Kenilworth Castle to sensationally interrupt Dudley's efforts to woo Elizabeth. However, the overall tone and feel of the work—its sweeping romance, mythical allusions, and its tales of unrequited desire—captures the ambience of this spectacular ruined palace.

No one, then, can stop time, but we can distill emotions felt hundreds of years ago. Today, seconds, minutes, and hours of our lives still pass as we wander around the awe-inspiring ruins of Kenilworth Castle. However, the beauty and extravagance of Queen Elizabeth's visit, around 430 years ago, still hangs heavy in the air.

Kenilworth Castle

Castle Green, Off Castle Road,
Kenilworth, Warwickshire, CV8 1NE
+44 (0)1926 852078
Official Website: **www.english-heritage.org.uk/daysout/properties/kenilworth-castle/**
Official Facebook: **www.facebook.com/kenilworthcastle**
My Website: **www.exploring-castles.com/kenilworth_castle.html**
Open every day in spring and summer; closed most weekdays during winter—check before you travel

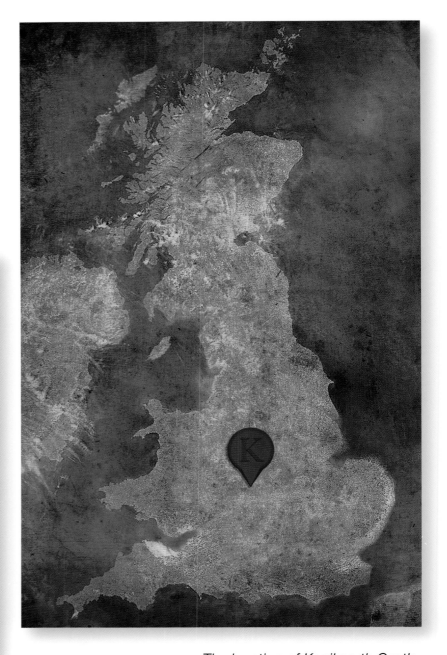

The location of Kenilworth Castle.

References and Bibliography

Recommended Books

There are many excellent texts about English castles. Here are some of the "must reads."

Brown, R Allen. *English Castles*. 2004 (Revised edition); ISBN-10: 1843830698. *To recognize the importance of this brilliant book, it was recently rereleased under the title* Allen Brown's English Castles.

Goodall, John. *The English Castle: 1066–1650*. 2011; ISBN-10: 0300110588. *A beautiful book—both in terms of the prose and the photography.*

Hull, Lise. *Understanding the Castle Ruins of England and Wales: How to Interpret the History and Meaning of Masonry and Earthworks*. 2009; ISBN-10: 0786434570. *Lise Hull has written many other books about Welsh and English castles, and has also created* **www.castles-of-britain.com.**

McNeill, Tom. *The English Heritage Book of Castles*. 1998; ISBN-10: 0713470259. *English Heritage also produces an excellent series of guidebooks to each of the castles it manages.*

Morris, Marc. *Castle: A History of the Buildings that Shaped Medieval Britain*. 2002; EAN 9781446492796. *See also Marc Morris's collections of essays on British castles, and his superb biography of Edward I.*

Toy, Sidney. *Castles: Their Construction and History*. 1986 (Revised edition); ISBN-10: 0486248984. *Probably the definitive book on castles in Britain, and further afield.*

Recommended Websites

Castles

Castle Wales, **www.castlewales.com.** *Self-evidently, this website doesn't cover that many sites in England (although it* does feature a few!)—even so, it's an outstanding resource for anyone interested in castles.

English Heritage, **www.english-heritage.org.uk.** *There's a lot of information about castles on the English Heritage site, although it's somewhat buried. Try searching by individual property and delving down into the linked resources.*

Gatehouse Gazetteer, **www.gatehouse-gazetteer.info.** *An exceptionally comprehensive database of castles in Britain, alongside links to academic studies on each. If you're interested in a particular castle, I'd recommend you start by looking for any listed periodical articles by G. T. Clark or R. Allen Brown.*

Of note, too, is the sister site to the Gatehouse Gazetteer: **www.castlefacts.info.** *Castle Facts shares the same underlying database as its older sibling but also contains a vast quantity of photography and mapping data.*

Don't forget to stop by at **www.exploring-castles.com,** too—or "like" us on Facebook.

British History

British Civil Wars, Commonwealth and Protectorate, **www.bcw-project.org.** *The definitive resource on the series of conflicts commonly called the English Civil War.*

British History Online, **www.british-history.ac.uk.** *This is an electronic library, filled with digital copies of primary and secondary sources, many of which relate to the medieval period. It's an unrivaled resource for anyone researching British history.*

Acknowledgments

Many people have kindly supported me in the production of this book, including historians (professional and armchair), writers, heritage agencies, graphic designers, and photographers. In particular, I'm indebted to Nicole Frail (my editor at Skyhorse), Alice Natali, Abby Letchemanan, Amy Morris and Vivien Morris, and Mark Willetts.

Glossary

ASHLAR: Fine jointed, closely worked stone. Used in some of the most prestigious of castles, including Bodiam.

BARBICAN: A fortified, often tortuous passageway, often added onto the castle gatehouse to provide another layer of defense.

BASTION: A sharp-angled firing platform, protruding from a curtain wall. Bastions (also known as bulwarks) were typically a feature of military forts built after the medieval period.

BATTLEMENT: The sawtooth fortifications traditionally found atop of the outer walls of the castle. Technically speaking, the upward-pointing bits are merlons, and the gaps between them are crenels.

CONCENTRIC CASTLE: Effectively a "castle within a castle." These fortresses, widely regarded as the apex of medieval castle design, comprised of a loop of outer curtain wall, enclosing a further, taller loop of inner curtain wall. The residences of the castle were sequestered within.

CROSS WALL: A load-bearing wall running through the center of an early medieval keep; an architectural necessity to support the four outer walls.

CURTAIN WALL: The thick outer wall of a castle, which typically formed a complete loop of protection.

DRUM TOWER: A mighty tower, usually built into a gatehouse or curtain wall. The protruding face was rounded, and so these towers typically had a footprint shaped like a capital letter D.

EMBRASURE: An alcove cut into the inner wall of a castle, surrounding an arrow-slit. An archer could use the space to gain a better field of vision.

ENCEINTE: A continuous loop of outer walls, within which lies the body of the castle.

FOLLY: A mansion or stately home, usually built in the 1800 to 1900s and consciously designed to emulate architectural features of a medieval castle.

GATEHOUSE: The fortified entrance to a castle, which usually boasted strong wooden doors and at least one portcullis.

GUARDEROBE: A castle latrine. See page 62.

KEEP: The central stronghold in any castle, sometimes referred to as the Great Tower (or originally "don-jon," meaning "stronghold").

MACHICOLATIONS: A deathly balcony, overhanging parts of the castle vulnerable to attack. The floor of the balcony contained holes, through which rocks or other heavy items could be dropped.

MOTTE AND BAILEY: The original castle design, as conceived by the Normans. The motte was a tall mound; the flat-topped bailey was positioned adjacent. See page 23.

MURDER HOLE: A hole in the ceiling of a castle passageway. Items could be thrown through it (or poured down it) on to the heads of intruders below.

NORMANS: Led by William the Conqueror, the invaders from continental Europe who brought the first castles to Britain, and changed the course of English history forever.

PORTCULLIS: A crisscross grille, usually made of metal, and lowered on pulleys to protect an external door.

POSTERN GATE: A second gate into a castle. Postern gates were usually located at the rear of the castle, but they could very occasionally be concealed, permitting an inconspicuous exit.

SALLY-PORT: A small door or gateway within a castle wall. During a siege, those inside the castle could "sally out" through it to make a brief, unexpected strike upon those attacking the fortress. The purpose of a successful sally was to wear down the besieging side.

SIEGE: The technique of surrounding a castle and preventing food or fresh supplies from reaching those within. The intention was to force those inside to surrender, and to claim the castle as a result.

SLIGHTING: The technique of intentionally damaging or destroying the defensive elements of a castle; the goal was to render the fortress unusable in future siege. The Parliamentarians slighted many castles in the aftermath of the English Civil War.

TREBUCHET: A mighty, stone-lobbing catapult, often used to assault a medieval castle. See page 126.

WALL-WALK: A pathway around the top of a curtain wall, providing a wide view of the surroundings. Sometimes known as an *allure*.

WARD: An area of open space protected by the outer castle walls. Sometimes referred to as a *bailey*.

Index